F⬦CUS ON

Writing Composition

Introductory

Louis Fidge

| | FICTION | | | | | | | | | | | NON-FICTION | | | |
	Stories with familiar settings	Traditional stories	Stories from other cultures	Stories with patterned language	Stories by children's authors	Texts with language play	Poems with familiar settings	Poems from other cultures	Poems with patterned language	Poems by children's poets	Poems with language play	Instructions/directions	Alphabetically organised texts	Explanations	Information texts
	✓		✓	✓											
							✓		✓		✓				
	✓														
							✓		✓						
												✓		✓	
												✓		✓	
												✓		✓	
	✓		✓	✓											
			✓	✓											
									✓	✓	✓				
			✓												
							✓	✓	✓	✓					
												✓		✓	
													✓	✓	
													✓	✓	
	✓				✓										
						✓		✓		✓					
	✓														
					✓									✓	
														✓	
														✓	
														✓	

Contents

Writing Stories about Familiar Experiences (1)

In this story Emma and Tom take their dog for a walk in the park. Max is a naughty dog. He does not always do what he is told. What do you think happens?

When they got to the park, Emma bent down and stroked Max. "I am going to let you off your lead. Come when we call you," she said. Max licked her hand and wagged his tail.

As soon as Emma let Max go he shot off like a rocket. "Come back, Max!" Tom shouted, but Max did not come back. He kept running. Tom and Emma chased after him. Max ran behind the trees and over the bridge. Max ran past the swings, under the slide and through the flower bed. He stopped for a moment. Tom and Emma sneaked up behind Max. They tried to grab him, but Max jumped into the muddy pool with a splash.

Max enjoyed splashing about. Then he climbed out and ran back to the two children. When he got near to them he shook himself. Muddy water went all over them. Emma put the lead back on Max. "You naughty dog!" she said. Max hung his head and looked very sorry.

The two children and the dog set off for home. They were all dripping wet.

"What will Mum say when she sees us?" Emma asked. "Woof!" Max barked and wagged his muddy tail.

Thinking back

1 Who are the main characters in the story?
2 a) Where did the children take Max?
   b) Why did they take him there?
   c) What happened when Emma let Max off his lead?
   d) Make a list of the places where Max ran.
   e) What happened when the children tried to grab Max?
   f) What happened when Max came out of the water?
3 What do you think their Mum said when they got home?

Thinking about it

• Write a story about the day you took a dog for a walk.
• Use copymaster 1 to help you plan your story.

Thinking it through

Write a story about the day a pet got away.
– What pet was it? a dog? a rabbit? something else?
– Where did it escape from? home? school? somewhere else?
– How did it escape?
– What happened when you try to catch it?
– How did it all end? Did you manage to catch it? How?

Stepping Stones to help you

Characters
• Who will be in your story?
Setting
• Where will it take place?
Main events
• What happens at the beginning? in the middle? at the end?
(Use Copymaster A to help you.)

Writing Poetry (1)

Some poems are really like lists. What is this poem a list of?

My Pet Dinosaur

My pet dinosaur
Was getting thinner
And so I brought
Him home for dinner.

He ate as fast
As he was able;
He ate the food,
He ate the table.

He ate the fridge,
He ate the chair,
He ate my favourite
Teddy bear.

He is a very
Naughty pet.
He even ate
The TV set.

by Charles Thomson

Thinking back

1 What is the title of the poem?
2 a) How many verses does the poem have?
  b) How many lines are there in each verse?
3 Make a list of the things the dinosaur ate.
4 Do you think it is a funny or serious poem? Why?
5 Write what you thought of the poem. Give your reasons.

Thinking about it

1 What sort of pets do you think each of these people has?
  Make them rhyme!
  a) Mrs Pratt (has a cat)   b) Mr Trogg   c) Benjamin Blake
  d) Mrs Grouse   e) Carrie Carrot   f) Little Bo Peep
  g) Mrs Gorse   h) Gerald Groat   i) Uncle Ben
2 Make up rhyming sentences about each one, like this:
  Fancy that! Mrs Pratt has a cat.

Thinking it through

1 a) Copy this and finish the line with a suitable word.
    One little monkey swinging on a tree.
    Two little monkeys splashing in the _____ .
  b) Continue the poem up to ten.
2 For more list poems see copymaster 2.

Stepping Stones to help you

• Write your ideas down in rough first.
• Change them if you want to.
• Choose your best ideas.
• When you are happy, make a best copy.
(Use copymaster B to help you.)

Writing Stories about Familiar Experiences (2)

Have you ever been frustrated when you try to do something and you can't? What can we learn from the story?

"I'll try to draw a shipwreck," Mark said, "With a storm and raging waves."

But though he tried, and tried, and tried, it wouldn't come right. It was stiff – and it was dull!

"Oh," said Mark. And he tore the drawing up. "Oh," cried Mark. And he jumped on it. "Oh! Oh! Oh!" shouted Mark in a fury. And he ran out of the room and out of the house away into the garden. And he lay on his stomach under a bush.

"Whoosh!" said the wind. "I can help you! It's no good shouting and stamping, though; that's no way to learn. Now watch closely." And the wind began to blow.

The trees were blowing wildly and excitedly – bending, curving, swaying in the wind. The leaves were tossing and quivering all together – the clouds were drifting and racing in the sky. The flowers were nodding and shaking all their petals – seeds were floating everywhere and the grass was bending flat.

Mark ran to the water and he noticed how it rippled and flowed and splashed and raced with the movement of the wind.

"I'm a whirlwind!" cried the wind. "A tearing huge tornado! I'm a gale, a gust, a summer breeze! I'm very restless, changing, moving. And that's what you need in your pictures! MOVEMENT! The movement of the wind! Now, go home and try!"

Mark ran all the way back to his house, seized the paper and pencil, and drew ... and it was better!

From *Mark and his pictures* by Carol Odell

Thinking back

1 Who is the main character in the story?
2 What is his problem?
3 a) How does Mark behave when he fails to do
   what he wants?   b) What does he do?
4 a) Who helps Mark to solve his problem?   b) How?

Thinking about it

Instead of trying to draw a windy picture, imagine Mark
tried to draw either:
a)   a rainy picture *or*   b) a sunny picture.
Use the questions in the 'Thinking back' section to help you
write your story. (Use copymaster 3 to help you.)

Thinking it through

Write about a time when you started to learn a new skill.
Here are some ideas:
    cooking, swimming, whistling, reading, riding a bike.
– What did you find difficult?
– What did you do? What did you say? How did you feel?
– Who helped you overcome your problems?
– What happened in the end? How did you feel?

Stepping Stones to help you

• Check that your sentences make sense.
• Check that you have punctuated your sentences correctly.
• Check that there are no silly spelling mistakes.
• Check that your work is presented clearly.
(Use copymaster C.)

Writing Poetry (2)

Think ahead

*What do you notice about the lines in **bold** in this poem?*

Happy Birthday!

Wake up. Open my eyes.
It's a special day today.
Get out of bed. Yawn and stretch.
The postman's on his way.

Get dressed. Have a wash.
It's a special day today.
Clean my teeth. Brush my hair.
The postman's on his way.

Run downstairs. Pat the dog.
It's a special day today.
Stroke the cat. Feed the fish.
The postman's on his way.

Someone's knocking at the door.
It's a special day today.
Who's there? Let me see!
The postman's come my way!

Thinking back

1 a) What is the poem's title?
  b) Is this a good title? Why?
2 What is the poem all about?
3 a) How many verses does it have?
  b) How many lines are there in each verse?
4 Did you like the end of the poem? Give your reasons.
5 Write what you thought of the poem. Give your reasons.

Thinking about it

Copy the poem, but change the lines in **bold** like this:
  Get dressed. Have a wash.
  It's a holiday today.
  Clean my teeth. Brush my hair.
  My friends are on their way.

Thinking it through

1 Copy this verse about what you do after school. Make up
  two more verses. Repeat the lines in **bold**.
    School has finished. Run home fast.
    It's time to have some fun.
    Do my homework. Play with friends.
    The day will soon be done.
2 For more ideas see copymaster 4.

Writing Instructions

Think ahead

In the instructions below, how do the numbers and the diagrams help you?

Aim: to make a paper aeroplane.

What you need:

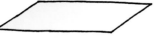  

• a sheet of A4 paper   • a pair of scissors   • some coloured pencils

What you do:

  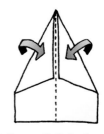

1 Fold the sheet of paper in half. Then unfold it.

2 Fold the two top corners into the middle.

3 Now fold them to the middle again (as shown).

 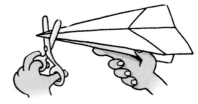

4 After this, fold along the middle.

5 Then fold the two flaps to make wings.

6 Cut off the point (so it can't go in anyone's eyes when you fly it).

 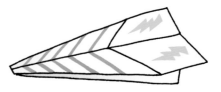

7 Decorate your aeroplane.

Thinking back

1 What are the instructions opposite for?
2 What do you need in order to follow them?
3 How many steps are there in the 'What you do' section?
4 Why do you think the steps are numbered?
5 How do the diagrams help you?

 Thinking about it

Write the instructions for having a bath in the correct order.
– Get in the bath
– Dry yourself on a towel
– Step out of the bath
– Put the plug in the plug hole
– Wash yourself thoroughly
– Fill the bath with warm water

 Thinking it through

1 Write some simple instructions for something you have made recently in school. Use the headings and layout of the instructions opposite to help you.
2 For more work on following and writing instructions, see copymaster 5.

Stepping Stones to help you

• Write the aim first.
• Next write what is needed.
• Then write clear steps on what you have to do.
(Use copymaster D.)

UNIT 6　Giving Directions

Think ahead

Why is it important to give directions clearly and carefully, and not to miss out any details?

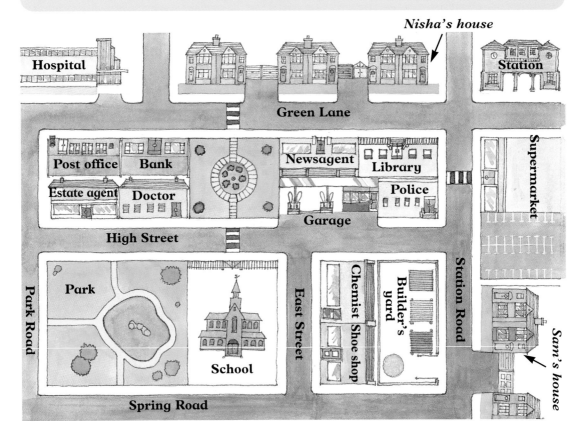

Nisha's mum takes her to school by car.
Nisha wrote down the directions.
Follow them and check they are correct.

- Turn right from my house along Green Lane.
- Go to the hospital and take the first turning on the left, up Park Road.
- When you come to the High Street turn left.
- Keep going along the High Street.
- You will pass the park on your right.
- The school is on the right-hand side, next to the park.

14

Thinking back

1 Where does Nisha live?
2 Name three things you will find along Green Lane.
3 Where does Sam live?
4 Where will you find: a) a chemist?   b) the station?
5 How many zebra crossings are there?
6 What is next to: a) the estate agents?   b) the park?

Thinking about it

1 Sometimes Nisha walks to school with her mum.
  Describe the safest way for them to go.
2 Write two ways Sam's dad could drive him to school.
3 Describe the safest way for Sam to walk to school?

Thinking it through

1 Use the map opposite to help you write some directions to
  other places. Give them to a friend to check.
2 Write directions for getting from your classroom to:
  a) the Head Teacher's room   b) the hall.
3 Write directions for getting to school from your house.
4 For more work on directions, see copymaster 6.

Stepping Stones to help you

- Begin by saying where the directions start from.
- Make it clear which direction to go in – turn right, go
  straight ahead, and so on.
- Don't miss out important details.
- Show or draw a map if possible.
(Use copymaster E.)

Writing Instructions (2)

Think ahead

What playground games do you like playing? What makes the instructions for the playground game below easy to follow?

These instructions tell you how to play a game called 'Drop the Jumper'.

What you need:
• eight or more players
• a jumper

Aim:
• to run faster than your opponent!

What you do:
1 Choose someone to be *IT*.
2 All the others stand in a circle, facing inwards.
3 *IT* walks round the outside of the circle, behind the others.

4 *IT* drops the jumper behind one person.
5 As soon as the jumper is dropped, *IT* runs quickly round the circle.
6 Whoever turns round and finds the jumper behind them, runs quickly round the circle in the *opposite* direction.
7 The one who gets back to the empty space first and picks up the jumper is the winner.

8 The loser now becomes *IT*, and the game continues.

Thinking back

1 a) What is the game called?
  b) Where is it usually played?
2 a) What is the aim of the game?
  b) What do you need to play it?
3 Why do you think you need at least eight players to play?
4 What is the first thing you need to do?
5 How is the game won?

Thinking about it

Make up instructions for a new playground game called 'Touch and Run'. Copy the instructions opposite and change the wording where you need to.
Instead of dropping a jumper behind someone, *IT* has to touch someone on the back and run. The person who is touched has to run in the opposite direction around the circle and try to get back to the empty space before *IT*.

Thinking it through

1 Write instructions for another playground game, such as 'Hopscotch'. Use copymaster 7 to help you.
2 Write instructions for a board game, such as 'Snakes and Ladders'.

Stepping Stones to help you

• Write the aim first.
• Next write what is needed.
• Then write clear steps on what you have to do.
(Use copymaster D.)

Story Settings (1)

Think ahead

All stories have a 'setting' – where the story takes place.
What is the setting of this story?

It's just a little garden. The peas and carrots and tomatoes grow in slightly crooked rows but the petunias around the edge have plenty of room to bloom pink and the marigolds marching down the middle almost make it look like two gardens.

Whose garden is it?

The wriggly brown earthworm thinks it's his garden because he lives there. He wriggles his way through the rich black earth, leaving it richer and softer.

Whose garden is it?

The yellow butterfly spends hours flitting among the marigolds. Sometimes it's hard to tell which is flower and which is butterfly. He is sure the garden belongs to him.

Whose garden is it?

The ladybird decided this was the perfect garden in which to raise her family. Now she has lots of little ladybird babies and she teaches them to look after the garden.

Whose garden is it?

From *Whose Garden* by Marilyn Kratz

Thinking back

1 Copy and complete these sentences about the garden.
   a) It is just a _____ garden.
   b) Around the edge of the garden there are some _____ .
   c) Down the middle of the garden there are some _____ .
2 Name some insects that you might find in the garden.
3 Write why each of these thinks the garden belongs to them:
   a) the earthworm   b) the butterfly   c) the ladybird.
4 Whose garden do you think it is? Give your reasons.

Thinking about it

The earthworm might say, "I love my garden. I love to wriggle around in the rich black earth, making tunnels." Write some things each of these might say about the garden: a) the butterfly   b) the ladybird.

Thinking it through

1 Here are some others who believe that the garden belongs to them: a) the bumble bee   b) the sun   c) the rain. Write some reasons why each one believes the garden is theirs. Then write some things each one might say.
2 For more work on writing about settings, see copymaster 8.

Stepping Stones to help you

• Try to picture the setting in your mind.
• Think about some things you see, hear, smell and feel.
• Use interesting words to make the description 'come alive'.
(See copymaster F.)

UNIT 9   Writing about Characters

Think ahead

Who are the three main characters in this traditional story from China?

Chen Ping was a poor boy. He lived in China. Chen was hard-working and honest. His master was lazy and greedy.

One day his master said, "Go into the forest and chop some wood." As he crossed the bridge over the river, he tripped, and his axe fell into the water. He began to cry.

Suddenly an old man with a long white beard appeared.

"Don't worry. I'll get your axe for you," said the old man. Then he jumped in the river and held up an axe. "Is this your axe?" he asked.

Chen Ping looked at the axe. It was made of silver. "No," he said, "that isn't it."

The old man held up another axe. This one was made of gold. "No," he said, "that isn't it."

The old man held up a third axe. It was made of iron. "Yes," said Chen Ping. "That's my axe."

The old man smiled and gave Chen Ping the axe. "You are an honest boy," he said, and then disappeared.

When Chen Ping began to chop wood in the forest the axe spoke. It said, "Sit down. I'll chop the wood for you." The axe worked hard for him and it had soon chopped a pile of wood. Chen Ping picked up the wood, took it home and told his master about the old man.

"You stupid boy," his master said angrily. You should have taken the axe made of gold."

Thinking back

1 Copy and complete these sentences about the story.
  a) The story takes place in _____ .
  b) Chen Ping was an _____ boy.
  c) Chen Ping's master was _____ and _____ .
  d) The old man had a _____ _____ beard.
2 Why did Chen Ping's master say he was stupid?

Thinking about it

1 Who said: a) "You are an honest boy."
  b) "You stupid boy."   c) "I'll chop the wood for you." ?
2 Write an ending for the story. Think about what each of
  these characters might say and do:
  a) Chen Ping's master   b) the old man
  c) Chen Ping   d) the magic axe

Thinking it through

Choose one of the three main characters and write a
description of him.
  – Use the information from the story.
  – Use your imagination.
Copymaster 9 will help you write some notes.

Stepping Stones to help you

• When describing characters write about:
  – their appearance   – things they do and say
  – other interesting facts.
• Use good describing words.
(See copymaster G.)

Writing Poetry (3)

What is the title of the poem? What do you notice about each verse of the poem?

If I were King

I often wish I were a King,
And then I could do anything.

If only I were King of Spain,
I'd take my hat off in the rain.

If only I were King of France,
I wouldn't brush my hair for aunts.

I think, if I were King of Greece,
I'd push things off the mantelpiece.

If I were King of Norroway*,
I'd ask an elephant to stay.

If I were King of Babylon,
I'd leave my button gloves undone.

If I were King of anything,
I'd tell the soldiers, "I'm the King!"

'If I were King' from *When We Were Very Young* by A A Milne

*Norway

22

Thinking back

1 In what way is this poem all about wishes?
2 What pattern can you find in this poem? Write it.
3 Do you think it is a funny or serious poem? Why?
4 Write seven pairs of rhyming words from the poem.
5 Did you enjoy the poem? Give a reason for your answer.

Thinking about it

1 a) Choose six of these countries. Write them in a column.
     Poland; Russia; Ukraine; Chad; Sudan; Hong Kong;
     Japan; Kuwait; Oman; Singapore; Chile; Peru; Mexico.
   b) Think of words that rhyme with each country, like this:
     Poland – hand, band, banned, canned, sand, stand.
2 Try writing some verses of your own, like this:
     If only I were King (or Queen!) of Poland
     I'd order school to be banned.

Thinking it through

1 Make up some more verses of your own for this poem.
     If my name were Fred,
     I'd say, "Jump on the bed!"
2 For more work on writing poems, see copymaster 10.

(Stepping Stones to help you)

• Write your ideas down in rough first.
• Change them if you want to.
• Choose your best ideas.
• When you are happy, make a best copy.
(See copymaster B.)

UNIT 11   Story Settings (2)

Think ahead

The description of the setting for this story is very vivid. When you read it, what picture does it make you think of?

The sun had hardly risen and already it was stronger than anyone could bear. For months there had been no rain and the land was dry. If nothing happened soon, maybe even their hope would dry out.

The crops had long since been eaten and nothing would grow in the cracked soil of Medina. Before the famine, Medina was an oasis in the desert, a fresh and vibrant spot in a stretch of scorching sand as far as the eye could see.

Now shops were shut, stalls folded away and merchants long gone. The town that had once been bustling and noisy was deserted and eerie.

From beneath a canopy on the flat roof of her home, Laila's eye caught something tiny shimmering on the horizon. She leapt up with excitement, pointing and shrieking, "Look!"

Making its way over the sand dunes was a heavily laden camel caravan of Utman, a rich and well-respected business man who had been on a shopping expedition.

"We are saved!" shouted Laila's thrilled parents.

'What it's worth' from *Faith Stories for Today* by Angela Wood

Thinking back

1 Where does the story take place?
2 The story says that 'Medina was an oasis in the desert'.
   Write what you think: a) an oasis is   b) a desert is
3 What is the weather like?
4 What is the problem?
5 Look at the picture and describe:
   a) what the houses are like   b) how the people dress

Thinking about it

Write an ending for the story. Use copymaster 11 to help you
plan your ending. Here are some things to think about.
– How did the people feel when they saw Utman coming?
– What did the people do when they saw Utman coming?
– What was Utman bringing with him?
– What difference did the arrival of Utman make to the
  village in the end?

Thinking it through

1 We can learn a lot about Medina by reading the passage
  carefully. Draw a chart in your book. Write down all the
  things you can find out about Medina before the famine,
  and what the village was like during the famine.

Before famine	During famine
People were able to grow crops because they had water.	It was very hot. There had been no rain for months.

2 Use the notes from your chart to write a description of
  Medina before and after the famine.

Writing Poetry (4)

What do you notice about the way this poem is written?

The Sun Wakes Up

The sun wakes up
Yes, the sun wakes up.

The sun it smiles
Yes, the sun it smiles.

The wind it blows
Yes, the wind it blows.

The clouds come over
Yes, the clouds come over.

The rain falls down
Yes, the rain falls down.

The earth dries up
Yes, the earth dries up.

The sun lies down
Yes, the sun lies down.

The dark moves in
Yes, the dark moves in.

The moon looks up
Yes, the moon looks up.

The night lies still
Yes, the night lies still.

The sun wakes up
Yes, the sun wakes up.

From *The Sun Wakes Up* by John Rice

Thinking back

1 What is the title of this poem?
2 What do you notice about the second line of each verse?
3 In what ways is the poem a bit like a circle?
4 Did you like the poem? Give a reason for your answer.

Thinking about it

1 Make a list of things that you do regularly each day, such as: *I wake up*; *I get up*; *I have a wash*; and so on.
2 Choose eight of these things and turn them into a poem. Do it like this: *I wake up.*
                    Yes, I wake up.
(Remember to repeat the first verse at the end of your poem!)

Thinking it through

1 Make a list of things you see, hear, smell, touch or do at the seaside. Turn them into a poem, like this:
    Gulls in the air –
    The sea, the sea.
    I hear them squeal.
    The sea, the sea.
2 For more work on writing poetry, see copymaster 12.

Stepping Stones to help you

- Write your ideas down in rough first.
- Choose your best ideas.
- When you are happy, make a best copy.
(See copymaster B.)

Think ahead

As part of their topic on 'Transport', Shireen and Tom are making a dictionary. Unfortunately, they have put two things in the wrong order. Which ones are they?

I wrote the names of some types of transport in *alphabetical* order.

I wrote a *definition*, explaining each type of transport.

aeroplane

bicycle

canoe

dinghy

ferry

escalator

hang-glider

An *aeroplane* has an engine and wings and flies in the sky.

A *bicycle* is a two-wheeled vehicle, which you ride by pedalling with your feet.

A *canoe* is a light, narrow boat, which is moved with a paddle.

A *dinghy* is a small boat.

A *ferry* carries people and vehicles across a river or a stretch of water.

An *escalator* is a moving staircase.

A *hang-glider* uses the wind. It does not need an engine.

Thinking back

1 How are the words in a dictionary arranged?
2 What is a 'definition'?
3 Where should the word 'ferry' come in the dictionary?
4 Which word comes first? Why?
5 What is: a) a dinghy?   b) an escalator?

Thinking about it

1 Shireen and Tom have put the wrong definitions with each
  word. Match up the correct definition with each word.

ambulance   This carries goods on rivers and canals.
engine   This carries people up and down mountains.
barge   This is a type of fishing boat
drifter   This takes sick and injured people to hospital.
cable car   This is the part of a train that pulls the
            carriages.

2 Now arrange the words with their definitions in
  alphabetical order, as they would appear in a dictionary.

Thinking it through

1 Think of six other types of transport. Make up a definition
  to explain each one. (Use a dictionary to help if you need
  to.) Arrange the words with their definitions in alphabetical
  order.
2 For more work on dictionaries, see copymaster 13.

UNIT 14 Flow Diagrams

Think ahead

We sometimes use a 'flow diagram' to explain how something works. In the flow diagram below, how do you know where to begin? How do you know in which direction to go?

The story of our water

1. The water we use comes from lakes and rivers. (Much of this water comes from the rain.)

2. Water is collected from rivers and stored in huge artificial lakes called 'reservoirs'.

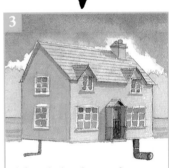

3. After it is cleaned, water comes from the reservoir into our homes through pipes under the ground.

4. Dirty water leaves our homes and goes into different pipes underground called 'sewer pipes'. These pipes take the water to the sewage works.

5. At the sewage works the dirty water is cleaned with chemicals.

6. The clean water is then put back into the rivers or lakes.

Thinking back

1 What is the title of the flow diagram?
2 Why is it helpful: a) to have the pictures numbered?
   b) to have arrows?
3 How helpful are the pictures?
4 What is a reservoir?
5 What happens at the sewage works?

Thinking about it

Here is a flow diagram of what Katie did yesterday – but it is in the wrong order. Set it out in the correct order. (Use copymaster 14 to help you.)

When I got home I had tea and watched TV.
↓
I had fish fingers for lunch.
↓
I went to school with my friend.
↓
In the morning we did English and maths.
↓
In the afternoon we had art.
↓
I had a bath and went to bed at 8 o'clock.

Thinking it through

Use a flow diagram to help you explain either:
a) how you wash your hair *or*
b) how to make a cup of tea.
(Use copymaster 14 to help you plan it and get all the steps in the correct order.)

Using Diagrams

Labels on pictures or diagrams can help explain things more clearly. How helpful are the labels on this picture?

Fighting fires

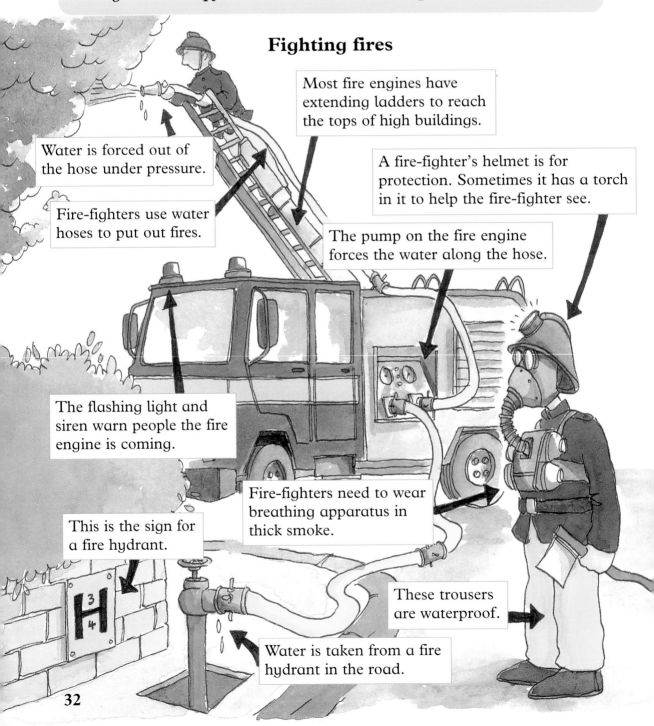

Most fire engines have extending ladders to reach the tops of high buildings.

Water is forced out of the hose under pressure.

A fire-fighter's helmet is for protection. Sometimes it has a torch in it to help the fire-fighter see.

Fire-fighters use water hoses to put out fires.

The pump on the fire engine forces the water along the hose.

The flashing light and siren warn people the fire engine is coming.

Fire-fighters need to wear breathing apparatus in thick smoke.

This is the sign for a fire hydrant.

These trousers are waterproof.

Water is taken from a fire hydrant in the road.

Thinking back

1 Why does a fire-fighter need: a) a helmet?
  b) breathing apparatus?
2 The fire-fighter is carrying an axe. Write a sentence explaining what you think it is used for.
3 Why does a fire engine have a siren and a flashing light?
4 Use the diagram to help you explain where the water comes from that fire-fighters use.
5 Look at the diagram and explain what you think 'extending' means.

Thinking about it

Use this description to help you draw an apple tree.
  The main part of a tree is the *trunk*. From the trunk *branches* grow. From each branch smaller branches grow called *twigs*. *Leaves* grow from the twigs. In summer, red and green *apples* grow from some twigs. Trees have *roots* which grow deep underground. These keep the tree firm and suck water from the soil to feed the tree.
Label these parts on your picture:

trunk	a branch	a twig
an apple	a root	a leaf

Thinking it through

1 Draw a picture of a bicycle. Label the handlebars, brakes, saddle, pedal, chain, wheel and tyre. Explain what each part is used for. (Use copymaster 15 to help you.)
2 Draw a picture of a car. Label five different parts of the car. Explain what each part is used for.

UNIT 16 Writing Longer Stories (1)

Think ahead

Can you work out who Mossop is in the story below?

Farmer Rafferty always liked to sing as he worked. He sang in a crusty, croaky kind of voice. That morning though, as old Farmer Rafferty went into the tumble-down barn to fetch corn from the corn bin, he suddenly stopped singing.

The animals crowded into the barn to find out what was the matter. They found Farmer Rafferty standing by the corn bin holding a mouse by its tail. "Have we, or have we not, got a cat on this farm?" said Farmer Rafferty in the nasty, raspy voice he kept for special occasions.

"We have," said Auntie Grace, the dreamy-eyed cow.

"Fetch him," ordered old Farmer Rafferty. "Fetch that Mossop here. I have a thing or two to say to him." But at that very same moment Mossop wandered into the barn, yawning hugely.

"MOSSOP! Everywhere I go these days there's mice or rats. There's mice in my barley sacks, there's rats in my roof and now there's mice in my corn bin. I've warned you before and this time I've had enough. If you aren't up to the job, you will have to go. That's all there is to it."

From *Mossop's Last Chance* by Michael Morpurgo and Shoo Rayner

Thinking back

1 Who are the two main characters in the story?
2 Where does the story take place?
3 Is Farmer Rafferty usually in a good mood?
4 What problem has made him angry?
5 a) Who is he angry with?   b) Why is he angry with him?

Thinking about it

1 What is Mossop like? Think about these things.
  – Who is he? What is his job?
  – What does he look like?
  – What sort of things does he like to do?
2 Stories often contain 'dialogue' (things people say).
  This makes them more interesting.
  a) Write something Farmer Rafferty said.
  b) Write something he might say when he is happy.

Thinking it through

1 Write an interesting end to your story. Here are some ideas
  to help you.
  – What does Mossop say to Farmer Rafferty?
  – What does Mossop do?
  – How does he get rid of the mice?
  – What sort of problems does he meet?
  – How does it all end?
  – What does the farmer say and do?
2 For more work on writing a longer story, see copymaster 16.

UNIT 17 Playing with Words

Think ahead

We can have lots of fun, playing with words.
Which of these do you like the best? Why?

1 A tongue twister

The rain comes pittering pattering down,
Plipperty, plipperty plop!
The farmer drives his horse to town,
Clipperty, clipperty clop!
The rain comes pattering
Horse goes clattering,
Clipperty, plipperty, plop!!

2 Some jokes

What kind of dog has no tail?
  A hot dog!
What falls but never gets hurt?
  Rain!
What do you call a gorilla
who never changes his socks?
  King Pong!
What do gorillas use to wash
dishes?
  Hairy Liquid!

3 A nonsense rhyme

Have you ever seen
  a blue frog?
Have you ever seen
  a flying dog?
Have you ever seen
  a walking fish?
Have you ever seen
  a singing dish?
Have you ever seen
  a monkey swimming?
Have you ever seen
  a tortoise grinning?

4 A riddle

You can feel me, but you
can't touch me or see me.
I am very strong. What am I?

Answer to riddle: the wind.

Thinking back

1 Write the words from number 1 beginning with 'p' and 'c'.
2 Which joke did you like best?
3 Why do you think number 3 is called 'A nonsense rhyme'?
4 Try and explain what a riddle is.

Thinking about it

1 Copy this tongue twister and underline all the 'b's in it:
   If Billy Button bought a buttered biscuit, where's the
   buttered biscuit Billy Button bought?
2 Write a tongue twister you know, or make one up.
3 Write a joke you know and draw a picture to go with it.
4 Write a riddle of your own. Give it to a friend to solve.

Thinking it through

1 Copy this nonsense rhyme. Fill in the gaps with suitable
  words. Add four more lines of your own.
   Have you ever seen a running snail?
   Have you ever seen a _____ whale?
   Have you ever seen a _____ hopping?
   Have you ever seen a giraffe _____ ?
2 For more work on nonsense rhymes, see copymaster 17.

Stepping Stones to help you

- Write your ideas down in rough first.
- Change them if you want to.
- Choose your best ideas.
- When you are happy, make a best copy.
(See copymaster B.)

Writing Longer Stories (2)

One of the main characters in this story is Henry.
How old do you think he is?

Henry picked up the parcel from the sideboard and read the address again. 'Henry Timms, 7 Goldthorpe Avenue.' The present was a parcel from Aunt Georgiana. She was such fun and she always sent him amazing birthday presents. Last year it had been a skateboard, with its own wind-up motor, and the year before that a personal stereo that recorded as well. He'd been able to tape his friend's conversations without them even knowing. So what fantastic present had she bought him this year? It was so small and it didn't even rattle.

"Henry!"

Henry dropped the parcel with a thud. He and his mum stared in horror.

"Oh Henry!" she said.

Henry gently picked it up. "It probably wasn't breakable," he said to his mum.

Henry frowned. If he'd broken Aunt Georgiana's present he'd never forgive himself. "Shouldn't we open it to check?" he asked.

"No!" said his mum, smiling. "Try whatever tricks you like, but you are not opening that present until your birthday."

So there it sat, taunting him.

From *Some Birthday Present* by Elizabeth Dale

Thinking back

1 Who are the two main characters in the story?
2 Where does the story take place?
3 What do you think would be a good title for the story?
4 What does Henry want to do?
5 Why won't Henry's mum let him open the present?

Thinking about it

What do you think Henry is like?
- What does he look like?
- What sort of a boy do you think he is?
- What sort of things does he like to do?

Thinking it through

1 Make up a good beginning and ending to the story.
Here are some ideas to help you.

Beginning
Why is Henry getting excited? What is he thinking about? What does he say to his mum? Does the parcel come while Henry is at home or at school? Where does his mum put the parcel?

Ending
Does Henry try to look in the parcel again? When does Henry find out what's in it? What is it? How does Henry react? Is he happy? disappointed? What does his mum say and do?

2 For more work on writing a longer story, see copymaster 18.

Writing about Books

When you have read a book you have enjoyed it is helpful to tell others about it. What do you think of Tahmina's book review?

Book Review by _____Tahmina_____
Title   Master Salt the Sailor's Son
Author   Allan Ahlberg

Favourite character
My favourite character is Mr Salt, because he leads an exciting life as a sailor, and has lots of adventures.

Mr Salt

What the book is about
The book is about Mr Salt the sailor, Mrs Salt his wife, Sally Salt his daughter and little Sammy Salt his son. Mr Salt thinks Sammy is too young to go to sea. One day Sammy sneaks on board without anyone knowing. The story is about the adventures the family have.

Favourite part of the book
My favourite part of the story is when Mr and Mrs Salt and Sally Salt fall overboard and Sammy saves them.

Opinion of the book
I really enjoyed the book. I thought it was exciting and funny.

Star rating (Colour how many stars you would give the book.)

Thinking back

1 a) What is the title of the book?   b) Who is the author?
2 Name two characters from the book.
3 Where does the story take place?
4 What happens in the book?

Thinking about it

Write a review of a book you have read and enjoyed recently.
Give your review to a friend to read. (See copymaster 19.)

Thinking it through

1 Make up your own front cover for a book you have read.
  Remember to include the title and name of the author.
  Include a colourful picture about something in the book.
2 Use the Stepping Stones below and make up your own
  book review.

Stepping Stones to help you

- Give the title and author.
- Give your opinion of some of the characters.
- Say where the story is set.
- Describe something that happens.
- Say what you think of the book and the way the author
  has written it.

(See copymaster H.)

Writing a Report

Mrs Lee asked Erica to write a report on polar bears.
How well has Erica kept to what she was asked to do?

Where do polar bears live?
Describe what they are like.
What do they eat?
Find out something else of interest about them.

Polar bears

Where they live
Polar bears live in the Arctic where it is very cold and icy.

What they are like
Polar bears are large animals (twice as big as tigers) and are very strong. They have thick, warm fur which helps to keep out the cold. Their fur is white which makes them difficult to see against the snow.

What they eat
Polar bears are good hunters and eat mainly seals. The bear waits by the seal's breathing hole in the ice until it comes up for air. When it does, the bear then gives the seal a blow with its powerful paw to kill it.

Some interesting facts about them
Although the bears spend much of their time on land they are very good swimmers. Their toes are partly webbed to help them swim well.

Thinking back

1 Use Erica's report to answer these questions.
   a) Where do polar bears live?   b) What do they eat?
2 What did you find most interesting about polar bears?
3 What do you notice about the way Erica set out her report?

Thinking about it

1 Write a report on walruses. Use the same headings as Erica.
   Walruses can grow up to four metres long.
   Walruses live along the coasts of the Arctic Ocean.
   They hunt for food on the seabed.
   They have small eyes and can't see very well.
   Walruses have two long tusks, which are long teeth.
   Sometimes they sleep in the sea and hook themselves
   onto the ice with their tusks.
   They eat clams, crabs and sea urchins.
2 For more work on writing reports, see copymaster 20.

Thinking it through

Choose any animal you wish. Use Mrs Lee's questions.
Find out some information about your animal. Write a
report. Set it out like Erica.

Stepping Stones to help you

- Write notes on all you know, or can find out, about the
  subject.
- Organise your notes under suitable headings.
- Write a few sentences for each heading.
(See copymaster I.)

UNIT 21 Writing Notes

Think ahead

When we write notes we only write down the most important words. Can you think of times when we could use notes?

Here are some notes that Samir wrote after reading some information on wild cats that live in rainforests. What do you notice about the notes?

Rainforest cats
1 wild cats – good eyesight – hearing – sense of smell
2 move very quietly
3 sleep during day – hunt at night
4 hard to spot – markings on coats help to
   camouflage them

Here is the information from which Samir made his notes. What has he done?

Rainforest Cats
1 <u>Wild cats</u> have <u>good eyesight</u> and <u>hearing</u> and a keen <u>sense of smell</u>.
2 They can <u>move very quietly</u> through the rainforest, without making a noise.
3 They <u>sleep</u> a lot <u>during</u> the <u>day</u> and <u>hunt</u> when it gets cool <u>at night</u>.
4 In spite of their size, wild cats are always <u>hard to spot</u> because the <u>markings on</u> their <u>coats help to camouflage them</u> (help them blend into the background).

Thinking back

1 Make these notes into a proper sentence.
  wild cats – good eyesight – hearing – sense of smell
2 Copy this sentence.
   Wild cats sleep a lot during the day and hunt when
   it gets cool at night.
   a) Underline the important words in it.
   b) Now write some notes on the sentence.

Thinking about it

1 Copy these sentences about a tiger. Underline the most
  important words in each sentence. Then write some notes
  on each sentence. (The first one is done for you.)
  a) A <u>tiger</u> is the <u>largest</u> and <u>strongest wild cat</u> in the world.
     tiger – largest – strongest wild cat
  b) The tiger is also the only wild cat with a striped coat.
  c) A tiger does not live in a group but lives on its own.
2 Write out this passage in note form.
  An <u>ocelot</u> is a <u>good climber</u> and <u>spends</u> a <u>lot of time</u> above
  ground, <u>sleeping in trees</u>. It <u>prefers to hunt</u> for its food <u>on</u>
  <u>the ground</u>. The <u>markings</u> on the ocelots' <u>coats vary</u>.

Thinking it through

1 Copy this passage about jaguars. Underline the most
  important words. Then write notes on it.
   A jaguar likes the water and will often live close to a
   river. A jaguar is a good swimmer. It catches fish and
   turtles in the water. Young jaguars stay with their mother
   for up to two years, while she teaches them to hunt.
2 For more work on writing notes, see copymaster 21.

Writing an Information Text

What makes the information on this page clear and easy to read?

Cereals

Introduction

Many of the cereals we eat come from the seeds or grains of different types of grasses. These are used to make a lot of the food that is eaten every day.

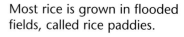

Most rice is grown in flooded fields, called rice paddies.

An ear of wheat

Wheat

Wheat is grown all over the world. It is ground into flour and is used for making bread. Pasta and noodles are also made from wheat flour.

Oats

Oats grow in countries where the weather is cool. They are often eaten in the form of porridge.

Rye

This grows in cold countries where other cereals will not grow. It is made into heavy, dark bread.

Maize

There are two types of maize. One type produces juicy corn on the cob. The other type is more starchy and dry and can be ground into flour. In South America it is made into a flat bread like a pancake, called a tortilla.

Rice

Rice grows best in warmer countries. Over half the people in the world eat rice at every meal. Enormous amounts of rice are eaten in India and China and throughout the rest of Asia.

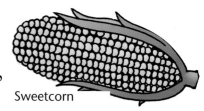

Sweetcorn

Thinking back

1 What is the title of the passage?
2 a) How many different sections is the passage divided into?
　b) List the headings of the sections.
　c) How can you tell when a new section begins?
3 Why do you think pictures are included?

Thinking about it

1 Write some information about fruit and vegetables. (Use copymaster 22 to help you.) Copy the introduction to start your piece of work.

　All fruit and vegetables come from plants. Fruit and vegetables contain vitamins, minerals and fibre which are important for keeping us healthy.

2 Sort this information into two sections.

　We eat many parts of vegetable plants.
　Different types of fruit can be found all over the world.
　We eat the leaves of some vegetables like cabbages.
　We eat root vegetables such as carrots.
　Many fruits contain seeds or pips.
　Fruit can be eaten raw, cooked or dried.

Thinking it through

Write an information text on either:
a) cats and dogs or
b) air and water transport.
Include an introduction, and two sections, each with its own heading. Also include some pictures with captions.

Paint Shop Pro® 9: Photographers' Guide

Diane Koers

THOMSON

COURSE TECHNOLOGY

Professional ■ Trade ■ Reference

SVP, Thomson Course Technology PTR: Andy Shafran

Publisher/Acquisitions Editor: Stacy L. Hiquet

Senior Marketing Manager: Sarah O'Donnell

Marketing Manager: Heather Hurley

Manager of Editorial Services: Heather Talbot

Associate Marketing Manager: Kristin Eisenzopf

Marketing Coordinator: Jordan Casey

Project Editor/Copy Editor: Marta Justak

Technical Reviewer: Sonja Shea

PTR Editorial Services Coordinator: Elizabeth Furbish

Interior Layout Tech: Bill Hartman

Cover Designer: Mike Tanamachi

Indexer: Katherine Stimson

Proofreader: Gene Redding

ISBN: 1-59200-661-2

Library of Congress Catalog Card Number: 2004114409

Printed in the United States of America

04 05 06 07 08 BU 10 9 8 7 6 5 4 3 2 1

THOMSON

COURSE TECHNOLOGY

Professional ■ Trade ■ Reference

Thomson Course Technology PTR, a division of Thomson Course Technology
25 Thomson Place ■ Boston, MA 02210 ■ http://www.courseptr.com

Dedication

To James Hutchinson

James, without your talent, guidance, friendship, and photographs, this book would never have come into its existence. Thank you.

You can see more of James Hutchinson's work at http://www.pbase.com/myeyesview or http://www.myeyesviewstudio.com/ and if you are ever in the Cedaredge, Colorado area, you can see his work in print at both the aGalleria and the Apple Shed Arts Complex.

Acknowledgments

In a book such as this one, it's hard to know where to start. There are so many people working behind the scenes, each one as valuable as the next. First, I'd like to thank Stacy Hiquet for believing in me enough to let me write this book. To Marta Justak, whose patience and sense of humor (not to mention her wonderful grammatical skills) kept me going through the process. To Sonja Shea, also known as Bonesy (www.psptoybox.com), who once again, used her incredible knowledge of Paint Shop Pro to keep me on track. To Brian McDonald and Peter Mayer for their assistance in keeping Sonja on track! To Bill Hartman, for exercising all his layout talents in making this a beautiful book. To Katherine Stimson, Mike Tanamachi, Gene Redding, and all the others working madly behind the scenes to get this book into print. To all of you, thank you from the bottom of my heart.

A special note of gratitude also goes to all the nice people at Jasc Software, especially Nancy Peterson, Gregory Beltz, and ElShaddai Edwards, who rushed to answer all my pesky e-mails.

Thanks to David Busch, who originated this series, for his help on Chapter 7. David has written a number of similar books, including *Photoshop 7: Photographers' Guide, Adobe Photoshop CS: Photographers' Guide, Adobe Photoshop Elements 3.0: Photographers' Guide, Digital Retouching and Compositing: Photographers' Guide.*

There were a number of people who provided the photographs you see in this book. It was often difficult for all of them because I frequently needed "less than perfect" images to work with. When you're a professional photographer, "less than perfect" sometimes is easier said than done. A special thank you to all photograph contributors:

James Hutchinson
Gary French
Tim Koers
JP Kabala
Patti Wavinak
Antonio Soberon

And finally, a huge thanks goes to my husband of 36 years. Vern, thank you for your patience and understanding of the late night hours, for fending for yourself or both of us at suppertime, and for keeping me encouraged and supplied with Diet Coke and working chocolate. I love you.

About the Author

Diane Koers owns and operates All Business Service, a software training and consulting business formed in 1988 that services the central Indiana area. Her area of expertise has long been in the word-processing, spreadsheet, and graphics areas of computing, as well as providing training and support for Peachtree Accounting Software. Diane's authoring experience includes over 30 books on topics such as PC Security, Microsoft Windows, Microsoft Office, Microsoft Works, WordPerfect, Paint Shop Pro, Lotus SmartSuite, Quicken, Microsoft Money, and Peachtree Accounting, many of which have been translated into other languages, such as Dutch, Bulgarian, Spanish, and Greek. She has also developed and written numerous training manuals for her clients.

Diane and her husband enjoy spending their free time traveling and playing with her grandsons and her Yorkshire Terriers.

Contents

Introduction

Designed for any photographer, professional or amateur, this book came into existence to show you how you can put the incredible power of Paint Shop Pro into play with your images. Whether you use a film or digital camera, you'll find instructions, tips, and tricks designed around you, the photographer.

This book cuts right to the chase of the Paint Shop Pro tools that are best used when working with photographs. You won't learn much about creating Web graphics here, although that is also certainly a strong feature of Paint Shop Pro. You will learn about photographs and how to correct and enhance them, making them better than they appeared out of your camera. There's even a chapter dedicated just to color and understanding how it works.

You'll learn about using layers to make adjustments, such as brightness, hue, color contrast, and many others. This book covers the often misunderstood topic of resolution and how it applies to your monitor, your images, and your prints.

It's not all work, though. You'll learn about many of the fun things you can do with your photographs, such as putting digital picture frames around them or creating digital scrapbook pages with them. Discover how you can make composite images, retouch, and repair damaged photographs and how you can create works of art with the special effects provided with Paint Shop Pro.

The best way to absorb a feature is to jump in and try it. Taste is relative. What you like about an image may be completely different than the person next to you. We are confident that as you make your way through this book, you will gain a good feel for the awesome power of Paint Shop Pro.

Assumptions

We make a couple of assumptions about our readers in this book. First of all, and most obviously, since you're reading this right now, we assume that you want to know more. Okay, we are going to try and fill you with knowledge. Secondly, we assume that you have certain skills with your camera and understand basic photography terms. And we assume that you know the basics of working with a computer, such as using the mouse, making menu selections, and opening, saving, and closing a file. If you know those basics, you can find your way around Paint Shop Pro.

Book Structure

This book contains 10 chapters, two appendices, and a glossary:

- **Chapter 1—Digital Imaging Basics.** We all have to start somewhere, so this chapter acquaints you with the basic Paint Shop Pro tools and how to use them. You'll also discover a few photography tips, generously provided by the professionals.

- **Chapter 2—Quick Fixes.** In a hurry and don't have a lot of time to spend correcting your image? In this chapter, you will learn how Paint Shop Pro can do many image corrections, mostly with a single click of the mouse.

- **Chapter 3—Retouching Tools.** In Chapter 3, we'll show you how to fix scratches, dust, red-eye, and image distortion. We'll show you how to correct lighting issues and use the numerous Paint Shop Pro retouch brushes.

- **Chapter 4—Selecting and Layering.** Selections, layers, and blending modes are what you'll discover in Chapter 4.

- **Chapter 5—Compositing.** Learn how you can combine all or part of multiple images together to create new images.

- **Chapter 6—Special Effects.** Allow yourself to go crazy experimenting with this chapter by applying the many different special effects included with Paint Shop Pro.

- **Chapter 7—More About Color.** In this chapter, you'll learn about color models and how color is perceived by the human eye and by a computer.

- **Chapter 8—Digital Scrapbooking.** Chapter 8 illustrates some of the fun things you can do with your images after you've enhanced them and don't know what else to do with them.

- **Chapter 9—Special Projects.** This chapter covers some of the time-saving features in Paint Shop Pro and also explains working with RAW image files.

- **Chapter 10— Resolutions, Resizing, and Printing.** This is the chapter where you'll uncover the secrets behind the horribly misunderstood topic of resolution.

- **Appendix A—Paint Shop Pro Web Links.** This appendix lists pages and pages of (hopefully) helpful links to Paint Shop Pro related items, including tutorials, fonts, and lots of free stuff.

- **Appendix B—Keyboard Shortcuts.** If you are a keyboard person and like shortcuts, this appendix lists all of the Paint Shop Pro keyboard shortcuts.

- **Glossary.** This expansive glossary lists many of the terms used in this book and how they relate to photography and Paint Shop Pro.

Throughout the book, we've also included various tips, notes, and warnings that are designed to alert you to special considerations.

Download Sample Images

If you'd like to follow along with the examples we've used in this book, the images are available online at www.courseptr.com/downloads. Locate the downloads by entering Paint Shop Pro or Diane Koers in the search book. Each file is listed separately by the chapter name and the image description. For example, in Chapter 6, we add a motion blur to a red car, so the downloadable image is called *CH06-red car*.

Corel Acquires Jasc

Just days before this book went to press, Jasc Software was acquired by Corel Corporation. Corel promises to actively support new initiatives for the Paint Shop products and pledges that they will continue to provide worldwide service and support to customers under the Corel brand. The combination of the two firms should deliver a powerful software portfolio for consumers and businesses seeking a proven digital photography solution at a competitive price.

In the words of Mr. Robert Voit, founder and former owner of Jasc Software Inc., "I believe that this acquisition will give Jasc the opportunity to continue to provide new and improved products along with being able to serve a greater range of international markets and business graphics users."

Only time will tell the result of this merger, but it's an exciting time for Paint Shop Pro and its users.

Contacting the Author

I am a teacher and a writer, a computer geek, and a Paint Shop Pro enthusiast. With those tools and a lot of help and research, I have written this book with the intention of helping you get the most you can out of Paint Shop Pro. I hope you enjoy learning from it as much as I enjoyed writing it.

If you have any comments about this book, please feel free to contact me at diane@thepeachtreelady.com.

May God bless all of you.
Diane

1

Digital Imaging Basics

This is a great time to enjoy digital imaging. Whether you're a professional photographer or a novice who wants to take family vacation shots, digital photography has changed our lives, and we are all finding it's more enjoyable than ever. With digital cameras you get instant feedback on the photo you just took, and often, if the picture isn't right, you can take another one that hopefully is better. However, even the best of shots sometimes need a little adjusting. Enter your computer and Paint Shop Pro, an award-winning image editing software.

Until recently, photographers had to use scientific processes when developing photographs, making sure that the images received the correct chemical exposure and timing. It was messy, expensive, time consuming, and very tricky to achieve just the right effect on each and every photograph. With today's digital imaging tools, however, you can transfer your photographic skills and knowledge to the digital palette and develop your photos with software, instead of gloves, developer, and other solvents.

Paint Shop Pro tools are priceless for fine-tuning digital photographs, whether they are images you took with your digital camera or scanned images you want to enhance from your film camera. Paint Shop Pro is also a huge favorite with graphic artists who work with a digitized canvas and other drawing platforms. But this book is about photographs: perfect photographs and not-so-perfect photographs. You, as a photographer, have at your fingertips the tools to enhance, edit, color tune, and totally manipulate your images, making them the best ever. Think of Paint Shop Pro as your Swiss Army Knife for photographs.

This chapter will provide some tips for photographing with your digital camera and getting acquainted with the basic Paint Shop Pro tools. Understanding how to get around in Paint Shop Pro will make editing your photographs faster and easier.

Taking Better Digital Photographs

If you buy the very best digital camera available, will you take better photographs? Not necessarily. Certainly having a decent camera affects the outcome of the image, but more importantly, it's your photography skills that count the most. There are lots and lots of books and classes available to teach you to shoot better pictures. This book is mainly about what you can do with those photos after you have taken them. I do, however, include a couple of quick tips, graciously shared with me by professionals.

All digital cameras have certain basic features, while more advanced ones (usually the more expensive ones) may have a plethora of additional features. Consult your user manual for instructions on using your specific camera. Which leads me into my first topic.

Read the Manual

Shooting fireworks with a digital camera can be a real challenge since the light dissipates quickly, making it difficult to capture fireworks in their brilliance. When I bought my first digital camera, the salesperson told me it had a setting for fireworks, and since I was going to a fireworks show the very next day, I was sold! Unfortunately, my camera wasn't as intuitive as I thought it was going to be, and I couldn't figure out which setting was for fireworks. Had I read the manual before I tried to use this feature, I probably could have captured some spectacular shots. Instead, I got lots of blurry light bursts. Read the user manual and make sure to take it with you everywhere you take your camera. Believe it or not, the manuals contain lots of useful information.

Take More Photos

As a rule of thumb, the more photos you take, the more likely you are to get a good one. With a film camera, it becomes expensive to take a single shot, but with a digital camera you are limited only by the amount of storage space in the camera memory card. Not enough? Pick up extra memory cards, keeping them handy for those photographic moments. You can reuse memory cards over and over again.

Go ahead! Snap away! Even a small change in the angle, position, or lighting can make a dramatic different in the resulting photo.

TIP

Because taking lots of shots drains your batteries, you'll want to make sure you have additional batteries on hand.

Concentrate on Composition

Compose your picture for interest. When composing a photograph, take a look at more than just the subject. Become aware of shape, form, color, and light—all of which combine to make your photograph more interesting. If the surrounding shapes and details complement your subject, include them. Busy backgrounds can sap pictures of their power by competing with the subject. Move the subject or yourself to position a plain background such as grass, a wall, or the sky behind the main subject. If that is impossible, then get closer to the subject to prevent it from being lost against a distracting background. Try to fill the picture area with a subject so that it stands out and grabs the viewer's attention.

A picture with a single dominant subject makes its point quickly and clearly. When you look through the camera's viewfinder, it is just human nature that your eye and mind will see only one subject, even if there are many objects. This lack of focus often results in cluttered pictures with unclear intent. When you take a picture, carefully arrange the scene so that one subject stands out.

Follow the "Rule of Thirds," where you imagine that your picture area is divided horizontally and vertically into thirds (see Figure 1-1). Any of the four points where the lines intersect forms a good location for your subject.

Figure 1-1 *Each imaginary line forms a good location for important structural elements in your composition. (Photo by Gary French)*

TIP

As important as the Rule of Thirds is, it's still just a guide to taking more interesting pictures, so don't feel you always have to use it. Sometimes you have to bend the rules a little!

When choosing your viewpoint, make sure there is a strong foreground, which provides your subject with depth and distance. For example, if you want a shot of the town canal, try and capture the bench setting on the grass as well. Your viewers see the bench before they see the canal, providing a sense of distance. Try changing your perspective by raising your viewpoint and angling your camera down.

Emphasize the size of a subject by including something to compare it to. For example, if you are trying to illustrate a tall tree in the redwood forest, place a vehicle or a person in the image for a comparative scale purpose.

Take Advantage of the Light

Make the best of available light and know where light is coming from. Harsh sunlight casts deep shadows. Cloudy daylight evenly illuminates scenes so that everything is clearly visible. Low lighting reveals textures, while overhead lighting reduces textures. Observe the light and change your position to get a better angle or wait for the sun to disappear behind a cloud to get better results. Pay close attention to the time of day. There are three times of day in photography: the right time of day, the wrong time of day, and the time of day you happen to be there to get the shot. The light direction, amount, type, and colors change as the day changes. If you're shooting pictures of Bryce Canyon, you'll find the image of truer color in the morning or late afternoon. Shooting photographs in incorrect lighting can make images appear washed out and faded like the one you see on the left in Figure 1-2.

Figure 1-2 *The image on the left is the original, while the one on the right was corrected in Paint Shop Pro. (Photo by Gary French)*

With a digital camera, you can compensate for various types of lighting when you're shooting by changing a setting on your camera. A digital camera can also change its sensitivity to light. A film with greater sensitivity to light is referred to as *faster film*; therefore, the greater the light sensitivity, the faster the film. Fast film allows you to shoot photos under low-light conditions without using a flash. With a digital camera, you can let the camera automatically change the equivalency of the camera film speed, or you can do it yourself. Or...you can use Paint Shop Pro to edit the image, making it just look like you picked the perfect lighting.

Keep the Camera Steady

A blurred image may come from a focus issue, but more than likely, it's from slight movements in the camera as the photograph is snapped. The best way you can control movement is, of course, to use a tripod. In a pinch, find a bench, fence post, or any other nearby stable object to steady the camera. Additionally, try squeezing the shutter button instead of pressing it. The softer touch from squeezing can eliminate some camera movement. Holding the camera steady is especially important on very cloudy days outdoors.

Be Prepared

This probably will sound superfluous to some of you, but a great shot could appear at any moment. Keep your camera with you at all times, keep the batteries charged, and make sure the lens is clean.

Many digital cameras can add special effects such as solarizing or using sepia. I don't recommend that you apply these special effects with your camera; instead, apply them after the shot by using Paint Shop Pro. You'll be happier with the results since you can undo unwanted effects with Paint Shop Pro.

How Does the Digital Camera Take Pictures?

While both traditional and digital cameras use some of the same equipment such as a lens, aperture controls, and a shutter, traditional cameras store their images on light-sensitive, chemical-coated film. In contrast, the digital camera doesn't use film, but instead uses electronic information to record the photograph on a silicon chip, floppy disk, or CD-ROM.

With a film camera, when the light hits the film, the chemicals react, causing the image to be stored on the film. The digital camera silicon chip is considered an *image sensor array,* approximately the size of a fingernail. It contains millions of light-sensitive computer chips called *photosites.* If an image scene is divided up in a checkerboard fashion, each resulting square is known as a *pixel,* which stands for picture element and is a single point in a graphic image that is similar to a colored square in a mosaic. Each photosite of an image sensor array detects a specific pixel. The more photosites there are, the more pixels there will be in the end image.

When the camera shutter opens, light enters through the lens and falls on the image sensor. Each photosite records the brightness of the light that falls on it by accumulating electrical charges and storing the information as a set of numbers. When you download that information to your computer, the computer reassembles the information and displays the image on your screen.

Pros and Cons of Digital Imaging

Every tool has its pluses and minuses, and using a digital camera is no different. On the plus side, you can get instant feedback after you take a picture. You can view it immediately after you shoot it, on the *liquid crystal display* (LCD). If you are not happy with the shot, you can delete it immediately and hopefully take another one. Additionally, you may be able to rescue a less than perfect image by using Paint Shop Pro. Finally, you save money because you don't have to keep buying film and paying for developed prints.

On the down side, because digital cameras require a short time lapse, usually a few seconds, to store an image after shooting it, many digital cameras are not well suited for capturing action shots. Likewise, printing at home is very expensive, and some lower-end cameras cannot produce the resolution you get with film cameras. Also, due to the constant changes in technology, which grows at an almost mind-boggling speed, you may find yourself constantly wanting to exchange your current digital camera for the "new and improved" model. That can translate into big bucks! There go your savings on film costs.

Using Your Photography Skills

As a photographer, you can transfer many of the photography skills you've acquired over a period of time. Skills you already have such as composition, lighting, exposure, and focus can be put to good use with image editing software. Here are just a few of the photography skills you will use with Paint Shop Pro:

Composition: Ansel Adams once said, "A good photograph is from knowing where to stand." As a photographer you decide what you want to include in the photo, where to place it, and how much space the subject occupies. You understand the Rule of Thirds and other basic composition skills needed for lining up exactly the right shot in the camera. Take that to the next level. With Paint Shop Pro, you can make compositional adjustments after you take your shot. Figure 1-3 shows a photograph both before and after compositional modifications. The original image, as taken, resembles lots of family snapshots that are boring, centered, and have no visual tension, but try recomposing it, and it becomes much more interesting.

Figure 1-3 *Change the focus from a stately statue to the hands of a worried mother. (Photo by JP Kabala)*

Filters: As a photographer, you probably have a number of lens filters that produce a variety of special effects. Paint Shop Pro includes dozens of effects filters that you can apply to all or a portion of your image. See Figure 1-4, where the photograph was aged about 30 years by adding a sepia effect.

Lenses: You probably have a variety of lenses, some of which may have been quite expensive. With Paint Shop Pro, you can achieve special lens effects by applying different lens effects filters such as fisheye, barrel, and pincushion to a straight photo.

Figure 1-4 *Applying a special effect may be a way to salvage a bad photo.*

Focus: With this feature, you can selectively focus part of your image after the fact. Notice in Figure 1-5 how the background is softened to bring the statue into better focus.

Exposure: Use this feature to compensate for over or under exposed images and shady areas.

Figure 1-5 *Use the Paint Shop Pro tools to sharpen and bring better focus to your images.*

Retouching: With Paint Shop Pro, you can retouch photographs by removing or disguising blemishes, repairing scratches, or touching up dust spots or digital noise (see Figure 1-6).

Figure 1-6 *Make scratches and fold marks disappear with the clone tool. (Photo by James Hutchinson)*

A large number of standard darkroom techniques are available with Paint Shop Pro tools, including masking, burning, dodging, and toning.

Basic PSP Tools

We know you understand photography. And we assume you know the basics of working with a computer, such as using the mouse, making menu selections, and opening, saving, and closing a file. If you know these basics, you can find your way around Paint Shop Pro. This section shows you the basic Paint Shop Pro window and where to locate many of the commonly used tools.

Toolbars

Toolbars are buttons that perform common functions. Of the eight Paint Shop Pro toolbars, Paint Shop Pro displays five of them by default. Toolbars can be either docked in the window margins or made to float over the workspace. To move a toolbar, place the cursor over the handle (you'll get the four-sided mover icon) and drag the handle to move the toolbar away from the window margin. Drag the toolbar back along a window margin to return it to a docked position.

Here's a list of the Paint Shop Pro toolbars and their basic functions:

- **Browser:** Includes tools used when the file browser window is open, such as copy, move, delete, or rename file.
- **Effects:** Includes commonly used effects such as drop shadows, bevels, hot wax, or fur.
- **Photo:** Includes common photo enhancement and corrections such as One Step Photo Fix, adjust colors, and repair red-eye.
- **Script:** Includes sets of instructions that produce a series of actions or effects. Buttons include run, stop, edit, record, and save.
- **Standard:** Includes common file function tools such as open, print, and save.
- **Status:** Displays text about the selected tool or menu command, as well as image information including the dimensions, color depth, and cursor position.
- **Tools:** Includes basic drawing and editing tools such as zoom, straighten, crop, and brushes and selection tools.
- **Web:** Includes Web object function tools, such as optimizing, image slicing, and seamless tiling.

Figure 1-7 shows the default toolbars. You control which toolbars are displayed by clicking the View menu, selecting Toolbars, and clicking any toolbar choice to toggle it on or off.

TIP

In Chapter 9, "Special Projects," you'll learn how to customize any PSP toolbar or create your own Paint Shop Pro toolbar.

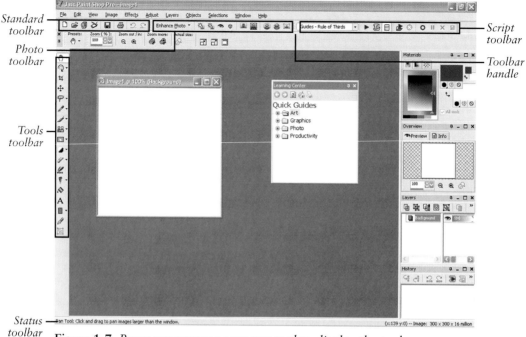

Standard toolbar

Photo toolbar

Script toolbar

Toolbar handle

Tools toolbar

Status toolbar

Figure 1-7 *Pause your mouse over any tool to display the tool name.*

Palettes

While the toolbars display the program's main tools, the palettes display the options. For example, the Materials palette displays available color choices for a selected tool, while the History palette displays the recent steps you have taken on a project. When working with layers (which you will discover in Chapter 4), the Layers palette will be a valuable asset.

Like toolbars, palettes can be docked along the edge of your Paint Shop Pro window, or you can drag them to any location over the workspace. Paint Shop Pro includes 10 different palettes to assist you when working on a project, but only six are displayed by default. To hide or display any palette, click the View menu, select Palettes, and then click any palette choice to toggle it on or off.

Additionally, click the pushpin on any palette to make it roll up when not being used. Called "auto-hide," if the palette is docked, and the pushpin button is pointing down, the palette will remain fully displayed in its docked position when you move the cursor away from it. If the pushpin is pointing to the left, the palette will slide into the area on the right side of the Paint Shop Pro window. You'll then see a tab with the palette name. To display the palette again, move the cursor over the tab.

The pushpin action changes a little if the palette is floating. If the pushpin is pointing down, the palette will remain fully opened when you move the cursor away from it, but if the pushpin is pointing to the left, the palette will roll up so that only its title bar is visible.

Here's a list of the palettes and their basic functions:

- **Brush Variance:** Controls how a selected brush behaves, such as how much paint is applied each time you make a brush stroke.

- **Histogram:** Displays the color and brightness values of the active image.

- **History:** Displays a list of each command that you apply to the active image.

- **Layers:** Displays the individual layers that make up an image.

- **Learning Center:** Contains quick and simple tutorials designed to get you acquainted quickly with Paint Shop Pro.

- **Materials:** Contains options for canvas material, colors, patterns, and styles.

- **Mixer:** Contains tools to mix any number of colors into a single paint swatch in a manner similar to a traditional artist's palette.

- **Overview:** Displays a thumbnail view of your current image.

- **Script Output:** Displays the result of a script as it runs.

- **Tool Options:** Displays options relevant to the currently selected tool.

Figure 1-8 illustrates the default palettes.

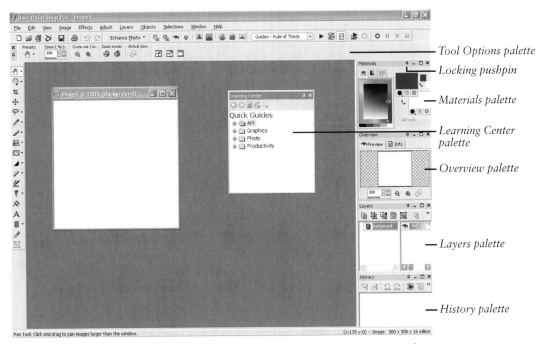

Figure 1-8 *Palettes provide access to controls used with various Paint Shop Pro features.*

Rulers, Guides, and Grids

When working on an image, it is often difficult to keep everything in the proper perspective. Using rulers, guides, and grids can help you keep precision in your work and increase your productivity.

Rulers

Rulers are displayed along the X and Y axes of the image window. You can turn the display of the ruler on or off through the View menu or by pressing the shortcut key combination of Ctrl+Alt+R.

Depending on your preference, you can display the ruler in inches, pixels, or centimeters. Click the File menu, select Preference, and then General Program Preferences. You set your preferred unit of measurement from the Units tab.

Guides

Guides are horizontal or vertical lines that you drag onto your image, that enable you to mark precise image areas. To place guides, you must display the rulers; then to toggle the guides on or off, click the View menu and select Guides.

To place a horizontal guide, position the mouse pointer over the top ruler until it appears as a black cross; then click and drag down into the image until the guide is at the desired position.

To place a vertical guide, position the mouse pointer over the left ruler until it appears as a black cross; then click and drag to the right onto the image until the guide is at the desired position. Figure 1-9 illustrates an image with both the rulers and the guides displayed.

Figure 1-9 *Use guides for positioning items or aligning brush stokes. (Photo by Gary French)*

You can place as many guides as desired. Each guide displays a small handle on the ruler indicating the guide position. Click and drag the guide handle to move a specific guide. To remove a guide, click and drag the guide handle beyond the outside border of the ruler.

TIP

To position a guide more precisely or change a guide color, double-click the guide handle to display the Guide Properties dialog. Type a value in pixels in the guide position box or click the color box to select a different guide color. Click OK to close the Guide Properties dialog box.

Grids

Similar to a guide, a grid provides for even positioning. While you can precisely position where you want guide lines, a grid by default lays both horizontal and vertical alignment lines across the entire image in the shape of a, well, a grid. Grids help you position objects for more precise layer or picture element alignment. Like rulers and guides, you control the display of grids through the View menu. Select View, Grids or press the keyboard shortcut of Ctrl+Alt+G.

If the grid is too small or too large, double-click the ruler to display the Grid, Guide, and Snap Properties dialog box. From there you can change the grid size and color.

Paint Shop Pro Browser

Many people consider the Paint Shop Pro Browser window to be a hidden jewel. As more and more digital images are stored on your computer, it becomes more difficult to remember where you put them and which images are which. You could open and close each file individually, but the Paint Shop Pro browser makes finding your images much easier. It's a visual picture manager that provides a simple way to view and manage your digital images.

Open the Browser in Paint Shop Pro by any one of three methods. (It's such a great tool, you'll want to learn all three.) Click the File menu and select Browse or click the Browse button on the Standard toolbar. Additionally, as a keyboard shortcut you could press Ctrl+B to open the Browser window.

As you can see in Figure 1-10, when you activate the Browser window, the menu bar changes to items that are relevant to the Browser. The menu bar now provides a variety of options for selecting files to open and for renaming, moving, copying, and deleting files. Additionally, with the Browser active, you can sort images by several different criteria.

On the left side of the Browser window you see a list of folders, similar to the Windows Explorer window. Click any of the + symbols to open a folder and display the image files within that folder. The Browser window displays only image and PDF files and doesn't list spreadsheets, program files, or other types of computer files.

Figure 1-10 *Navigate among your folders and locate your photos visually, rather than by filename.*

The Image Browser contains two tabs, Find and Info, in the left side of the Browser window. The Find tab contains the familiar Windows Explorer–like navigation view, and the Info tab displays image information, creator data, and EXIF data.

When you find a file you want to open, double-click the image, and it will appear in the Paint Shop Pro screen. The Browser window will remain open under your current image until you manually close it.

TIP

Drag an image thumbnail from the Browser into the Paint Shop Pro workspace to open the image for editing.

Comparing File Formats

In the film world, format refers to the size of the film you use, such as 35mm or APS. In the digital realm, there are many format types. A digital format refers to the way the software stores digital data. File formats are identified by the three letter extension at the end of the identifying filename: filename.ext. Every format has its own characteristics, advantages, and disadvantages. You cannot just change the name of the file extension to another set of letters; it must be converted for use in different programs. Many digital cameras, as well as Paint Shop Pro, offer several different file formats for saving your digital images.

Let's take a brief look at a few of the popular formats:

JPEG (Joint Photographic Experts Group) is one of the most common file formats. JPEG files can be used on both Mac and PC computers and are most commonly used for images on Web pages or in e-mail. JPEG uses a lossy compression scheme, which means it throws away some of the graphic data every time you save your file using the JPEG format. There are varying levels of compression with varying loss of detail. With a higher compression, a number of unwanted noise artifacts begin to appear on the image, giving a substantial loss of quality. At the highest compression (lowest quality), it can reduce files sizes to about 5% of their normal size. Merely opening a JPEG file, as on the Internet, does not result in any loss of data.

PNG (Portable Networks Graphic) is a format similar to a JPEG file, but it produces higher quality pictures and supports transparency and other features. PNG is a relatively new format, and if you are putting a PNG image on a Web site, the visitor must have a newer (V5 or above) Web browser. Also, PNG files are typically a little larger in file size. Like a JPEG, PNG formats use a lossy data compression for color images with varying levels of compression and with varying loss of detail.

TIFF (Tagged Image File Format) is another widely supported file format for storing images on a computer (both PCs and Macs). TIFF graphics can be any resolution, and they can be black-and-white, grayscale, or color. Additionally, TIFF files use a nonlossy format so that no data is lost when you save and resave files in a TIFF format. Files in TIFF format end with a .tif extension.

GIF (Graphics Interchange Format) is a Web standard file format that typically is small in file size and usually quick to load. GIF images also support transparency. GIF files use a lossless compression scheme and retain all the image information, but they store only 256 colors, so the prints might look rough, blotchy, jagged, or banded because they don't include enough shades of color to accurately reproduce an image. A GIF format is not a good choice for color photographs.

RAW file format, while the largest in file size, includes all information regarding a photograph, sort of a "digital negative" containing all the original information gathered by your camera with no compression or other processing. While every camera takes an image in a RAW format, you might need special software from your camera vendor to save an image in RAW format. Although RAW files are the largest in size, they are the most accurate representation of your image in terms of white balance, color, sharpening, and so forth.

pspImage (Paint Shop Pro) is a proprietary format native to Paint Shop Pro images. While you can open, save, and close the PSP file without losing any special features, the file can only be opened with the Paint Shop Pro program. Therefore, it probably won't be the final format in which you save your file, but it's a great format to use while working on an image.

NOTE

Paint Shop Pro version 7 and earlier used .psp as the file extension. Newer Paint Shop Pro versions can work with either .pspImage files or .psp files.

BMP (bitmap) files consist of rows and columns of dots. The value of each dot (whether it is filled in or not) is stored in one or more bits of data. For simple monochrome images, one bit is sufficient to represent each dot, but for colors and shades of gray, each dot requires more than one bit of data. The more bits used to represent a dot, the more colors and shades of gray that can be represented. The density of the dots, known as the *resolution*, determines how sharply the image is represented. This is often expressed in dots per inch (dpi) or simply by the number of rows and columns, such as 640 by 480. To display a bitmapped image on a monitor or to print it on a printer, the computer translates the bitmap into pixels (for display screens) or ink dots (for printers). Bitmapped graphics are often referred to as *raster graphics*. Bitmapped graphics become ragged when you shrink or enlarge them, and they are not a good choice for photographs or Web graphics.

Most digital cameras, by default, save images as JPEG files because of the JPEG efficient use of size, although some of the better cameras allow you to change formats. Both JPEG and TIFF files are quite different from the original information captured by your camera. After the image is snapped, the data is taken from a RAW format into a processed JPEG or TIFF format.

TIP

You'll learn about working with RAW files in Chapter 9, "Special Projects."

What's Next?

In Chapter 2, we'll take a look at many of the "quick and easy" photo repair tools included with Paint Shop Pro. You'll also learn how to calibrate your computer monitor to get the best display possible, which will be essential when working with digital images.

2

Quick Fixes

Using Paint Shop Pro isn't going to make you a better photographer. That only comes with knowledge, time, talent, and lots of practice. In most cases, however, Paint Shop Pro can help you make your photographs look like they should, in other words, look more perfect than they were when you took them.

There is a difference between photo correction and photo enhancement. If you need to make the image look like it should, say for example to remove digital noise or adjust the color, that's known as a *correction*. If you want to actually modify the contents of the photograph, that is called a *photo enhancement*.

Paint Shop Pro includes a number of automatic correction tools for working with your digital photos. Some of these tools are quite easy to use, such as the One Step Photo Fix, while others, such as Automatic Color Balance, need some input from you. Many are "one-click" tools that provide a number of resourceful features that are sufficient for most photo editing problems. Each of these tools offers basic settings, but you should know that these aren't the only tools to work with your images. Paint Shop Pro includes many in-depth tools, allowing you to get to the very heart of your images and make the most minute changes you can imagine. However, most people find the automatic tools work quite to their satisfaction.

If you can identify the parts of your photo that need improvement, Paint Shop Pro can provide ways to make these improvements, from automatically balancing your color or contrast to making very specific, detailed adjustments, such as working with channel mixers, thresholds, and histogram modifications.

This chapter deals mainly with the Paint Shop Pro "quick and easy" photo correction tools. In later chapters, you'll learn more about the detailed photo correction and enhancement tools.

Calibrating Your Monitor

Before you begin manipulating your images, you should calibrate your monitor. Calibrating conforms your monitor to widely accepted standards of image display, which enables others to view your images as you want them to be viewed. Calibrating also improves the quality of how *you* see your photos.

Like most of us, you probably took your monitor out of the box and made little or no effort to calibrate the monitor in order to get the best image possible. There are software programs available for purchase to help you with calibration, or you can tune up your monitor visuals without spending a dime. A few simple adjustments to your graphics card and other Windows settings can ensure peak visual performance. Let's look at some of the areas that you can change to enhance your calibration.

> **TIP**
>
> A shaking or shimmering image on your screen may be due to nearby magnetic fields. Keep clocks and other appliances that use a lot of electricity away from your monitor. Power lines behind walls can cause interference, so try moving the display away from nearby walls.

Update the Graphics Driver

Your computer graphics card is controlled by its Windows driver, so make sure that you always have the latest driver release for your card. To see what version you have, right-click the desktop and choose Properties to open the Display Properties dialog box. Then click Settings, Advanced, Adapter, Properties and look on the Driver tab. To download the most recent version of your graphics driver, visit your graphics card vendor's Web site or the Microsoft Windows Update site.

Once you've verified you have the most recent graphics driver, you can begin optimizing your monitor's resolution, color-depth, and refresh-rate settings in Windows.

Typically, monitors take a little time to warm up, so you shouldn't attempt to adjust your display until it has been running for at least 30 minutes. Make sure you position the screen to avoid reflections and glare, and it helps if you reduce (but not eliminate) the quantity of light in the room.

Resolution

Resolution is the number of pixels displayed on your screen. The higher the resolution, the more pixel dots per inch, and the sharper the displayed image. Although higher resolutions increase the processing demands on your graphics board and computer, you need the higher resolution for working with digital images.

Most of today's graphics cards support resolutions of at least 1024 by 768, meaning the screen image is composed of an array that is 1,024 pixels across and 768 pixels tall, although some graphic cards support much higher screen resolutions.

To adjust screen resolution, open the Display Properties dialog box and click the Settings tab (see Figure 2-1). Slide the Screen Resolution bar to the resolution you want. The resolution you find that works best for you will also depend on your monitor size. For example, many people using a 17-inch monitor prefer a 1024 by 768 resolution. Higher resolutions improve image quality, but they also shrink icons, text, and other on-screen objects, so if you suffer from the "over-forty" vision problems, you may need to experiment to find the setting that's right for you.

Figure 2-1 *Finding the right setting for you may also involve changing the Display Properties Appearance Settings.*

Color Quality or Depth

Color quality or depth is the number of colors that your graphics card supports. The more colors available for use, the more realistic the image, but like higher resolutions, the more colors on your screen, the greater the processing demands on your system.

The color quantity options you have available vary, depending upon the graphics card and version of Windows on your system. You can access the color quality setting by opening the Display Properties dialog box and clicking the Settings tab. From the Color quality drop-down menu, you will see your choices. You may see options such as True Color, High Color, Highest, or Medium. Each is named for the number of bits it assigns to each pixel: 24-bit color makes 16,777,216 colors available, while 16-bit color supports 65,536 colors. 32-bit color offers the same 16 million-plus colors as 24-bit color, and it uses the extra 8 bits to control image opacity. Don't use less than 16-bit color because your images will look terrible onscreen.

Refresh Rate

The refresh rate tells how often the phosphors that glow to create an image on a CRT screen are reenergized; that is, the times per second that the screen's image is redrawn. Expressed in Hertz, or cycles per second, a refresh rate that's too low can cause annoying screen flicker and can result in eyestrain and headaches. If your refresh rate is too high, you could lose image opacity. Typically, your refresh rate should be between 72Hz and 80Hz. Try different refresh rates until you find the one that works for you.

To adjust your screen's refresh rate, open Display Properties and click Settings, Advanced, Adapter, List All Modes (see Figure 2-2). Pick a combination of refresh rate, screen resolution, and color depth from the list of supported values.

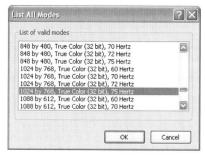

Figure 2-2 *Try different refresh rates until you find the one that works for you.*

TIP

Refresh rate, screen resolution, and your color depth setting all compete for graphics-processing capacity, so if your graphics system is running at its maximum but you're not happy with it, try increasing one setting and lowering another.

Brightness and Contrast

You can improve the image quality of your monitor via its built-in controls. The options vary by display manufacturer and model, but you should find brightness and other controls on most monitors. If all else fails, locate and <gasp> read the manufacturer's manual.

To calibrate your monitor, you need an onscreen aid that helps you adjust the monitor's brightness and contrast. The Jasc Web site provides a free onscreen aid, as well as detailed instructions for calibration. Visit http://www.jasc.com/support/kb/articles/monitor.asp or go to the Support section of www.jasc.com, click the Knowledge Base link, and use the keywords "monitor calibration" in the Search field.

The brightness setting actually controls the darkness, or black point, of your monitor. If the black point is too low, dark shades of grey will appear black, but if the black point is too high, your darkest blacks will look grey. Using a greyscale chart, lower the brightness until the last two dark shades on the chart are black and then increase the setting until the first shade of grey emerges next to the pure black area.

After you've set your black point, adjust the display's contrast, which actually sets the lightness intensity. Pick a setting that's pleasing to your eye. Brighter isn't always better; contrast settings that are too high can cause blurring on some CRT monitors, as well as increase eyestrain.

Gamma Correction

Without getting too deep into the technical aspects of gamma, almost every computer monitor has one thing in common. They all have an intensity to voltage response curve, which is roughly a 2.5 power function. Simply put, this means that if you send your computer monitor a message that a certain pixel should have an intensity equal to x, it will actually display a pixel that has an intensity equal to x to the power of 2.5. Because the range of voltages sent to the monitor is between 0 and 1, this means that the intensity value displayed will be less than what you wanted it to be. Monitors, then, are said to have a gamma of 2.5.

Gamma correction matters in displaying an image accurately on a computer screen because it controls the overall brightness of an image and the ratios of red to green to blue.

Paint Shop Pro includes a monitor gamma setting that adjusts how colors display in Paint Shop Pro. This setting does not affect how your monitor displays colors in other applications. Also, you should use caution when adjusting gamma controls, especially when an image needs to look good on different systems or platforms. While most monitors work in about the same way with respect to gamma correction, some computer systems do not work in exactly the same way.

To adjust the Paint Shop Pro monitor gamma, click the File menu and select Preferences, Monitor Gamma. The Monitor Gamma Adjustment dialog box you see in Figure 2-3 opens.

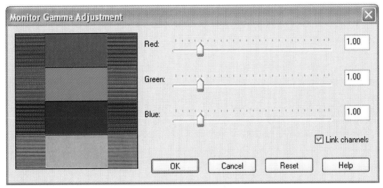

Figure 2-3 *Correcting monitor gamma helps ensure that what you see on the screen is what you get in your prints.*

Stand back from your monitor and look at the red, green, blue, and grey rectangles. Each color contains an inner, solid color rectangle and outer patterned rectangles. On a correctly adjusted monitor, the inner rectangles are difficult to distinguish from the outer rectangles.

If you need to adjust the values, drag the slider until the inner rectangle seems to blend into the outer rectangle; then click OK.

TIP

To return to no gamma adjustment (1.00), reopen the Monitor Gamma Adjustment dialog box and click Reset.

Photo Improvement Steps

Throughout this entire book, you'll find a number of steps you can take to improve your images. However, most photographic improvements will fall into a few general categories, with some photos requiring multiple steps:

- Focus adjustments
- Color, contrast, and saturation adjustments
- Image clarity and sharpness
- Noise and scratch removal
- Color aberrations
- Correct flash problems
- Lens distortions
- Red-eye removal

WARNING

Before you begin correcting a photograph, you should duplicate the image and work on the duplicate. That way, if you are unhappy with your results, you still have the original image to work with, and you can start over. Duplicate an image by clicking the Window menu and selecting Duplicate. Additionally, you can compare the original image and the duplicate image side-by-side to get a better view of your changes (Window, Tile Vertically).

Cropping

Use the Crop tool to permanently remove unwanted portions of an image. Cropping an image can create stronger compositions and change the image focus. Cropping also reduces the image file size and the computer memory needed to edit the image.

Cropping is one of the first steps in correcting a photograph because any subsequent color changes you make might be affected by objects you may not even want in the photo. Many features such as the One Step Photo Fix or Color Balance use the entire image to make the feature changes. By eliminating superfluous areas of color, cropping can make color corrections more accurate.

If you do want to crop your photo, first decide what the subject should be and remove anything that detracts from the photo or distracts the eye from the subject. You don't have to crop all your images; in fact, many images would lose their composition if extra space around a subject were cropped off. Remember the Rule of Thirds and avoid creating a photo with the subject in the dead center.

If you are planning on printing the image, don't crop it too small. Depending on the source of the original photograph, your image may lose some resolution if you try to make it larger for printing. If you used a good resolution digital camera when taking the image, this would be the time when all those extra pixels produced by the camera come in handy, because the remaining cropped image would still be large enough to print at a reasonable size.

The Crop tool is one of the easiest Paint Shop Pro tools you can use, and you can crop your image to any size you want, or you can have Paint Shop Pro constrain the crop so that you can use one of many standard sizes such as 4 × 6 or 5 × 7. The Crop tool is the third tool on the toolbar, or you can just press the letter R to activate the Crop tool.

Cropping Tool Options

Before you actually crop the image, you should become familiar with cropping options. Each time you select a tool from the toolbar, the Tool Options palette displays options specific to the selected tool. Click the Crop tool, and Paint Shop Pro displays the Crop tool options as seen in Figure 2-4.

Apply   Reset

Figure 2-4 *Pause your mouse over each tool option to see its name.*

The following list explains some of the tools on the Crop Tool Options palette:

- **Presets:** Selects from standard print sizes. See "Cropping to a Specific Size" later in this chapter.

- **Apply:** Accepts the cropping selection and crops the image.

- **Reset:** Removes the cropping selection without cropping the image.

- **Width:** Enters a specific width for cropping, based on units.

- **Height:** Enters a specific height for cropping, based on units.

- **Units:** Specifies the unit of measurement in centimeters, inches, or pixels. If the Specify Print Size option is checked, you can only select from centimeters or inches.

- **Resolution:** Displays the image resolution, based on the crop selection size, along with your unit of measurement.

- **Specify Print Size:** Allows a change in the resolution of the crop area to a value that will result in a specific printable size. There are no more or fewer pixels in the crop rectangle, but by changing only the resolution of the image, the default print size will be different than if this check box is not pressed.

- **Maintain Aspect Ratio:** Checking this box constrains the crop area to keep its current proportions. If using a Preset size, this box is unavailable.

- **Left, Top, Right, Bottom:** Use these boxes to enter exact pixel locations for the top, bottom, left, and right sides of the crop area.

Cropping to Your Selection Size

If you want to exactly control the crop of your image, you can specify the crop size either in measurements or by drawing a boundary selection box. Select the Crop tool from the Tools toolbar. Notice how the mouse pointer changes to match the cropping tool with a small cross on the end of it. The cross indicates your starting point.

Click and drag around the area of the photo you want to keep. As soon as you click in the image, the entire original image becomes shaded, and the selected area you are drawing around brightens up so you can get a better idea of what your image will look like after cropping (see Figure 2-5).

If you didn't select exactly the right size or location you want, you can adjust the cropping selection by clicking and dragging the handle boxes located on the sides or corners until the cropping selection is the size you want. As you position your mouse pointer over the selection box handles, the mouse pointer turns into a double-headed arrow.

Figure 2-5 *Cropping permanently removes the image area outside the crop selection box. (Photo by James Hutchinson)*

If you want to move the selection box, place the mouse pointer inside the rectangle to move the entire rectangle around. If you are having difficulty getting the selection box exactly the size and location you want, you can start over by clicking the Reset Crop Rectangle tool on the Tool Options palette.

When you're happy with your selection area, click the Apply button on the Tool Options palette or double-click inside the selection area.

> # TIP
>
> If the requested cropping size is larger than the selected photo, the Crop tool will change the resolution of the image to make it fit. The Tool Options bar displays the resolution.

If you change your mind after you crop the image, click the Edit menu and select Undo Crop or click the Undo button on the Standard toolbar.

> # NOTE
>
> After cropping an image, you may notice that the Width and Height values in the Crop tool options are set to 1 if you are measuring in pixels and .100 if you are measuring in inches. No one seems to be sure why the values change to 1, but this is not a reflection of the cropped image size. To see the image size dimensions after cropping, click Image, Image Information and look at the Dimensions field.

Cropping to a Specific Size

In the previous section, you discovered how to crop an image to any size you want, but to help you keep the image perspective and use a common print size, Paint Shop Pro includes 16 preset image sizes and orientations.

Follow these steps to crop your image to a preset size:

1. Select the Crop tool.
2. Click the small arrow next to the Presets button. A list of available preset sizes will appear. Preset sizes are measured in centimeters or inches.

> # TIP
>
> Click the Category arrow on the Presets button to segregate the options by measurement type.

3. Select the finished size from the Presets button. A crop selection box of the selected size will appear in the upper left corner of the image.

4. With the mouse pointer inside the crop selection box, click and drag the box until it is positioned over the image area you want to keep.

5. Click the Apply button.

Figure 2-6 illustrates the image after cropping to a 5×7 image.

Figure 2-6 *Cropping an image can change image composition.*

Rotating Images

Some images lend themselves to turning the camera on its side and taking the image in portrait orientation. If the subject matter is taller than it is wide, you'll want to shoot it in portrait, and if it's wider than tall, use landscape orientation.

When you open any photograph in Paint Shop Pro, you see it in landscape orientation. If it was taken in portrait orientation, you'll need to rotate the image to view it properly in Paint Shop Pro. In Figure 2-7 you see a picture of a beautiful chocolate lab desperately trying to reach a chipmunk in a tree. This picture was best portrayed by rotating the camera to make a portrait shot.

When you open any photograph in Paint Shop Pro, you see it in landscape orientation. If it was taken in portrait orientation, you'll need to rotate the image to view it properly in Paint Shop Pro. You have three rotating options available, all of which are available by clicking the Image menu and selecting Rotate:

- Rotate 90 degrees clockwise
- Rotate 90 degrees counter-clockwise
- Free Rotate

The first two are self-explanatory in that they rotate your image exactly 90 degrees. You can also use the Free Rotate command to specify exactly how much you want to rotate the image. After you select Free Rotate from the menu, you'll see the Free Rotate box seen in Figure 2-8. From this dialog box you can select one of the preset rotations or enter a custom value to rotate it at any angle.

When you rotate an image in straight 90 degree angles such as 90, 180, or 270 degrees, Paint Shop Pro rearranges the order of the image pixels, and since only the order of the pixels is being modified, no quality is lost. If you rotate an image in anything other than a 90-degree increment, Paint Shop Pro must re-create all the pixels to create the rotation, which results in minor image quality degrading. If you rotate again on top of a previous rotation, you may see the image quality decline and the image distort.

Figure 2-7 *Kinda makes you wonder if the dog ever managed to get the chipmunk, doesn't it? (Photo by James Hutchinson)*

Figure 2-8 *Use this dialog box to enter a custom rotation angle.*

> **TIP**
>
> Avoid adding rotation to rotation. If the first non 90–degree rotation didn't give you the results you want, undo the rotation before trying another one. Click Edit, Undo Rotate to undo the rotation.

Because of the possible image degradation, I'd like to offer a word of advice here. With a seriously crooked scanned image, if at all possible, rescan the image. If you cannot rescan the image but don't need to fully rotate it, try straightening it with the Straighten tool.

Straightening

Sometimes a photo may not be as straight as you intended, and there's nothing quite as distracting as a photo that's slightly crooked. This commonly occurs in action shots where the camera wasn't quite level with the horizon. If an image is crooked, the best thing to do is retake the photograph or rescan the image. Often though, those are not options. In that case, or if the image is only slightly crooked, Paint Shop Pro includes a toolbar tool that helps align crooked photos and scanned images. Like the Rotate feature, if the picture is seriously crooked, you may see some image distortion. The Straighten tool works best when the image has a strong vertical or horizontal feature, such as a building or a horizon.

 On the Tools toolbar, click the Straighten tool. The Straighten tool is in the menu on the second toolbar tool (with the Deform tool). You may have to click the arrow next to the Deform tool to select the Straighten tool. The Straighten tool places a straight line through the middle of the frame.

To illustrate this, we'll use a beautiful, serene fall lake scene, but one in which the water line isn't quite straight with the horizon. This picture needs a little straightening (see Figure 2-9). Drag the straightening line to the area on which you want it to align. In our example, we want to straighten it to the water line, so we'll drag the straighten line down to the water level. Click and drag one of the bar end handles to align it with the part of the image that you want to be straight.

On the Tool Options palette, besides the typical Presets, Apply, and Reset tools, choose from these options:

- **Mode:** Auto, Make Vertical, or Make Horizontal: Paint Shop Pro automatically straightens the image based on the position of the straightening bar, rotates the image to make the straightening bar vertical, or rotates the image to make the straightening bar horizontal, respectively. Usually, you will use the Auto mode.

- **Crop Image:** Use this option to have Paint Shop Pro crop the edges of the image to make it rectangular after straightening. If you do not select this image, Paint Shop Pro attempts to fill the blank rotated area with a solid background color.

- **Rotate All Layers:** Mark this check box to have Paint Shop Pro straighten all layers in the image. (You'll discover more about layers in Chapter 4, "Selecting and Layering.")

Figure 2-9 *Drag the straightening line along the image section that you want to straighten. (Photo by James Hutchinson)*

■ **Angle:** Instead of visually aligning to the straightening bar, use this box to enter a specific angle for the straightening bar.

Like many other Paint Shop Pro tools, click the Apply button to apply the straighten feature.

One Step Photo Fix

Paint Shop Pro has many tools you can use to help fix your photos. You can manually adjust the color balance, contrast, clarity, and saturation, smooth the edges, and sharpen the edges on each and every image. While you can open, close, and use each of these tools independently, Paint Shop Pro also includes a One Step Photo Fix command that can automatically apply these features for you. It's a totally automatic feature, so you don't get to select any options, but most of the time it does a good job getting the most out of the photo without having to select and use each tool manually.

With the image open on your screen, you can access the One Step Photo Fix from the Photo toolbar or from the menu. From the Photo toolbar seen in Figure 2-10, click the Enhance Photo button, which drops down a menu of options, and then select One Step Photo Fix.

Enhance Photo button

Figure 2-10 *The Photo toolbar includes buttons for frequently used photo correction tools.*

Figure 2-11 illustrates an image both before and after using the One Step Photo Fix.

Figure 2-11 *The image on the top is before using the One Step Photo Fix, while the image on the bottom is after using the One Step Photo Fix. (Photo by Tim Koers)*

Using Paint Shop Pro Dialog Boxes

Before we actually go into using the different automatic tools provided with Paint Shop Pro, let's take a brief look at how the photo adjustment dialog boxes work. The controls in the adjustment dialog boxes operate in a similar manner to each other.

Figure 2-12 shows the Automatic Color Balance dialog box. You'll discover Automatic Color Balance in the next section. For now, let's review the controls that many Paint Shop Pro dialog boxes have in common.

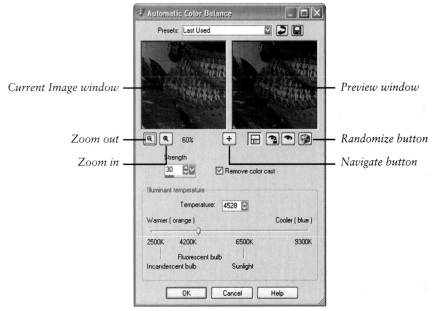

Figure 2-12 *The top half of the dialog boxes offers common controls, while the bottom half contains controls specific to the adjustment you are making.*

- **Presets:** Choose from a variety of preset control options.

- **Save Preset:** Click this to save your customized settings for future use.

- **Reset to Defaults:** Click this button to reset the control options to the factory default settings determined by Paint Shop Pro.

- **Current Image window:** Displays your image before you make any changes with the dialog box.

- **Preview window:** Displays the effects of your changes on your image.

- **Zoom out:** Zoom out on your image. When you zoom out, both the Current Image window and the Preview window zoom out.

- **Zoom in:** Zoom in on your image. When you zoom in, both the Current Image window and the Preview window zoom in.

- **Navigate button:** Click and hold this button to display another window containing a small version of your image, with the zoomed area indicated by a rectangle. Drag the rectangle to a different part of the image you want to preview.

- **Show/Hide Previews:** Hides and redisplays both the Current Image window and the Preview window.

- **Auto Proof:** Lets you see the current changes as you make them on the actual image (under the dialog box) without accepting the changes until you click OK. It locks the proof on so that you can see each change you make without having to click the regular Proof button each time.

- **Proof:** Click this button to see the current changes you make on the actual image (under the dialog box) without accepting the changes until you click OK. Unless you use Auto Proof, you'll need to click this button each time you want to see the results on your image.

- **Randomize:** Each time you click the randomize button, it "rolls the die" and randomly changes all of the settings pertaining to the feature you are working with. It's a fun feature, but generally not very practical.

Now that you understand the way the Paint Shop Pro dialog boxes work, let's take a look at using one of them—the Automatic Color Balance.

Automatic Color Balance

When you use the One Step Photo Fix, it modifies a number of different components, including color, saturation, contrast, clarity, and others. But what if your image doesn't need adjustment in all those areas? You can implement each correction independently of each other.

Photos taken indoors tend to look more orange, while photos taken in bright sunlight tend to have a bluish tint to them. To create natural-looking colors and remove any stray or odd color cast commonly found in digital images, try the Automatic Color Balance command. Follow these steps:

1. Access the Automatic Color Balance from either the Photo toolbar or the Adjust menu, which displays the dialog box you see in Figure 2-13.

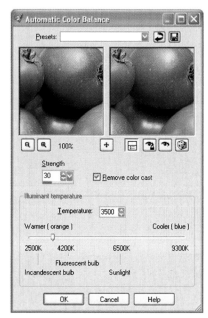

Figure 2-13 *Balance your color temperature with this dialog box.*

> **TIP**
>
> You can apply this command to a selection or an entire image. You'll learn about making selections in Chapter 4, "Selecting and Layering."

2. In the Current Image window, center an important part of the image. If needed, use the Navigate button to locate the desired area. Zoom in or out, as necessary.

3. Set the Strength of correction for the image, from 1 (the least) to 100 (the most). Generally, you can start with 30 and then adjust the strength until the image looks the most natural.

4. If there is a strong color cast to the image (a particular color added to all colors in the image), mark the Remove color cast check box to remove it.

5. In the Illuminant temperature group box, set the image temperature by entering a value or dragging the slider to change the temperature from warmer orange tones to cooler blue tones. The default setting is 6500K, which gives the effect of a photo taken in typical daylight. Adjust the value to achieve the desired effect or until the colors look the most natural.

6. Click OK. The dialog box closes, and Paint Shop Pro makes the image corrections per your specifications.

Figure 2-14 illustrates an image before and after using the Automatic Color Balance feature. As you can see, the original is way too cool and has a bluish tint. Setting the color temperature to warm at 3500 did the trick. After adjusting the color, these tomatoes look ripe, juicy, and ready to eat.

Figure 2-14 *The image on the top is before the Automatic Color Balance correction, and the image on the bottom is after the Automatic Color Balance correction. (Photo by James Hutchinson)*

Automatic Contrast Enhancement

The Auto Contrast Enhancement feature offers an instant contrast boost for those photos that may have too much darkness in them, perhaps from not enough flash or an incorrect light perspective. Contrast is defined as the measure in a picture of the tonal scale between black and white or the distribution of lightness values.

Typically, images with fewer tones have higher contrast. In most images, objects in the distance can be lower in contrast than the foreground objects, but all foreground objects should display the same contrast you'd expect from objects lit by the same illumination source.

The important thing to remember when choosing a subject for a high contrast image is to make sure that the most important part of the subject matter has one of the lightest tones in an image. If most of the tones in an image are too similar to each other, then the image has a low contrast and appears flat or dull. If the tones are spread widely across the scale, then its contrast is high.

As the contrast is boosted, the dark tones and most mid-tone areas will become black, while the very lightest tones will remain white. If your key subject matter is too dark, it will turn black along with the other mid and deep tones and not be visible in your finished image.

Paint Shop Pro's Automatic Contrast Enhancement feature is useful for improving the tone distribution of your image. The following steps show you how to use the Automatic Contrast Enhancement feature:

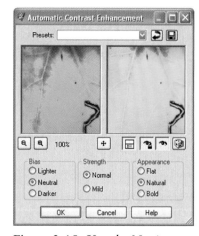

Figure 2-15 *Use the Navigate button to view different sections of your image.*

1. Access the Automatic Contrast Enhancement feature from either the Photo toolbar or the Adjust menu, which displays the dialog box you see in Figure 2-15.
2. In the Current Image window, center an important part of the image. If needed, use the Navigate button to locate the desired area. Zoom in or out, as necessary.
3. Set the Bias (Lighter, Neutral, or Darker), which is the overall brightness.
4. Set the Strength of the correction to either Normal or Mild, depending on your preference.
5. Set the Appearance (Flat, Natural, or Bold), which is the overall contrast.
6. Click OK.

TIP

Typically, the Neutral, Normal, Natural setting can improve the look of most photos, but if you want a little more contrast, try the Bold appearance setting. Be cautious with Bold, though, because it can also cause details in the shadows to turn too dark.

In Figure 2-16, the image on the top is before using Automatic Contrast Enhancement, and the image on the bottom is after using Automatic Contrast Enhancement. The default settings of Neutral Bias, Normal Strength, and Natural Appearance gave this image the correction it needed.

Figure 2-16 *Using Automatic Contrast Enhancement brought out the natural translucent quality of the leaves. (Photo by James Hutchinson)*

Automatic Saturation Enhancement

One of the more common problems faced by photographers is photos with colors that are dull, appear washed out, or both; and yet when you took the image, you saw the image in vibrant, beautiful color. The reason this happens is quite simple. The human eye dynamically allows you to see a greater range of colors than your camera. Cameras only record a fixed amount of red, green, and blue. Often, these dull drab images can be corrected by adjusting the saturation. Typically, you'll want to adjust saturation after you have adjusted the contrast of your image.

Just what is saturation? If hue is the expression of color values within a picture, then saturation is the intensity illustrating how much of the hue is composed of the pure color itself and how much is diluted by a neutral color such as black or white. Saturation is more a measure of how different a color is from a neutral grey of the same brightness.

An image with good color saturation can display subtle color changes distinctly so that the human eye perceives them as being different from one another. If similar colors blend together, or if colors appear dark, they are oversaturated. Colors that appear washed out are under-saturated. If a color image is completely desaturated, it appears to be a greyscale image. Increasing saturation can give your image brighter, more vibrant color.

Paint Shop Pro includes an Automatic Saturation Enhancement command that is useful for improving the saturation of your image by automatically adapting to the color content of each image. This feature is most effective when used across an entire photo without any selections, because then the entire range of colors is available for analysis.

The following steps show you how to use the Automatic Saturation Enhancement feature:

1. Access Automatic Saturation Enhancement from either the Photo toolbar or the Adjust menu, which displays the dialog box you see in Figure 2-17.
2. In the Current Image window, center an important part of the image. If needed, use the Navigate button to locate the desired area. Zoom in or out, as necessary.
3. Set the Bias, which is the overall saturation.
4. Set the Strength of the correction to Weak, Normal, or Strong.
5. Mark the Skintones present check box if your image has people in it. With this check box selected, Paint Shop Pro modifies the saturation adjustment algorithm in a way that produces more natural-looking skin tones and keeps skin color from becoming oversaturated and looking red and blotchy.
6. Click OK.

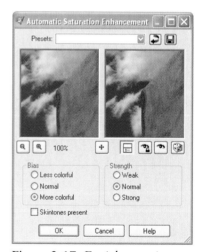

Figure 2-17 *Enrich your image colors through this dialog box.*

In Figure 2-18, auto saturation livened up the sky and brought a warmer feeling to the stucco by setting the Bias to More colorful and the Strength to Strong.

Figure 2-18 *This photo displays the stark contrast of the billowing cloud and the hard lines of the building. (Photo by James Hutchinson)*

Removing Noise

I'm one of those people who don't like a lot of noise. When I'm driving, I rarely listen to the radio or play CDs, as I prefer the silence of my thoughts and the ability to absorb the beauty around me. Similarly, I don't like the distraction of having the television going when I'm trying to read or write. In photographic images, the same idea applies. Keep the noise and distraction away. Digital noise appears as tiny speckles that appear on the image and distract from the subject matter.

Most digital images contain some noise, some more than others, and this noise usually results from taking photos with the camera set at extreme high speed levels but with longer than normal exposure. Many high-end digital cameras offer noise reduction features, but you can remove most unwanted noise with Paint Shop Pro. A noise reduction tool should remove objectionable noise but still retain a natural low level of noise.

NOTE

Noise filters work on 16 million color and greyscale images only. You can increase your color depth by making selections from the Image menu.

Digital Camera Noise

In reality, there are several types of digital noise, and before you determine which Paint Shop Pro feature you use, you need to determine the type of noise you want to get rid of. If the image noise is relatively constant throughout the image, similar to sensor noise or film grain, the Digital Camera Noise Removal (DCNR) is the tool best suited for you. Generally, the DCNR does not remove impulse noise, JPEG artifacts, or moiré patterns.

Overall, the DCNR feature works like this. The filter automatically scrutinizes the image to determine uniform areas in shadow, mid-tone, and highlight regions. Each pixel is examined and compared to what is expected for a noise-free image having that particular color and lightness. This is done for every scale of image noise, taking image texture into account. By a complicated mathematical calculation, a result pixel is computed as a combination of the original image along with different proportions of luminance and chrominance smoothed at different scales. During this process, edges in the image are smoothed so as to preserve the edge information. The result is an image in which each pixel has its own unique combination of luminance and chrominance.

To launch the DCNR filter, click the Adjust menu, select Photo Fix, and select Digital Camera Noise Removal. You'll see a DCNR dialog box like the one seen in Figure 2-19.

TIP

The Photo toolbar also contains a button for Digital Camera Noise Removal.

First you need to select sampling areas, which are indicated by white crosshairs in the Sampling regions window. In each sampling area, Paint Shop Pro makes a separate analysis of the noise, determining whether it is a small scale, medium scale, or large scale noise. We'll learn more about noise scale a little later in this section.

By default, Paint Shop Pro places some sampling markers on the image, but you can add more or move the existing sampling markers to other areas of the image. Click a crosshair in the Sampling regions window, and you can see the area in the Current Image window and the results in the Results window.

The DCNR filter works best with at least three noise samples in the image. Place one in the shadow areas, one in the mid-tone areas, and one in the highlight area. In other words, select a sampling from a dark area, a light area, and an area in between. One other trick in DCNR sampling is if the image contains large distinct regions of different hue, such as red, green, blue, or yellow, it may be helpful to place a sample in each hue region, even though these regions may have similar brightness values.

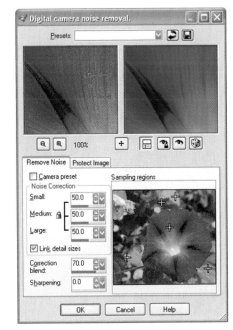

Figure 2-19 *Like many other Paint Shop Pro dialog boxes, the DCNR filter provides a range of settings to control the quality of the result.*

If you want to move a sampling area, drag the crosshair to a new position, and the sampling region will move accordingly. If you want to create more crosshairs, in the Current Image window, drag the cursor over the areas you want to apply correction, which creates a correction box in the Current Image window and places the additional crosshair in the Sampling regions window. You can have a maximum of 10 sampling regions, although typically three or four is sufficient.

TIP

Avoid sampling pure black and pure white areas of the image, as these areas may result in underestimated noise. Also, avoid sampling image edges, as this can result in excessive smoothing.

Now you need to select the setting for the sampling areas. There are three levels of noise details: Small, Medium, and Large. Each visual noise level equates to audio noise levels of "fairly quiet," "busy noise," and "rambunctiously loud," or as they would be known around my house, "the dog snoring," "the television on," and "the kids fighting over a crayon" type noise.

Take a look at the following five samples. The images on this row show the original image and an image after running the DCNR.

But if you look at the following images, you see the image with only certain noise levels removed. The image on the left shows only the small noise removed, the center image shows only medium noise removed, and the image on the right shows only large noise removed.

Each of the Small, Medium, and Large detail sliders in the Noise Correction group controls how much noise is removed at each of the scales. You can control each noise level independently or keep them linked together. Most of the time, keeping the levels linked together produces the best result. The higher the setting of each slider, the more noise of that scale is removed, but higher settings can also destroy image detail.

The next setting is the Correction blend setting. During the correction process, the DCNR creates a de-noised image, which is then blended with the original image. The Correction blend setting determines how much of the corrected image and the original image you want to blend together. Values range from 0 percent, which is no noise reduction, to 100 percent, which is full noise reduction; the default is 70 percent. If you were to blend at 100 percent, your image would have no natural noise in it, resulting in an overly smoothed image.

The last correction setting on the Remove Noise tab is the Sharpening setting. Just like it sounds, this setting controls the percentage of sharpening you want to add back to the image after the noise reduction. The control does not function like a conventional sharpening filter, so typically this control is best left at around 10.

Finally, if you have specific areas of the image that you want to protect from noise correction, click the Protect Image tab and, while holding down the Ctrl key, drag the cursor over the region you want to protect.

Click OK to accept your DCNR settings. Figure 2-20 illustrates an image before and after using the DCNR.

Figure 2-20 *A properly de-noised image should be free of grainy noise, but the detail is still preserved. (Photo by James Hutchinson)*

Impulse Noise

Sometimes, image noise occurs in specific parts of the image rather than over the entire image. This is known as *impulse noise*, and examples of impulse noise might be stuck sensor pixels, hot pixels visible at very long exposures, or specks of dust on a print or a slide. To remove impulse noise, you might want to take a look at one of Paint Shop Pro's many other noise removal features. The noise removal features are available under the Adjust, Add/Remove Noise menu. Here are just a few of them:

- **Despeckle**: The Despeckle command can remove subtle graininess from an image. It works by examining the brightness of each pixel in comparison to surrounding pixels.

- **Edge Preserving Smooth**: Use the Edge Preserving Smooth command to remove noise in an image without losing edge details. This command finds details such as object edges and preserves them while smoothing the areas between the edges. When selecting Edge Preserving Smooth options, it's best to choose the smallest amount of smoothing that removes the specks while retaining image detail. For example, in Figure 2-21, Edge Preserving Smooth got rid of the small reflections caused from crystallized ice/snow that appear as noise in this brightly lit snow scene. The Edge Preserving Smooth command is also helpful to minimize film grain.

Figure 2-21 *Edge Preserving Smooth changes are best viewed under a high zoom ratio. (Photo by James Hutchinson)*

- **Median Filter:** The Median Filter command is similar to the Despeckle command in that it subtly removes areas of noise in the image. The difference between the Despeckle command and the Median Filter command is that instead of comparing neighboring pixel brightness, it calculates an average value of the nearby pixels and applies the result to the area in question.

- **Texture Preserving Smooth:** Use the Texture Preserving Smooth command to remove noise or specks in an image while preserving texture details. This command examines an image's pixels to determine if they display textured or smooth areas. Few noise adjustments are made in textured areas, and smooth areas are adjusted to remove noise. For example, if you are looking at a prairie scene, noise may be excessive for a face or a sky, which we know to be smooth in real life, but in the grassy areas, we expect to have some texture or noise. The Texture Preserving Smooth command can remove the noise from the sky but leave it present in the grassy area.

Sharpening Your Images

High acutance, or sharpness, is a photography fundamental. Photography awards are won and lost because of sharpness. A problem arises with digital photography or scanning that can make edges appear blurred because of detail being lost during the digitization process.

Can you ever recover the lost detail? Not really, but through sharpening, you can make it appear as though you have. By increasing differences between neighboring pixels, Paint Shop Pro enhances image edges, thereby making the edges appear sharper, whether they really are or not.

You can use sharpening commands to enhance detail in photos, but remember that none of the sharpening commands can add detail that was not saved in the original image. Paint Shop Pro includes a number of different tools you can use to sharpen your images, including Sharpen, Sharpen More, Clarify, and Unsharp Mask. Each has a specific use; however, most professionals prefer the Unsharp Mask tool over the others.

TIP

You should not apply sharpening effects until you are finished with other corrections, including color and tone. Sharpening should be the last effect you should apply. This general rule applies to all sharpening tools.

The Clarify feature can make hazy, slightly blurry objects, those ones that are just a tad out of focus, look clearer. Clarify works more with the detail in the shadow and highlight areas of a photo, making objects stand out and giving the image a crisper, more focused look, which then adds a sense of depth and clarity to the image. You can access the Clarify function through the Adjust menu, Brightness, and Contrast; then click Clarify. For strength of effect, use the smallest value that gives your image the result you need.

Sharpen and Sharpen More improve image clarity by increasing the contrast between adjacent pixels where there are significant color contrasts, usually at the mid and high contrast image edges. Just like it sounds, the Sharpen More command sharpens with a stronger effect than the Sharpen command. Paint Shop Pro automatically applies these commands to the image without any input from you, but also tends to tweak the wrong parts of a picture and make it look grainy, like an old 35mm photo. While the Sharpen commands may be faster and easier, you lose a great deal of control over the sharpening, so a lot of photographers don't use them anymore. Access the Sharpen and Sharpen More commands by clicking the Adjust menu and selecting Sharpness.

Unsharp Mask, like Sharpen and Sharpen More, works more on the mid to high contrast edges of an image, but you have much more control over the process. Despite what its name indicates, Unsharp Mask actually sharpens your image. The principle behind it lies in exaggerating the light-dark contrast between the two sides of an edge.

The process actually mimics a traditional film compositing technique by taking two or more copies of the image, manipulating them, and then merging them back together. One copy is translated into a negative image, while the others are slightly blurred. The images are then combined together; the light areas of the blurred images cancel out the dark areas of the negative, but the blurring around the edges has nothing to cancel it out, which results in lighter and darker lines on either side of the edges. That, in turn, adds the appearance of sharpness.

You access the Paint Shop Pro Unsharp Mask feature by clicking the Adjust menu, clicking Sharpness, and selecting Unsharp Mask. You'll then see a dialog box like the one in Figure 2-22.

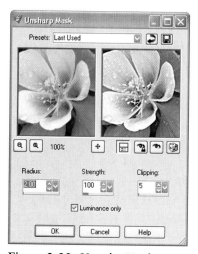

Figure 2-22 *Use the Unsharp Mask dialog box to sharpen your image.*

TIP

The Photo toolbar also contains a button for Unsharp Mask.

There are three settings for the Unsharp Mask feature: Radius, Strength, and Clipping. Let's take a look at what each of these settings does.

- **Radius:** The Radius setting determines the number of pixels to adjust around each edge. The practical effect of this is to specify how large a region is darkened or lightened. As this number increases, so does the apparent sharpness of the image. Setting too high a number, though, can result in harsh edges with lighter pixels around all the edges, especially if you also increase the Strength setting. The range is from .01 to 100, but the default setting is only 2.

  Lower values sharpen only the edge pixels, while higher values sharpen a wider band of pixels. The effect is much less noticeable in print than onscreen because a small radius (for example, 1 pixel) represents a smaller area in a high-resolution printed image. Therefore, use lower values for onscreen images and higher values for high-resolution printed images.

  The main thing to keep in mind is the original resolution of your image. Low-resolution images can't benefit from much more than one to three pixels worth of edge sharpening, while higher-resolution images can accommodate values of 10 or more. You'll know right away if you have set your values too high because you will see thick, poster-like edges that aren't realistic, accompanied by a high degree of contrast.

- **Strength:** The Strength setting refers to how much sharpening you are applying. In other words, it controls the contrast change along the edges in your photo, making dark colors darker and light colors lighter. The Strength range is from 1 to 500, with 100 being the default. As a general rule, 100 to 150 percent is the most useful range for this variable. Start with the default and see if you like the effect; if not, increase it gradually. But be careful about increasing it too much because you can end up with a noisy photo with harsh edges and too much contrast.

- **Clipping:** The Clipping setting determines how much contrast must exist between the pixels before the filter will be applied to an area. Low contrast equals a blurry, soft image, whereas high contrast tends to mean a sharp, hard image. A very low setting value means that edges with relatively small contrast differences will be accentuated. High setting values mean that the difference must be very great before any additional sharpening is applied.

  The Clipping setting has a range of 0 to 100 with a default setting of 5. Normally, you'll need to change the clipping only when the default value produces an image with excessive noise or some other undesirable effect. Try setting the Radius and Strength settings first and then experiment with Clipping to see if you like the results any better.

Also, remember that all three of these values work together. If you use a high Clipping value because your picture was taken in low light and suffers from some digital noise, you may want to increase the Strength to 150 percent to beef up the sharpening effect. Figure 2-23 illustrates an image before and after applying the Unsharp Mask function.

Figure 2-23 *Unsharp Mask shows more detail in the flower petals and makes the water drops crisper. (Photo by James Hutchinson)*

What's Next?

Chapter 3 takes what you've learned even further. Next, you'll discover more about image retouching tools, including getting rid of pesky red-eye, removing unwanted objects with the Clone tool, eliminating dust and scratches, and correcting distortion and lighting problems.

3

Retouching Tools

Previously, photographic technicians and specialists, called *retouchers*, worked directly on film negatives and other media with brush and color. It was a time-consuming and expensive process, but an important piece of photography. Most published photographs and other media images were retouched in some manner. Today, virtually all the images you see in advertising and magazines have been retouched and manipulated digitally.

Paint Shop Pro provides you with the tools you need to retouch images in resourceful and creative ways. You can remove or disguise blemishes, touch up dust spots, repair scratches, and perform many tasks that were once available only through the realm of the film retoucher.

In this chapter, you'll discover methods to correct those types of image defects, as well as correct perspective, remove red eye, and rectify lighting and distortion problems. We'll also delve into the Clone Brush, which you can use to remove unwanted subject matter, and we'll take an in-depth look at the many different retouch brushes you can use to modify your image details. Many photos need multiple corrections, so you should look at each image as a project.

> ## TIP
>
> Before you begin retouching a photograph, you should duplicate the image and work on the duplicate. That way if you are unhappy with your results, you still have the original image to work with and start over. Duplicate an image by clicking the Window menu and selecting Duplicate. Additionally, you can then compare the original image and the duplicate image side by side to get a better view of your changes (Window, Tile Vertically).

Removing Red Eye

We've all seen it. You snap a photo of friends, loved ones, or even your dog, only to find that their eyes have taken on an eerie red glow. Red eye is a basic fact of human biology because the pupils expand and contract in response to light exposure. In bright light, the pupils are small; in low light they can get really big. When the camera flash goes off, it travels through the dilated pupil and reflects light off of the blood vessels behind the retina inside the eye. The camera picks it up as a distracting red spot.

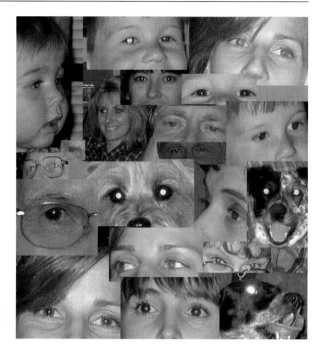

The term red eye is particularly appropriate for people. The lighter the eye color, the more pronounced the effect can be. The red eye effect can have a different appearance with animals. Many animals have a reflective layer in the back of their eyes that enhances their night vision. Studies have shown that the color of the reflective layer varies to some extent with the animal's coat color. For example, a black dog will have a green layer, producing a vivid green-eye effect. No matter what the color, it still makes the person or animal look possessed.

The best thing you can do is to prevent red eye from happening when you take the photo. Here are a couple of tips:

- Move the flash away from the lens altogether.

- Use the red eye reduction feature on your camera, which fires a few quick bursts of light that cause the pupil to react before the real camera flash goes off.

- Turn on a light or move the subject to a brighter area. The pupils become smaller, and the red eye reaction is reduced.

- Have the subject look away from the lens, either above the camera or to the side opposite the flash, to reduce the reflection.

If your image does have red eye, you can use the Paint Shop Pro Red-eye Removal tools to make a correction and return the eyes to their natural look.

There are a couple of parameters you must meet before you can use the Red-eye Removal command. First, your image must be in 16 million colors or greyscale, and secondly, the image must have no selections. (You'll learn more about selections in Chapter 4, "Selecting and Layering.")

The following steps guide you with the Red-eye Removal command:

1. Click the Adjust menu and select Photo Fix.
2. Click Red-eye Removal, which displays the Red-eye Removal dialog box you see in Figure 3-1.

TIP

You can also select the Red-eye Removal button on the Photo toolbar.

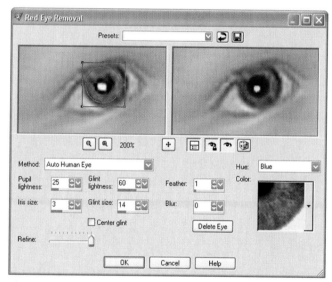

Figure 3-1 *Use this dialog box to remove red eye from human or animal photos.*

3. In the Current image window, center the subject's red eye. If needed, use the Navigate button to locate the desired area. Zoom in or out as necessary so the red eye is large enough to work with.
4. From the Method drop-list, select whether you are working with a human eye or an animal eye. Try the Auto selections first, but if the pupil is partially hidden, you can manually select the correction area with the Freehand Pupil Outline or the Point-to-Point Pupil Outline option.

5. Click the Hue drop-down list and select an eye hue. If you are working with animal eyes or the Freehand Pupil Outline and Point-to-Point Pupil Outline methods, this option will not be available.

6. Click the Color drop-down list and select an eye color or, in the case of an animal eye, an eye style. The animal choices include one cat eye option and two dog eye options.

7. Click anywhere inside the red area of the eye to select the eye automatically. You can also click and drag from the center of the eye to the outside edge of the red area. A circle appears around the selected area, and a control box for making adjustments encloses the circle. The Preview window displays the corrected eye.

   For the Auto Animal Eye method, drag the center rotation handle to rotate the selection. You can also reshape the eye from a circle to an ellipse by dragging its side handles.

TIP

To move the selection, drag it to a new location. To remove a selection, click the Delete Eye button.

---

8. In many cases, you won't need to do anything else, but if necessary, the Red-eye Removal dialog box contains a number of additional adjustments tools:

   ■ Adjust the value for Pupil Lightness so that the corrected eye matches your perception of the natural color. Increasing the number makes the pupil lighter.

   ■ Change the iris size. Increasing the iris size decreases the pupil size. (Animal eyes don't have an iris.)

   ■ Adjust the lightness of the glint. A glint makes the eye look natural and lively. Lower values darken the glint; higher values lighten it.

   ■ Adjust the glint size. Larger values make the glint larger.

   ■ If desired, center the glint in the eye by checking the Center Glint check box.

   ■ Use the Feather setting to adjust how much feathering surrounds the corrected eye. Smaller values make the edges more defined; larger values blend the edges to the surrounding image areas.

   ■ If the photo is rather grainy, you can increase the blur to blend the eye with surrounding pixels.

TIP

If the eyelid covers part of the eye, you can use the Refine option to reduce the amount of correction and minimize its overlap with the surrounding skin area.

---

9. Repeat this process for the other eye and then click OK.

Figure 3-2 illustrates how the Red-eye Removal tool removed the red eye from the baby's eyes.

As mentioned earlier in this section, red eye isn't always red, especially in animals. Take a look at Figure 3-3. On the left, you can see the dog's eyes glaring in vivid green, but using the red eye reduction feature, the Yorkie on the right looks quite friendly.

TIP

As an alternative to the Red-eye Removal tool, try using the Saturation brush or the Hue brush. You'll learn more about these brushes later in this chapter.

Figure 3-2 *Removing red eye makes the eyes look natural.*

Figure 3-3 *Animal red eye can have different colors due to the animal's fur color.*

Removing Unwanted Objects

Sometimes, an image has undesirable elements such as a telephone pole, debris, scratches, dust, or even ex-wives/husbands/boyfriends/girlfriends and so forth. Paint Shop Pro has a number of tools to remove the unwanted elements and, if desired, replace the space with other elements.

Using the Clone Brush

Paint Shop Pro includes a tool called the *Clone Brush* that provides a unique way to edit your images by using other parts of an image as a paint source. The Clone Brush creates a brush that automatically matches the color and texture of an area you select. Using the Clone Brush, you can remove unwanted items or add additional items.

Here's how the Clone Brush works: You choose a source location somewhere in the picture. The source location can be part of the same image layer, another layer in the image, or an area from another image. When you paint with the Clone Brush, you paste copies of pixels from the source location wherever you click.

In this first example, you see a beautiful field of poppies, but there is an unsightly pole right in the middle of the picture. We'll use the Clone Brush to remove the pole.

 The Clone Brush is the eighth icon down from the top of the Tool palette. Since it shares this space with the Scratch Remover, you may need to pick it from the list. Just click the drop-down arrow on the right side of the tools and select Clone Brush. A shortcut to selecting the Clone Brush is to just press the letter C.

There are a number of selections available on the Clone Brush Tool Options bar. Let's take a look at the available options:

TIP

Several of the Paint Shop Pro brushes use many of the same options.

- **Shape:** Choose from square or rounded edges when painting.
- **Size:** Select the brush pixel size from 1 to 500.
- **Hardness:** Pick how sharp you want the edges of the tool to be. Settings are from 0 to 100, with 100 giving you the sharpest, hardest edge and lower values giving softer, fading edges.
- **Step:** Select a value from 1 to 200 that determines the distance placed between applications of paint during a paint stroke. Using a lower number gives a smoother, more continuous appearance.
- **Density:** Sets the paint coverage. From values of 1 to 100, you'll usually want a higher number for more complete coverage. Using a lower number results in spotty paint coverage.

■ **Thickness:** Works with the brush shape setting and controls how wide the brush is. With values of 1 to 100, a round brush and a setting of 100 provide a perfect circle, while a lower value with a round brush sets the brush to an oval. As you decrease the thickness, the brush becomes narrower.

■ **Rotation:** Determines the rotation of the brush. Measured in degrees, select from 0 to 359.

■ **Opacity:** Establishes how well the paint covers the image surface. At 100 percent opacity, the paint covers everything. Use opacity numbers less than 100 percent if you want some of the underlying pixels of the original area to show through. At 1 percent opacity, the paint is almost transparent.

■ **Blend mode:** Select from options that determine how painted pixels are blended with pixels on underlying layers. (You'll learn more about layers in Chapter 4, "Selecting and Layering.")

■ **Stroke:** Specify whether you want the paint to build up as you apply multiple strokes over the same area. If checked, the paint maintains a continuous color, and repainting an area has no effect. If not checked, each brush stroke over the same area applies more paint until the paint coverage reaches 100 percent opacity.

■ **Aligned mode:** Check this box to have the Clone Brush paint from the point of the source area relative to the first point you clicked on the target area each time you stop and start painting again. If the option is not selected, every stroke you paint will have the same as the source data.

■ **Sample merged:** Use this when working with multiple layers. If checked, the Clone Brush will gather information from all the layers merged together, but if unchecked, the Clone Brush will only use the information on the current layer.

Let's begin by using the Clone Brush to remove the unsightly telephone pole from the image you see in Figure 3-4. We'll also remove the small sign from the hill on the left.

Figure 3-4 *Remove unwanted image elements with the Clone Brush.*
(Photo by Patti Wavinak)

You can use the default settings on most of the Clone Brush options, but you'll definitely want to set the size, which determines the diameter of the paintbrush. If you make the brush too small, the cloning won't look natural, and it will take a long time to completely erase the unwanted element. If it's too large, you won't be able to get an accurate, natural-looking brush stroke.

Start with a size that looks like it will allow you to erase in realistic looking pieces. For the sample picture, we set the size to 40 pixels. On some images, you'll need to change the size, depending on the area you are working in. For this example, we also clicked the Aligned mode option.

Right-click the mouse on an area you want to paint over the affected area *with*. You won't see anything happen, but you may hear a slight tone from your computer. In the sample, since we want to get rid of the pole and replace it with sky on the top and poppies on the bottom, we need to right-click the mouse on the area to the left, next to the pole (see Figure 3-5).

Next, you need to hold down the left mouse button and paint over the pole. As you paint, Paint Shop Pro replaces the pole with the pixels just like the ones in the area where you right-clicked. Release the mouse button periodically and begin again, occasionally reselecting the source area. You could simply click, hold, and drag, creating one long brush stroke, but that method usually creates noticeable irregularities. You'll get a better look with less streaking if you erase parts of the pole one click at a time. Zoom in and out, as necessary, to easily see the area you are erasing. If you look at Figure 3-6, you'll never know the pole was there in the original image.

Figure 3-5 *After selecting the source area, paint over the area you want to cover.*

Figure 3-6 *Notice the sign that was on the hill on the left is gone, also courtesy of the Clone Brush.*

Figure 3-7 also illustrates an example where the Clone Brush was used to add to the picture. On the top, you see the original image, which began as a great shot of a dog sitting in a creek, but notice the unsightly black plastic areas around some of the rocks. Painting the black plastic, using the Clone Brush with the grassy areas as the source area, made the black plastic disappear. The retouched image on the bottom also has a little green grass added to some of the dead grass areas.

Figure 3-7 *We even added a few new flowers growing by the rocks on the bottom. (Photo by James Hutchinson)*

Removing Dust and Scratches

Many of us have boxes full of old photos that we will "someday" put into beautiful albums. Unfortunately, since the images are not generally protected, they are inclined to get dust, scratches, tears, or creases. When you scan those images digitally, you pick up the same blemishes as are on the original. Fortunately, Paint Shop Pro includes several tools to remove some of these marks from the digital image.

Removing Scratches

You can use the Scratch Remover tool to remove scratches, cracks, and other defects from your images, but you should know this tool works best if the image background is relatively smooth. The Scratch Remover tool can be used only on backgrounds and only with images that are 16 million color or greyscale.

Take a look at the image in Figure 3-8, which has a large scratch along the top of the photo. If you look closely, there is also a long thin scratch running down the groom's face. We'll use the Scratch Remover tool to remove both blemishes. The image also has a lot of dust spots, including one on the bride's eyebrow and in her hair. You'll learn in the next section how you can use the Salt and Pepper filter to remove dust.

Figure 3-8 *Although this bride and groom look very happy on their very windy wedding day, they wouldn't be pleased with all the scratches, dust, and noise in this image.*

TIP

To limit the correction to a specific area, first make a selection. This step works well when you need to be careful *not* to remove important details near the scratch.

Follow these steps:

1. Zoom in to the area you want to work with. When working with the retouching tools, it's important to get in very close to the damaged area. When you've finished retouching an area, zoom back out to view the overall image changes.

2. Select the Scratch Remover tool. Like the Clone Brush, it's the eighth icon down on the toolbar and shares space with the Clone Brush. The Scratch Remover icon looks like a trowel, the kind used to fill in cracks before you paint.

3. On the Tool Options palette, set the following options:

   ■ **Width:** When you choose the tool and drag it along the scratch or crease, the length is determined as you drag, but you need to set the width, which is measured in pixels. Choose a width that is about 3 or 4 pixels wider than the scratch. If the width is considerably larger than the scratch, you will lose image detail.

   ■ **Selection boxes:** There are two different shapes you can use with the Scratch Remover tool. Select the flat-end option to correct scratches that are perpendicular to object edges in the image or are in an open area. Select the pointed-end option to correct scratches at an angle. The pointed-end setting gets into small spaces and tight corners more easily than the blunt-end version.

4. Center the cursor just outside one end of the scratch; then click and drag the bounding box over the scratch. When the rectangle properly encloses the scratch, release the mouse button, and the scratch is removed (see Figure 3-9).

TIP

Press the arrow keys to move the starting point of the bounding box by 1 pixel. Press the PageUp or PageDown key to increase or decrease the width of the box by 1 pixel.

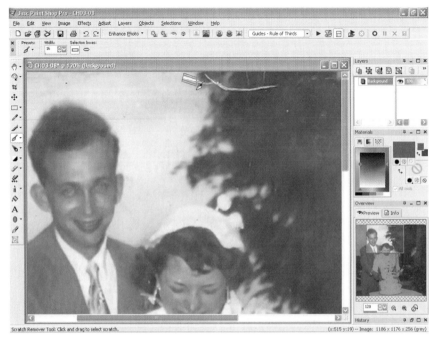

Figure 3-9 *We'll need a wider scratch removal width for the top scratch but a very thin width for the scratch on the man's face.*

For the best results, follow these tips:

■ Before using the tool, select the area that contains the scratch. If there is an abrupt change in color, you are often better off to make multiple shorter selections than one long one.

■ Choose the smallest possible width that completely encompasses the defect inside the inner borderlines without touching the scratch or cut at any point. If your selection touches the scratch, you'll get unattractive smearing.

■ For scratches over several different backgrounds, try removing the scratch a section at a time.

■ Work in the direction of the scratch or crease.

■ You'll get a smoother repair if you stop and make a new selection when the angle of the scratch changes.

Removing Dust Spots

Many images pick up dust spots that need touching up. The spots could come from dust on a scanner bed, the camera lens, or any number of places. The bottom line is that you will want to clean those up.

Paint Shop Pro includes a wonderful noise filter, called the *Salt and Pepper filter,* which can remove black or white specks, such as those caused by dust. The Salt and Pepper filter works by comparing an area of pixels to the surrounding pixels and adjusting an area that is a speck to match those surrounding pixels.

You can remove the dust from a selected area of your image or from the entire image. To illustrate this, we'll use the old wedding photo again in which we previously removed some scratches.

You'll find the Salt and Pepper filter under the Adjust menu and the Add/Remove Noise submenu.

The Salt and Pepper filter uses the following options:

- Speck size, which is the minimum size in pixels of the largest speck that you want Paint Shop Pro to remove. The value is always an odd number.

- Sensitivity to specks, which is how different an area must be from its surrounding pixels in order to be considered a speck.

- Select the Include all lower speck sizes check box to have Paint Shop Pro remove all lower speck sizes. Results are usually better if you mark this check box.

- The Aggressive action check box determines how hard you want Paint Shop Pro to work in correcting the spots.

For the photo we are working with, we need to set the Sensitivity option to 5 and select both the Include all lower speck sizes and the Aggressive action check boxes. Figure 3-10 shows the image as it was first scanned (left) and the final, cropped, de-noised, scratches and dust removed image.

Figure 3-10 *Using the Clone Brush, we can even tame down the groom's windblown hair.*

Removing JPEG Artifacts

When you save a file to the JPEG format, the file information is compressed to create a smaller file. Often, using compression produces unwanted image problems known as *JPEG artifacts* that can appear as halos or color leakage beyond the edges of objects, checkerboard problems on smooth backgrounds, or blocky-looking areas in an image.

Use Paint Shop Pro's JPEG Artifact Removal command to restore a JPEG image to its original appearance. Because JPEG compression is a lossy compression method, the saving process actually discards image information. As a result, there are limits as to how well the image can be restored.

Use the following steps to remove JPEG artifacts from your image:

1. Make sure the image has no selections. The JPEG Artifact Removal command doesn't work if the image contains a selection.

2. Click the Adjust menu, select Add/Remove Noise, and then click JPEG Artifact Removal. You'll see the dialog box shown in Figure 3-11.

3. In the Current View window, select an area of the image where the artifacts are very apparent.

4. Set an option for the correction Strength. Choices include Low, Normal, High, and Maximum. For best results, try each option and examine all areas of the image to see which Strength setting works best.

5. Select the amount of Crispness, which determines how much fine-detail information the artifact removal should attempt to restore. Values are 0 (the least) to 100 (the most). It's only a guess because the original information is lost, so you should typically start in the middle and adjust the value until the image looks the most natural. Setting the Crispness too high can add additional noise to the image.

6. Click OK.

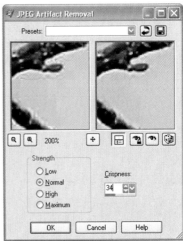

Figure 3-11 *Setting the Crispness too high can add additional noise to the image.*

See Figure 3-12, which illustrates an image both before and after JPEG artifact removal.

Figure 3-12 *Luckily, when this photo was taken, it was fall, and the hornets were all gone!*

Bettering Perspective

When you take pictures of tall objects, the results may have a perspective illusion; that is, the objects seem to be leaning or angled. This happens when the camera is at an angle to the subjects. The best remedy is to take the picture with a longer lens or a perspective control lens, but that's not always an available option. Sometimes, you just need to tilt the camera upward to capture your subject.

Unfortunately, that can give you a result similar to what you see in Figure 3-13. In this image, you see a very unique building that captured the photographer's interest when touring along the Chicago River. Besides all the unwanted extraneous elements in the photo, the subject building appears to lean, due to a bad perspective when shooting the photograph.

Figure 3-13 *Looks like a long way to the top.*

Paint Shop Pro can help correct perspective problems with the Perspective Correction tool. The Perspective Correction tool is the second tool on the toolbar and shares a space with the Straighten tool, the Deform tool, and the Mesh Warp tool.

 When you select the Perspective Correction tool, Paint Shop Pro places a grid on the image, which you can then use to specify the image (such as the building) that is supposed to be rectangular but is angled.

You can change the size and number of gridlines through the Gridlines box on the Tool Options palette.

The Crop image check box is very important. You select this option to have Paint Shop Pro crop the image back to its original size after the perspective is applied. Areas of the image that fall outside the original image size are deleted. In Figure 3-14, you can see both options.

Figure 3-14 *The image on the left did not have the Crop image option selected, while the image on the right does have the Crop image option.*

Drag each handle to the corner of the feature you want to straighten. Make sure that the outside gridlines run parallel with the subject. From the Tool Options palette, you can fine-tune the position of the box by specifying the X and Y positions of the four corner handles. Figure 3-15 shows the image with the gridlines applied. When you are satisfied with the grid lines, click the Apply button.

TIP

If the correction causes some image data to fall outside the image canvas, you can restore that data by increasing the size of the canvas.

In Figure 3-16, we corrected the perspective; then using the Clone Brush, we liminated the extra unwanted areas.

Gridlines

Figure 3-15 *Drag the gridlines until they are parallel with your subject.*

Figure 3-16 *Straightening and removing the extra elements drew the focus back to this building.*

Correcting Distortion

Sometimes, pictures can suffer from lens distortion issues, including barrel distortion where the subject lines bow outward, making the subject appear spherical, or pincushion distortion where the subject lines bow inward and look pinched at their center. Although distortion is frequently found in cameras with inexpensive lenses such as disposables, you'll sometimes find it in digital camera images, too. Digital camera lenses must be wider than their film counterparts to capture the same area. As a result, pictures taken with digital cameras can suffer from lens distortion. Typically, you'll find wide-angle lenses can cause barrel distortion, and telephoto or zoom lenses can cause pincushion distortion.

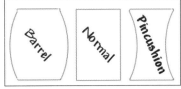

One other type of lens distortion is called *fisheye*. Fisheyed images look like they have been pasted onto a sphere or blown up like a balloon. Lines that should be straight are curved, and edges look compressed. Unwanted fisheye distortion is rare.

In general, distortion is most noticeable when you have a very straight edge near the side of the image frame. Take a look at the images in Figure 3-17. The image on the left shows no distortion, but the image on the right has quite a bit of barrel distortion. The street curb is curved, and the building almost looks full, like it could pop at any moment.

Figure 3-17 *Barrel distortion causes the subject to bow outward. (Photo by Gary French)*

Fortunately, Paint Shop Pro includes correction tools to manage image distortion. For the lens corrections to work properly, the axis of the camera lens must coincide with the center of the image; therefore, you should apply any lens distortion corrections before you crop your image. Additionally, the distortion correction tools work only on images in 16 million colors or greyscale.

Follow these steps to remove lens distortion:

1. Turn on the grid for a point of reference
2. Click the Adjust menu and select Photo Fix.
3. At the bottom of the Photo Fix submenu, you'll see the three lens correction options: Barrel, Fisheye, and Pincushion Distortion Correction. Select the option you want to use. A dialog box similar to the one seen in Figure 3-18 will open.
4. Look for horizontal or vertical elements that are curved and adjust Strength value until they become straight. Strength values range from 0 to 100, with 0 making no changes. The image is resized as you adjust this value.

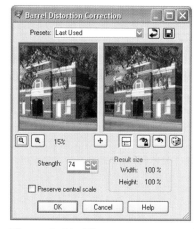

Figure 3-18 *The image is resized as you adjust the strength.*

TIP

Click the Proof button to see the effect on the image against the grid.

---

5. Select whether you want Paint Shop Pro to preserve the central scale of the image. This option determines whether the scale of the center of the picture remains the same or is adjusted. If you don't check the box, Paint Shop Pro will not change the image size, but if the box is checked, Paint Shop Pro adds or removes pixels to or from the image. The resulting size ratio is displayed in the Result size area.
6. Click OK.

Lighting

One of the hardest things to get right in a photograph is the lighting. Too much light, too little light, or a combination of the two can ruin an otherwise perfect photo.

But Paint Shop Pro can provide two lighting effects to repair an incorrectly lit image. Let's take a look at Backlighting and Fill Flash—first to understand what each type of lighting does, and secondly, how Paint Shop Pro can help.

Backlighting is just as it sounds: light that comes from behind your subject. This can make a beautiful photo or turn a beautiful photo into a disaster. Backlighting is what turns a palm tree into a silhouette against the sunset. In this case, that is a good thing that adds to the photograph.

But the same thing can happen if you want to take a photograph of a person who has a strong backlight behind them, such as the sun, sky, or bright lights. The camera reads the brightness behind the main subject and sets its internal meter to expose properly for the extra light. This underexposes your subject and will usually turn him into a silhouette. You can avoid this by using a fill-flash. A fill-flash will fill in the needed light, chasing away the shadows from your subject caused from the bright light behind.

Backlighting

When the sun is in front of the photographer, coming directly at the camera, you have what is referred to as backlighting; that means that the light is behind the subject. Backlighting can produce some wonderful images, but learning how to backlight can be tricky. This type of lighting can be very effective for pictures of people outdoors in bright sunlight because in bright sunlight, when subjects are facing the light, they may be uncomfortable and squint their eyes. Backlighting helps to eliminate this problem.

Backlighting is also used to produce a silhouette effect. If a subject is translucent or semi-translucent, like flower petals, delicate leaves, or even jellyfish, backlighting can reveal the object's internal details and often make it glow with beautiful iridescence.

However, too much backlighting can cause a problem by washing out the entire image. A similar problem involves photos with too much flash on the subject. If your images appear too dark or washed out to see all the details, chances are your digital camera captured all the information you needed to lighten or darken areas in your photos, and it pulled out the details in the process. Paint Shop Pro includes a backlighting filter to help you darken the bright, overexposed areas of a photo.

Click the Adjust menu, select Photo Fix, and then click Backlighting. Paint Shop Pro displays the Backlighting Filter dialog box you see in Figure 3-19.

The Strength setting determines how much you want Paint Shop Pro to darken the lighter areas. In the example you see in Figure 3-20, the image on the left is the original, and the image on the right is after applying the Backlighting filter.

Figure 3-19 *Experiment with the strength until you get the best result for your image.*

Figure 3-20 *A backlighting strength of 60 did the best job of correcting the almost washed-out mountains to the back left. (Photo by James Hutchinson)*

Fill Flash

Another lighting problem occurs when photos taken in bright light have little detail in the shadow areas because the camera is attempting *not* to overexpose the brighter areas. If you have taken outdoor photos of people without a flash, chances are the subject's face was too dark or had harsh shadows under the eyes.

But you already know that on a bright day, if you place the subject so that his back is to the sun, it keeps the subject from squinting. The problem arises that the existing daylight may not be enough to illuminate your photograph properly. A brief burst of light from a flash, called *Fill Flash*, can add sparkle to the eyes and soften harsh shadows.

The Paint Shop Pro Fill Flash filter lightens the darker, underexposed areas of a photo. If your photo's background is too dark, or you feel there's too much difference between the photo's light and dark areas, this filter is a good choice to help correct that problem. In people pictures, this usually means dark eye sockets and unattractive shadows under the nose and lips. The Fill Flash filter lightens these shadows to create more attractive portraits. See Figure 3-21.

Figure 3-21 *The Fill Flash brought out the sparkle in this woman's eyes.*

Fill Flash is not limited to people pictures. Take a look at Figure 3-22. Here you see a beautiful fall lane whose thick trees blocked out much of the sunlight from coming through, but after adding the Fill Flash filter, became a cheerier brighter path by illuminating the tree bark, eliminating some shadows from the lane, and bringing out the rich golden color of the leaves.

Figure 3-22 *The figure on the left is the original, and the figure on the right is after adding the Fill Flash filter. (Photo by James Hutchinson)*

To apply the Fill Flash filter, click the Adjust menu, select Photo Fix, and click Fill Flash. Paint Shop Pro displays the Fill Flash Filter dialog box, which is similar to the Backlighting Filter dialog box. Select the strength of the light you want to apply.

You may also run into a situation where a photo has just enough of a problem with too-dark areas as well as too-light areas. In that case, try running the Fill Flash filter on the photo and then using the Backlighting filter (see Figure 3-23). The image benefited from the Fill Flash filter to illuminate the darker, underexposed back porch area, but the Backlighting filter then darkened the bright, overexposed grassy area in front of the porch.

Figure 3-23 *Adjusting the lighting made this back porch look much more inviting. (Photo by Patti Wavinak)*

Using the Retouch Brushes

So far, the corrections we've been making have been to an entire image; however, sometimes you just need to make minor retouches to selected areas of your photograph.

Paint Shop Pro provides a variety of artistic brushes you can use to selectively retouch and enhance your images. Using brush tips, similar to the painting and drawing tools in Paint Shop Pro, these brushes have controls that enable you to dodge (lighten), burn (darken), soften, change the saturation or hue, and much more. These Retouch brushes take time and practice to master, but they are definitely worth the effort.

Due to the number of changes these tools can make, they appear as two different icons on the toolbar. Seven brushes are included on the first tool, which is the ninth icon on the toolbar. The tenth icon contains four additional brushes. Let's take a look at each brush and its task.

Icon	Brush Name	Function
	Dodge	Lightens shadowed areas to bring out more details.
	Burn	Darkens light areas it passes over and is commonly used to add depth to an image, as well as darkening light spots.
	Smudge	Intermingles colors as if you were running your finger through wet paint by spreading the color and details from the starting point and picks up new color and image details as it moves.
	Push	Pushes existing color and image details over the canvas from the starting point, but does not pick up any new color or details.
	Soften	Smoothes and reduces contrast on the edges, making them blend into the background better. It's a good tool to use for the edges on pasted areas.
	Sharpen	Brings an area into better focus by heightening the edges and creating greater contrast.
	Emboss	Causes the foreground to appear raised from the background by suppressing color and tracing edges in black.
	Lighten/Darken	Increases or decreases brightness by adding more light or darkness to a selected area. Using the left mouse button lightens the selected area, and using the right mouse button darkens the area.

Icon	Brush Name	Function
	Saturation Up/Down	Increases or decreases the saturation level by affecting the HSL value of pixels. Using the left mouse button increases saturation, and using the right mouse button decreases the saturation.
	Hue Up/Down	Adjusts the color shade of a selected image area by affecting the HSL value of pixels. Using the left mouse button increases the hue value, and using the right mouse button decreases the hue value.
	Change-to-Target	Changes pixels so they look like they are painted on a canvas or other material from the Materials palette.

Now that we know what each function of each brush performs, take a look at the available brush options that appear on the Tool Options palette. Earlier in this chapter, you learned how each of these options affects the Clone Brush. The options work exactly the same for the Retouch brushes.

There are a few extra choices, depending on the tool you select. For example, there is an extra option available for the Lighten/Darken, Saturation Up/Down, or Hue Up/Down brushes. It's the Swap Mouse Buttons option, and with the option not checked, the left mouse button does the first function (Lighten, Saturation Up, Hue Up), and the right mouse button does the second function (Darken, Saturation Down, Hue Down). If you check this box, the mouse button functions are reversed.

If you opt to use the Change to Target brush, you have an additional option to select the mode. If you choose the color as the target, the tool applies the foreground color without affecting the luminance. If you choose the hue, saturation, or lightness as the target, it applies the foreground color's hue, saturation, or lightness value without changing the other values.

TIP

When using the Retouch brushes, making smaller changes as you work enables you to make the changes less obvious. Try lowering the opacity to change the amount of effect a brush has.

What's Next?

In this chapter, you learned about some of the amazing retouching tools included with Paint Shop Pro with which you can enhance and correct your images. In Chapter 4, you'll learn about making selections so you can modify only a portion of your image and about working with layers, one of the most powerful features included with Paint Shop Pro.

4

Selecting and Layering

So far, you've become familiar with the basic photograph correction and enhancement tools by learning what they are and how to use them. Now it's time to advance to the next step.

In earlier chapters, you learned how to make enhancements and corrections to your photographs, but those changes were applied to the entire image. Making selections is an important step in working with images if you want only to modify a particular part of the image. You can use one of Paint Shop Pro's powerful selection tools to separate the fragment you want to change. After you create a selection, you can edit the selection while leaving the rest of the image unchanged, or you can reverse that thought and use the selected area to protect your selection from unwanted changes.

Another powerful feature involves layers, which are fundamental to creating and editing images in Paint Shop Pro. You use layers to blend image pixels in a variety of ways, creating color enhancements and great artistic effects that make editing images easier.

In this chapter, we will show you how to isolate the part of your image you want to modify, as well as using layers and masking to manage your image modifications.

Working with Selections

Most of what you've learned so far applies to working with the entire image. Occasionally, you only want to make changes to a portion of an image. Telling Paint Shop Pro *what* you want to change before you specify *how* you want it changed is called *making a selection*. You can then make your change to the isolated selected area without affecting the rest of the image. You also need to select an area if you want to copy or cut a portion of the image to the Windows Clipboard for use in other programs or images.

The Selection Tools

Paint Shop Pro includes several different selection tools called the *Shape Selection tool*, *Freehand Selection tool*, and *Magic Wand*. These three tools have one purpose, and that is to define the part of the image you want to work on. How they determine that area is what makes each of them unique. Let's begin by taking a look at what each tool does differently from the others. All three tools occupy the space of the fifth icon on the toolbar:

- **Shape Selection tool:** Use this tool to define a common geometric shape option.

- **Freehand Selection tool:** Use this tool to define an irregular shape selection.

- **Magic Wand:** Use this tool to define a selection based on color options.

The Shape Selection Tool

The Shape Selection tool is the fastest and easiest to use of the three tools. The Shape Selection tool selects a portion of your image in any one of 15 different shapes, including circles, rectangles, triangles, stars, and arrows.

TIP

Later in this chapter, we'll put selecting items into real use. For now, you can practice making selections by opening any existing file.

Click the Shape Selection tool or, as a shortcut, just press the letter S. When the Shape Selection tool is activated, the mouse pointer turns into a cross with a dotted box beside it. The Tool Options palette provides a number of different options for the Shape Selection tool:

- **Selection type:** Use the Selection Type drop-down list to choose from the list of available selection shapes.

- **Mode:** If you already have an area selected, Mode specifies whether you want to Replace, Add, or Remove from the existing selection.

- **Feather:** Feathering is a process that expands your selection and softens the edges of your selection. The higher the Feather value, the softer the selection edges.

- **Anti-alias:** Anti-alias is a graphics term that digital artists use to refer to mathematical calculations and pixels on a screen. When an image is aliased, it has a somewhat jagged edge. Therefore, using anti-alias smoothes the edges of slanted lines and curves by filling in the pixels, giving a smoother appearance.

- **Custom Selection:** Use the Custom Selection button if you want to make a selection of a specific size by entering the selection position in pixels for the left, top, right, and bottom positions.

■ **Create Selection From:** This option applies when adding to an existing selection, and it has three choices. The Surround Current button makes a new selection surrounding the current selection. The two opaque buttons select only the nontransparent opaque areas of the image, with the Layer Opaque button selecting from the current layer only and the Merge Opaque button selecting from all layers if the image has multiple layers.

Select your options from the Tool palette; then click and drag the mouse across the portion of your image window you want to select. As you draw, a solid line appears around the selected area, but as you release the mouse, the border of the drawn area is identified by bland and white dashes called a *marquee of marching ants*—moving dashed lines. The area within the marquee is your selected area. Figure 4-1 illustrates a rounded, rectangular shape selection around the fawn.

TIP

If, when working with a selected area, you find the marquee in the way, you can temporarily hide the "marching ants." Click the Selection menu and choose Hide Marquee.

Figure 4-1 *Remember that simply selecting an area does nothing to your image. It only tells Paint Shop Pro that this is where you intend to take some action. (Original photo by James Hutchinson)*

The Freehand Selection Tool

Selecting with the Freehand Selection tool gives you a great amount of freedom in drawing the area you want to select. Use this tool to select irregularly shaped areas of an image. Using your mouse with the Freehand Selection tool might feel a little clumsy at first. You'll find out later in this chapter how to add to and subtract from your selection if you didn't get it quite right with the Freehand Selection tool.

TIP

Selecting with the Freehand Selection tool is much easier if you are zoomed in on the area that you want to select.

 The Freehand Selection tool is also on the fifth tool of the toolbar.

Similar to the Shape Selection tool, with the Freehand Selection tool, the Tool Options palette provides a number of different options:

- **Selection Type:** Edge Seeker finds the edges between two areas with subtle color or light changes between them. Smart Edge lets you click along the edges of irregularly shaped areas with two areas of highly contrasting color or light. Use Point to Point to draw a straight border between selected points, which provides a selection with straight edges. With the Freehand Selection tool, you click and drag when you want to make a selection quickly.

- **Mode:** If you already have an area selected, Mode specifies whether you want to Replace, Add, or Remove from the existing selection.

- **Feather:** Just as with the Shape Selection tool, feathering expands your selection and softens the edges of your selection. The higher the Feather value, the softer the selection edges.

- **Range:** Range, available only when using a selection type of Edge Seeker, allows you to specify the distance (0 to 15) from the point you click that Paint Shop Pro should search for an edge.

- **Smoothing:** Specifies the amount of smoothing for sharp edges or jagged lines for the selection border. Smoothing has a range of 0 to 40.

- **Anti-alias:** Using anti-alias smoothes the edges of slanted lines and curves by filling in the pixels, giving a smoother appearance.

- **Sample Merged:** If the check box is marked, the tool searches for an edge in all layers of the area you select. If the check box is cleared, the tool searches for edges only in the current layer. It is available only when the image has multiple layers and when using the Edge Seeker and Smart Edge selection types.

When you select the Freehand Selection tool, the mouse pointer turns into a cross with a "lasso" beside it. Click and hold the mouse button and draw around the area you want to select. When using the Freehand Selection tool, it's best to take small multiple strokes. As you draw, a line will appear. Double-click the mouse when you are finished, and the marquee will appear around the selected area. Figure 4-2 shows how we used the Freehand Selection tool with the Smart Edge option to select the entire basket of tomatoes.

Figure 4-2 *With a Feather setting of 10, the selection marquee is drawn out an additional amount from the actual tomato basket.*

The Magic Wand Selection Tool

The third selection tool, the Magic Wand, works differently from the other two selection tools. The Shape and Freehand Selection tools select an area of the image, regardless of content, but the Magic Wand works by selecting pixels of equal or similar colors or brightness. Through the Tool Options palette, you control which types of pixels you want the Magic Wand to select.

- **Mode:** If you already have an area selected, Mode specifies whether you want to Replace, Add, or Remove from the existing selection.

- **Match mode:** The Match mode determines how the Magic Wand makes the selection. If you select *None*, the Magic Wand chooses all pixels. If you select *RGB Value*, the Magic Wand selects pixels based on the amount of color they contain. If you choose *Color*, it selects pixels of the same color you select. *Hue* selects pixels based on their position in the color wheel. With *Brightness*, the Magic Wand selects pixels based on the amount of white they contain. *All Opaque* chooses only areas containing pixels. No transparent areas are selected. Finally, *Opacity* selects pixels based on their opacity.

- **Tolerance:** Controls how closely the selected pixels must match the initial pixel you click. With a range from 0 to 200, at higher settings, the Magic Wand tool selects a wider range of pixels.

- **Sample merged:** With this box unchecked, the Magic Wand will search for matching pixels in the current layer only, but if checked, it will search in all layers.

- **Contiguous:** Mark this check box to select only matching pixels that connect to your original pixel. Unchecked, this option selects any image pixel meeting the other criteria you've set.

- **Feather:** Just like with other selection tools, feathering expands your selection and softens the edges of your selection. The higher the Feather value, the softer the selection edges.

- **Anti-alias:** Using anti-alias smoothes the edges of slanted lines and curves by filling in the pixels, giving a smoother appearance. If you choose to use anti-alias, you can then select whether you want to use anti-alias from the inside or the outside of the selection marquee.

When you click the Magic Wand tool, the mouse pointer turns into a black cross with a magic wand beside it. Click the mouse on an edge of the image you want to select, which makes the marquee appear around the area according to the options you selected. In Figure 4-3, we removed the Contiguous check mark, and with a single click of the Magic Wand, Paint Shop Pro selected all the light blue railing.

Figure 4-3 *Just like magic, Paint Shop Pro selects all areas displaying the similar pixels. (Original photo by Gary French)*

Modifying Selections

Unless you've got that perfect steady hand, your selection may not be exactly as you anticipated. Fortunately, Paint Shop Pro provides the ability to modify your existing selection or simply delete the selection marquee and begin anew.

Removing All Selections

If you've selected an area in error, or when you've completed whatever you wanted to do to a selection, you need to remove the selection marks. Removing a selection does nothing to your image—it only removes the selection marks. Click the Selections menu and choose Select None. Optionally, press Ctrl+D to remove all selections.

Reversing the Selection

Sometimes the easiest way to select a complicated part of an image is to select the part of the image that you *don't* want and then invert the selection. For example, if you have a picture of a tree silhouetted against a blue sky, use the Magic Wand tool to select the sky and then invert the selection to select the tree.

Often it's easier to select all the areas *except* the area that you want to edit. If that's the case, Paint Shop Pro includes a method that reverses your selection area.

Select the areas that you don't want. The marquee will appear around the selected area. In Figure 4-4, we want to change the area surrounding the basket of tomatoes, not the actual

Figure 4-4 *Notice the marquee around the entire perimeter of the image.*

tomatoes, but it's easier to use the Freehand Selection tool and select the basket. Next, we'll click the Selections menu and select Invert. The selected area reverses to the nonselected area. The entire image *except* the tomatoes is now selected.

Expanding a Selection Area

Did you make a complex selection only to find that you made it too tight or forgot to feather it? You can expand your selection with the Selections menu. You can expand the area that just stretches the selection without any feathering, or you can feather the area that both expands and feathers (softens the edges).

Make a selection and then click the Selections menu. Click Modify, which displays the Modify submenu. Click Expand or Feather and enter the number of pixels you want to expand or feather the selection. The selection area expands or contracts by the amount you specify.

Adding to or Removing from a Selection

For whatever reason—whether you have multiple objects to select, your hand wasn't quite steady enough when you made the initial selection, or you've just changed your mind—you might need to modify a selection. You don't need to deselect and start over. You can add to or subtract from your initial selection.

You can mix and match between all three selection tools when you're adding to a selection. Paint Shop Pro provides two methods to add to a selection, but we'll take a look at the easiest method.

First, using any of the selection tools, select the first area you want. Next, if desired, change the selection tool, but no matter which tool you use, change the mode on the Tool Options palette to Add (Shift). Select the second area you want to include. Both the original and the second area are marked with a marquee. You can continue to add as many areas to the selection as you need.

TIP

If you need to remove an area from the selection, use the above process, but change the mode on the Tool Options palette to Remove (Ctrl). Each time you select an area, Paint Shop Pro removes it from the selection.

Using a Selection

After you select an area, you can then delete the selection by pressing the Delete key (which displays a transparent area where the selection was located), move the selection by dragging it to another area of the image, or add an adjustment or effect to the selected area. To illustrate using a select, we'll use an image of a fawn and add a soft background to the area surrounding the fawn.

To begin, we'll use the Freehand Selection tool, set with Smart Edge, to select the fawn. Next, we'll expand and feather the selection with the Feather Selection dialog box, as you see in Figure 4-5.

Next, because it's not the fawn we want to soften but the background, we need to invert our selection through the Selections, Invert option.

Finally, we need to apply the soft focus to the selected area. We'll click the Adjust menu, select Softness, and choose Soft Focus. The Soft Focus command makes the image look as though it were taken with a camera using a soft focus filter.

Figure 4-5 *Using the Smart Edge option made selecting the fawn much easier.*

Like many other filters, Soft Focus displays a dialog box for you to select options, such as a percentage to soften the image, how much to soften the edges, and how much light halo you want to surround the image. At lower values, the halo effect is subtle. At higher values, the halo effect is more obvious.

For the image results you see in Figure 4-5, the softness was at 77%, edge importance 80%, and the halo amounts, size, and visibility were 60, 41, and 58, respectively. After making the selections and clicking OK, we need to deselect the background by pressing Ctrl+D or picking Select None from the Selections menu. Notice how in the image on the right, the fawn itself is still sharply in focus, while the background is dramatically softened.

Figure 4-6 *We added a little extra here to emphasize the concept, but you may not want as much soft focus as applied to this image.*

You can also use selections to protect a portion of your image from change. Remember our basket of tomatoes? By selecting the basket and then inverting the selection, we basically protected the tomatoes. In Figure 4-7, we used the paint brush to paint a yellow/orange/red gradient pattern over everything but the tomatoes. By painting within a selection (the inverted area), the paint brush could not go outside of the selection boundaries, thereby painting everything but the basket of tomatoes.

Figure 4-7 *Changes are applied only to selected areas.*

Understanding Layers

Layers is one of the best features of Paint Shop Pro, and once you start using them, you'll never want to be without them. Think of layering as putting each portion of your graphics image on a separate transparent sheet of paper, such as tracing paper. Layering makes it much easier to edit or move a particular portion of the image because, as you edit one portion of the image, you won't disturb the other portions. You can then shuffle the order of the layers (sheets). If you are making composite images, you'll find layers particularly helpful.

All images have at least one layer. When you open a digital photograph or a scanned image in Paint Shop Pro, the image is on the background layer. For most photographic enhancements, such as cropping, correcting colors, or retouching, you can work on this background layer without ever adding another layer; however, there are many ways to use layers with your photographic images to make changes easier and create interesting effects, especially when you intend to do more complex work such as adding elements to the image, creating photo compositions, adding text and other effects, and so forth.

Layer Types

There are many types of layers: Background, Raster, Vector, Art Media, Mask, Adjustment, Group, Floating Selection, and Edit Selection. Only greyscale and 16 million color images can have multiple raster layers; however, images of any color depth can include multiple vector layers. The layer type you use depends on your needs. Often, when working with photographs, you'll use adjustment layers, which enable you to make easily changeable modifications to your photographs. Paint Shop Pro supports up to 500 layers, but most images use only a few. Let's take a look at some of the different layer types.

Background Layers

Every image has at least one layer, appropriately called the *background layer*, and it is the bottom layer in an image. Background layers are a type of raster layer in that they contain raster data, but background layers have some limitations to them that regular raster layers do not. For example, you cannot change the background layer order in the stack since it's always on the bottom, and you cannot change a background layer blend mode or opacity. You can, however, change a background layer to a regular raster layer and then make any desired adjustments.

Raster Layers

Raster layers are layers with only raster data, which is individual pixels such as photographs. You can use raster layers for objects and raster text on which you want to apply raster-only commands and tools, such as items in the Effects menu or the Retouch tools.

Vector Layers

Vector layers are layers with only vector objects that are composed of geometric characteristics, such as text, lines, and shapes. When you edit vector objects and text, you edit these lines and curves, rather than editing individual pixels. Vector graphics and vector text maintain their clarity and detail when scaled to any size, making them easy to edit.

Art Media Layers

Paint Shop Pro automatically creates Art Media layers when you begin using any of the Art Media tools, such as the oil paint brush, pastels, or crayons. Art Media layers function similarly to vector layers because the objects on art layers are easy to move around.

Adjustment Layers

Paint Shop Pro provides adjustment layers to make color and tonal corrections instead of changing the image directly. Adjustment layers are correction layers that modify an image color or tone by making the same correction as you did with the Adjust menu, but do not change image pixels on the original layer. You can place each correction type on its own layer to test various color corrections or to see how several corrections look when you combine them.

Mask Layers

A mask layer is basically an adjustment layer that modifies opacity, which then shows or hides portions of underlying layers. Use masks to create sophisticated effects. For example, mask all details around the main subject in a photograph, or use a mask to create a picture frame that fades away at the center to reveal the subject. Mask layers cannot be the bottom layer in an image.

Using the Layer Palette

Most layer management is accomplished through the Layer palette. Displayed on the right side of your screen, the Layer palette shows you all the information about each layer in your image, as well as providing a place to create, delete, rename, hide, group, and generally manage your image layers. Let's take a look at a Layer palette for an image with multiple layers (see Figure 4-8).

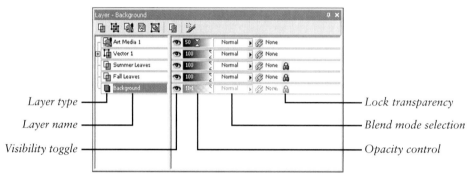

Layer type

Layer name

Visibility toggle

Lock transparency

Blend mode selection

Opacity control

Figure 4-8 *Pause the mouse over the layer name to see a representation of the layer contents.*

TIP

Press F8 to toggle the Layer palette display.

■ **Layer type:** Each type of layer represents a different layer type. In our example, you see a clear and a solid box, indicating that this is a raster layer.

■ **Layer name:** When you start adding lots of layers, you'll want to give each layer a unique name to quickly identify what each layer holds.

■ **Visibility toggle:** The eye icon indicates that the layer is visible. On occasion, you might want to hide one or more layers so that you can more easily view and edit objects on the remaining layers. Click the visibility icon to hide or display the selected layer.

■ **Opacity:** Opacity measures how much an object blocks light transmission (the opposite of transparency). When the opacity is lower, the resulting image is more transparent. Background layers do not have opacity control.

■ **Blend mode:** This feature displays a combination of pixels of the current layer with the pixels of all the underlying layers; however, it is for display only—the layers are not actually combined.

■ **Lock transparency:** This option lets you locks transparent pixels in an image so that only the nontransparent pixels can be edited.

Let's take a look at a simple image with layers. Figure 4-9 shows our image of the basket of tomatoes (the background layer), but we've added two new raster layers, which we've called *Summer leaves* and *Autumn leaves*. We added the leaves to each of these layers by using the Picture Tube tool, which you'll learn about in Chapter 8, "Digital Scrapbooking." The image on the top shows all the layers being visible, but in the image on the bottom, by clicking the Visibility toggle, we've hidden the Summer leaves layer so that Paint Shop Pro displays only the Autumn leaves layer and the background layer that includes the basket of tomatoes and the counter top on which they are sitting.

Figure 4-9 *The summer leaves aren't gone; they are only hidden.*

Creating Layers

Paint Shop Pro provides several methods to add new layers. The three common layer types, Raster, Vector, and Art Media layers, can be added by clicking an icon on the Layer palette. You can add any layer type, including adjustment layers, either through the Layers menu or by right-clicking any existing layer and selecting the type of layer you want to add.

When you add any new layer, Paint Shop Pro will prompt you for pieces of information such as a name for the layer, opacity, or blend mode. You can enter the information at the New Layer dialog box, or you can change the information after you add the layer. If you don't give the layer a name, Paint Shop Pro will name it for you, such as Raster1 or Vector3.

Naming Layers

As you add more layers, you might want to identify more easily what each layer represents, and you can do so by using the Rename feature to name each layer clearly. Background layers are already named, so you cannot rename a background layer, but to rename other layers, right-click on the layer name and select Rename. Paint Shop Pro then highlights the existing layer name, and you can just type over the existing name with a new descriptive name and then press Enter.

TIP

The currently selected layer name appears in the image title bar.

Duplicating Layers

For most simple image retouches and corrections, you do not have to add any layers. However, you can duplicate the layer before applying actions such as the photo correction commands. By applying any changes to the duplicated layer, you'll always preserve the original image on its own layer. Another example might be if you created a layer just the way you want it and you need another similar layer; then you can duplicate the existing layer and modify the new one rather than re-creating the layer. Either right-click the layer you want to duplicate or click the Layers menu and choose Duplicate. The new layer will appear on the Layer palette and be named *Copy of (layer you duplicated)*. You might want to rename the layer.

Reordering Layers

Paint Shop Pro displays layers based on how they are stacked in the Layer palette, with the layer name on top being the top layer of your image. If your layers are stacked differently than you want, you can change their order with the exception of the background layer, which is always the lowest layer. You can move layers up or down one layer at a time, or you can move a layer to the top or bottom of the stack. Reordering layers is an option under the Layers, Arrange menu, or you can simply place your mouse pointer on the Layer palette on the layer name you want to move and drag it to the desired stacking order.

As an example, take a look at Figure 4-10. The image on the top shows the fall leaves under the summer leaves, but the image on the bottom, after moving the Fall leaves layer, places the fall leaves on top of the summer leaves.

Figure 4-10 *By reordering the layers, you can have the fall leaves on top of the summer leaves or under the summer leaves.*

Moving Layers

If a particular layer isn't displaying the portion of the image where you want it, you can move the layer. We're not talking about changing the stack order, but actually moving the entire layer content into a new position.

From the Layer palette, click the layer name you want to move; then click the Mover tool on the Standard toolbar. When the Mover tool is selected, the mouse pointer turns into a four-headed arrow. Drag the layer and its contents around until it's in the position you want. In Figure 4-11, we moved the summer leaves to the lower left side of the image.

Background layers, however, cannot be moved, so if you want to move something residing on a Background layer, select the object and place it on its own layer. You can then move it as needed.

Figure 4-11 *Putting individual objects on their own layer makes moving the object independently of the other objects quick and easy.*

Deleting Layers

If you've created a layer you no longer want, you can easily delete it from the Layer palette. If you delete a layer in error, don't forget that you can click Edit, Undo (or press Ctrl+Z) to reverse your last action. One thing to remember about layers is that both Adjustment layers and Mask layers cannot be the bottom layer, so Paint Shop Pro won't allow you to delete other layers if deleting them causes an Adjustment or Mask layer to become the bottom layer.

Like other Layer commands, you can access the Delete command from the Layers menu or by right-clicking on the layer you want to delete and selecting Delete. Paint Shop Pro confirms that you're deleting a layer, but you can turn off the confirmation message if desired by clicking the "Don't ask about this" check box in the Delete dialog box.

TIP

If you delete the background layer, the background of the image will become transparent.

Layer Groups

After you merge layers, which you'll learn about in the next section, the elements are on a single layer and cannot be manipulated individually. Instead of merging the layers, you might want to group them. For example, you might want to group layers if you want to move items on one layer and want the items on some of the other layers to move along also. Each image can contain multiple layer groups. Think of grouping as a temporary way of merging layers.

Similar to creating a new layer, when you create a layer group, Paint Shop Pro assigns a number or name to the group that appears on the Layer palette. Add a layer group by right-clicking on one of the layers you want included in the group and selecting New Layer Group. This option is also available under the Layers menu. You have to start with one layer, but you'll see in just a moment how easy it is to add additional layers to a group.

Paint Shop Pro displays the New Layer Group dialog box, where you can optionally type a name for the group and then click OK. The new group will appear on the Layer palette above the currently selected layer (see Figure 4-12).

New Group ———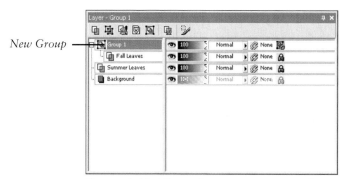

Figure 4-12 *If you do not type a name for the group, Paint Shop Pro automatically assigns it a number.*

A group isn't much of a group with just a single layer, so you'll probably want to add other layers to the group. In our example, we're going to group the fall and the summer leaves together. From the Layer palette, click the next layer you want to include in the group and drag it until it falls right under the group name. When you release the mouse button, you can see that the moved layer is now included in the group as in Figure 4-13.

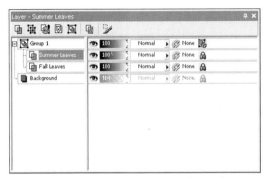

Figure 4-13 *To remove a layer from the group from the Layer palette, drag the layer name up or down the list until it is no longer part of a group.*

Merging Layers

After you get your images in the correct position on their individual layers, you might want to merge the layers. When you create multilayered images, you must save them in Paint Shop Pro's native format to maintain all layer information. When you save to most other file types, such as .JPG, .GIF, or .PNG, Paint Shop Pro prompts you that all layers are merged into one background layer since these formats allow only for a single layer.

NOTE

After you flatten and merge your layers, other than using the Undo command, you cannot restore the individual layers. You might want to keep a copy of your images with all the layers. Save a copy of the file as a Paint Shop Pro file before you merge the layers.

Paint Shop Pro provides several types of merging:

- **Merge Down:** Selectively combines two layers that are adjacent to each other. The merged layer retains the name of the lower layer and contains images from both layers.
- **Merge All:** When you merge all the layers (called flattening), the image becomes nonlayered. If you have transparent areas in the image, Paint Shop Pro fills them with white, and the image will consist of a single background layer with all the components.

- **Merge Visible:** Merges all nonhidden layers into a single layer but leaves any hidden layers separate. This is helpful if you want to pick and choose which layers you want to merge because the layers don't need to be adjacent to each other.

- **Merge Group:** Combines group layers into a single layer by merging the group. The single layer keeps the group name and contains the images from all the combined layers.

Promoting the Background Layer

As you've seen so far, a raster background layer, created when you open a new image with a nontransparent background, is a little different from the other layers. First, it is always the lowest layer in the stack. Second, it does not have opacity control like the other layers. If you want to control the opacity or transparency of the background layer, you must first promote it to a regular raster layer. Click the Layers menu and select Promote Background Layer. Paint Shop Pro assigns the new raster layer name to the former background layer name. From that point on you can apply blends, rename the layer, and do anything with it you do with a standard raster layer.

Working with Layers

OK, now that you've got a good grasp of what layers can do for you and how they operate, let's put it to some practical photographical use. For our first example, we'll show you how by using layers you can convert a color image into one that is a combination of color and greyscale like the image you see in Figure 4-14. We'll use a new tool, the Eraser tool, which erases pixels and makes them transparent.

The following steps walk you through the process of creating the combination image you see in Figure 4-14.

1. To begin this project, we need two copies of the same image. We'll need to change one of the copies to a greyscale image, so we can't just duplicate the layer, we need to duplicate the image. Click the Windows menu and select Duplicate to duplicate the open image.

2. Next, we'll take the duplicate image and change its color range to greyscale. You'll learn more about working with greyscale images in Chapter 7, "More About Color," but for now, make sure the duplicate image is the active window, click the Image menu, and select Greyscale.

Figure 4-14 *Use layers to create a multitonal image. (Original photo by James Hutchinson)*

3. Now we're going to take the greyscale image and make it a layer in the original image. Click the Edit menu and select Copy. It doesn't look like anything happened, but it did. Windows and Paint Shop Pro are keeping track of your steps.

4. Activate the original image, click the Edit menu, and select Paste, Paste as New Layer (or press Ctrl+L). The greyscale image appears as a new layer on the Layer palette. Your original image may look greyscale, too, but that's because the greyscale layer is on top of the background layer. That's OK...and as it should be.

5. Next, click the Freehand Selection tool and, using the Smart Edge as the Selection type, select the part of the image you want to be in color. (See Figure 4-15.)

Figure 4-15 *Select the area of the image you don't want to be in greyscale.*

6. Click the Eraser tool from the toolbar or press the letter X. The Eraser tool is the eleventh tool on the toolbar and...you guessed it...it's the one that looks like a pencil eraser.

7. From the Tool Options palette, make sure the hardness is set to 100 and make the size large enough that you don't have to spend too much time uncovering your colored image.

8. Using your mouse pointer, which now looks like an eraser, erase the complete area within the selection boundary. You don't have to worry about staying in the lines, because you selected the area you want to erase, and the eraser will not go beyond those boundary lines. As you run the eraser over the image, Paint Shop Pro replaces the grey pixels with transparent pixels, and the color from the background layer begins to show through.

9. Deselect your selection boundary by pressing Ctrl+D or clicking Selections, Select None.

Remember that if you save the image as anything other than a PspImage format, Paint Shop Pro will merge the layers, and you won't be able to come back and easily bring out other colors in the image. You should save the image first as a Paint Shop Pro image and then save it as another format, such as TIF or JPG.

Working with Adjustment Layers

We mentioned earlier in this chapter that the type of layer used most often by photographers is the Adjustment layer. What are Adjustment layers? Although similar to regular layers, Adjustment layers are correction layers that modify an image color or tone without directly modifying the image pixels. You can't paint or add anything to an Adjustment layer, but you can intensify or lessen its effect by adjusting its opacity or blend modes. (You'll learn more about blend modes in the next section.)

You can and should place each correction type on its own layer to test various color corrections or to see how several corrections look when you combine them. Falling into three main types of corrections, Paint Shop Pro provides nine different types of Adjustment layers. When you opt to add an Adjustment layer by clicking Layers, New Adjustment Layer, a submenu will appear with the nine choices.

To adjust Color Balance, select Color Balance, Hue/Saturation/Lightness, or the Channel Mixer Adjustment layers.

To adjust Brightness & Contrast, select Brightness/Contrast, Curves, or the Levels Adjustment layers.

To reduce or remove colors, select the Invert, Threshold, or Posterize Adjustment layers.

TIP

After you've created an Adjustment layer, you cannot change its type. Simply delete the unwanted layer and create a different one.

When you add an adjustment layer, you cannot add colors, so if you look at your Materials Properties dialog box, all you see are shades of grey.

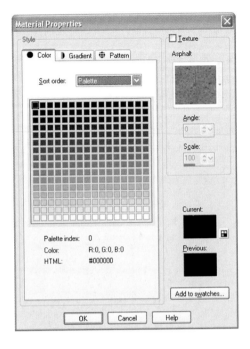

After you add the adjustment layer, Paint Shop Pro provides a dialog box from which you can fine-tune the adjustment. Figure 4-16 shows the Hue/Saturation/Lightness dialog box where, like other Paint Shop Pro dialog boxes, you see the Current view and the Preview windows so that you can observe the effect of your changes and adjust them until the image meets your preferences.

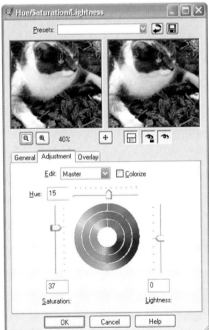

Figure 4-16 *Modify the hue, saturation, or lightness by using the slider bar for each setting or by manually typing in a value.*

In Figure 4-17, you see an image of a chili pepper, but the image definitely needs some corrections. It needs adjustments for brightness and contrast as well as color balance, and it could probably benefit from using the Unsharp Mask command.

Figure 4-17 *Experiment with the different settings to see what works best for your image. (Original photo by James Hutchinson)*

You learned in Chapter 2, "Quick Fixes," about making some of these changes, but in real life, modifying an image takes a lot of trial and error. Try a setting and see if you like it. If not, then undo it. You'll find yourself doing a lot of "what-if" scenarios, and working with each correction on its own Adjustment layer makes trying the "what-if" issue much easier.

Figure 4-18 shows the image after adding three Adjustment layers: Hue/Saturation/Lightness, Curves, and Brightness/Contrast. We also duplicated the background layer and used the Unsharp Mask feature on the duplicated raster layer. (You'll learn more about the color adjustment settings and curves in Chapter 7, "More about Color.")

Adjustment Layers

Figure 4-18 *This image has several different types of layers.*

Blending Layers

By blending layers, you can change the mood of a photograph or create very interesting abstract images. Just as the name implies, blends result from mixing. Mixing, in this case, refers to two or more layers together. Blend modes allow you to control how colors in one layer affect the underlying layers because the Blend layer's pixels are blended into underlying layers without actually combining the layers. The way the pixels blend together depends on which Blend mode you apply.

Paint Shop Pro includes a large variety of Blend modes. Table 4-1 lists each Blend mode and its effect:

Table 4-1 Blend Modes

Blend Name	Effect
Burn	The lightness values of the selected layer reduce the lightness of underlying layers, which results in darkening the overall image.
Color	Without affecting the lightness, Color applies the hue and saturation of the selected layer to the underlying layers. (Also has a Legacy mode.)
Darken	Displays pixels in the selected layer that are darker than the underlying pixels. Any pixels lighter than the underlying layers disappear.

Table 4-1 Blend Modes—continued

Blend Name	Effect
Difference	Subtracts the selected layer's color from the color of the underlying layers.
Dissolve	Creates a speckled effect by randomly replacing the colors of some pixels on the selected layer with those of the underlying layers.
Dodge	The color's lightness value in the selected layer increases the lightness of underlying layers, which results in lightening the overall image.
Exclusion	Similar to the Difference blend mode, subtracts the selected layer's color from the color of the underlying layers, but does so with a softer color difference.
Hard Light	Adds highlights and shadows by combining the Multiply and Screen blend modes, depending on the color channel.
Hue	Without affecting the saturations or lightness, applies the hue of the selected layer to the underlying layers. (Also has a Legacy mode.)
Lighten	Displays pixels in the selected layer that are lighter than the underlying pixels. Any pixels darker than the underlying layers disappear.
Luminance	Without affecting the hue or saturations, applies the lightness of the selected layer to the underlying layers. (Also has a Legacy mode.)
Multiply	Darkens the image by mixing the colors of the selected layer with the underlying layers. There are two exceptions: Multiplying any color with white leaves the color unchanged, and multiplying any color with black results in black.
Normal	The default option, displays pixels of the underlying layers based on the opacity of pixels on the selected layer.
Overlay	Shows patterns and colors of the selected layer, but preserves the shadows and highlights of underlying layers. Similar to the Hard Light blend mode in that it combines the Multiply and Screen blend modes, depending on the color channel value.
Saturation	Without affecting the hue or lightness, applies the saturation of the selected layer to the underlying layers. (Also has a Legacy mode.)
Screen	Lightens the colors of underlying layers by multiplying the inverse of the selected and underlying layers, resulting in a lightened color of the selected layer.
Soft Light	Adds soft highlights or shadows by combining the Burn and Dodge blend modes, depending on the channel value of the selected layer.

Four of the blend modes (Color, Hue, Luminance, and Saturation) also have Legacy blend modes that are more compatible with other applications.

In most cases, the order of the layers becomes an important issue because Paint Shop Pro blends the pixels of the selected layer with all the underlying layers. The exceptions to this are the Multiply, Screen, Difference, and Exclusion blend modes because they produce the same result no matter which layer is on top.

Let's take a look at a simple example. We'll begin with a photo of a lake and a plain light blue image, which we added as a solid color layer to the lake photo. For best results, the solid color image should be the same size as the photograph.

Next, we need to change the blend level on the blue layer. Double-click the layer name on the Layer palette, which results in the Layer Properties dialog box like the one you see in Figure 4-19.

TIP

You can also change the layer Blend mode from the Blend section on the Layer palette.

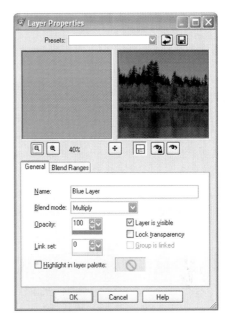

From the Blend mode drop-down list, try the different Blend modes until you find the one most appropriate for your image; then click OK. Figure 4-20 shows the lake scene and the blue layer blended in Color mode.

Figure 4-19 *The Layer Properties dialog box lets you preview your blend mode selection.*

Figure 4-20 *Without affecting the lightness, the Color blend applied the hue and saturation of the blue layer to the lake scene.*

You certainly don't have to apply a solid color layer to create blends. Let's take a look at another example, but this time we'll blend a beautiful sunset with our lake scene. *(Both original photos by James Hutchinson)*

When you are blending images, you should use photos of the same size or scale and one of which has an element that would look somewhat natural if placed in the second photo. In this example, we copied the sunset picture and then pasted it into the lake photo as a new layer. In Figure 4-21, you see three completely different results from using a blend mode on the copied sunset layer. The image on the top is in Overlay blend mode, the middle image is in Multiply blend mode, and the image on the bottom is the Soft Light blend mode.

Figure 4-21 *Each blend mode gives the image a different look.*

If you aren't quite satisfied with the blend mode defaults, you have the option of adjusting any or all of the Grey, Red, Green, or Blue color channels. You can adjust channels for any layer. The Blend mode adjustments are a tab on the Layer Properties dialog box as seen in Figure 4-22.

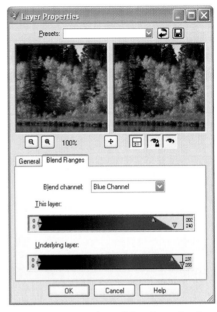

Figure 4-22 *Adjust blend modes by channel color.*

Masks

We use masks in a lot of places. Obviously, at Halloween you see masks that hide your face but still allow the eyes and mouth to show through. When you use a stencil to spray paint some letters onto a sign, you are using a mask. When you paint your living room and you don't want to get paint on the woodwork, you tape the area that you want to protect off with—what else—masking tape. In the art world, watercolor artists use a masking product to keep washes of color from bleeding into particular areas of a painting.

Similarly, Paint Shop Pro supports masks, which in reality are greyscale layers that hide portions of other layers without actually deleting them or modifying them. You can use mask layers to hide and show parts of a layer, fade between layers, and create other special effects. You can create a mask from a selection, an alpha channel, or an existing image, and the mask can completely cover a layer or cover a layer with varying levels of opacity.

You can create a new mask layer that you can paint on, use the mask layer to hide or show underlying layers, or create a mask layer from an image, a selection, or the luminance of an image. In addition, you can use one of the sample masks (stored in the Masks folder of the Paint Shop Pro program folder) and apply it as is or customize it.

Masks work with greyscale with transparency and 16 million color images only. And, like other types of layers, you can turn the visibility of the mask layer on or off, change the overall opacity of the mask layer, or link the mask layer to other layers.

When you save your image that includes a mask in a the .PspImage format, the mask is saved as well; however, if you save your image in another format such as JPEG or TIFF, Paint Shop Pro flattens the image and merges all layers together, including the mask layer. Additionally, you can save a mask to an alpha channel or as a separate image file on a disk, which is really beneficial if you plan on using the mask again.

Using Standard Masks

Paint Shop Pro includes over 30 uniquely designed masks that you can use on your images as a great timesaver. Additionally, you can add to the predefined mask collection by creating your own mask and saving it to a disk file, which you'll learn about in the next section.

If you apply a mask to a background layer, the area being masked out becomes transparent, and when you save it to a file format that doesn't support transparency, Paint Shop Pro turns the transparency to a solid color. For that reason, if you don't want transparency, you should start by creating a solid color background for your image. Make the background the same size as the photograph you are going to use.

Next, copy the photograph and paste it in as a new layer on the solid color background. (Edit, Paste as New Layer or Ctrl+L). Now you're ready to pick a mask. Make sure, from the Layer palette, that you have the raster layer selected and not the background. If you try to apply a mask to a background, Paint Shop Pro prompts you to first convert that background layer to a raster layer.

A mask layer applies to all layers below it that are at the same level, as follows:

- If a mask layer is in a layer group, it applies only to layers within the group that are lower in the stacking order.

- If the mask layer is at the main level (rather than in a layer group), it applies to all layers below it in the stacking order.

To change which underlying layers the mask applies to, on the Layer palette drag the mask layer to a new position in the stacking order. Mask layers can never be the bottom layer in the image or in a layer group.

To use a mask, click the Layers menu and select Load/Save Mask; then choose Load Mask from Disk. You'll see the dialog box seen in Figure 4-23.

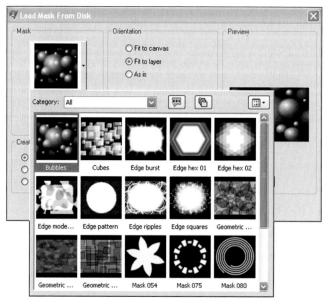

Figure 4-23 *When you create your own masks, they will also appear in the drop-down mask list.*

Click the down arrow next to the Mask preview box and select the mask you want to use. For Orientation, you will typically want Fit to Layer. Click Load, and Paint Shop Pro applies the mask to your image. Additionally, if you take a look at the Layer palette, a mask layer appears above your image layer, and the two are grouped together.

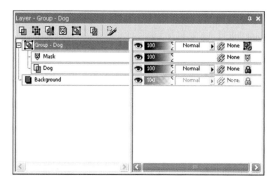

Figure 4-24 shows three different images with three different predefined masks applied. Each image has a different background color, each selected to blend with the image.

Figure 4-24 *Create some unique effects by using masks. (Original photos by James Hutchinson)*

Creating Your Own Mask

Paint Shop Pro certainly doesn't limit you to its selection of predefined masks. You can create your own and save it for future use. A mask can cover a layer completely or with varying levels of opacity. Where a mask is black, it completely covers the layer, and where it is white, it leaves the layer uncovered. If you use a grey value between black and white, the mask produces a semi-visible effect.

Although Paint Shop Pro includes a number of masks and hundreds more are available on the Internet, you might want to design your own mask.

TIP

It's easier to create a mask if you don't have any other images open when you're creating it.

The following steps take you through creating your own mask:

1. Create a new image with a black background. When applied, the black portion of a mask will block the image from showing. The size of the image isn't too important; when you load a mask, you decide then what size it should be. Just make the new image a size that's easy for you to work with.

2. Next, you need to delete a portion of the black layer so that when the mask is applied, part of the image can show through. Click the Shape selection tool and pick a shape. For the example you will see shortly, we're using the Ellipse shape.

TIP

Set the feathering to 4 or 5 for a nice edge-softening effect.

---

3. Draw a selection in the black image that displays the selection marquee. The size you select is the size of the masked area.

4. Click the Flood Fill tool and set the foreground color to white. Remember that whatever you paint in white will appear through the mask (see Figure 4-25).

5. Deselect the mask area by clicking Selections, Select None or by pressing Ctrl+D.

   So far, you have an image consisting of an oval. Next, you need to tell Paint Shop Pro that the image is intended for a mask.

6. Click Layers, New Mask Layer; then click From Image.

7. Because the image was originally created as a background layer, the background must first be promoted to a regular layer, so click OK to the Auto Actions dialog box. (You can click the Always take these actions button so Paint Shop Pro won't prompt you for future actions on converting background layers.)

8. The Add Mask from Image dialog box is asking which image you have onscreen is the one you want for a mask. (Now you know why the earlier Tip mentioned that it's easier to create a mask if you don't have any other images open.)

9. Click OK. Paint Shop Pro now knows that the current image is a mask and turns the black area into a transparency, indicated by grey-and-white checks. Masks are made up entirely of black, white, or shades of grey.

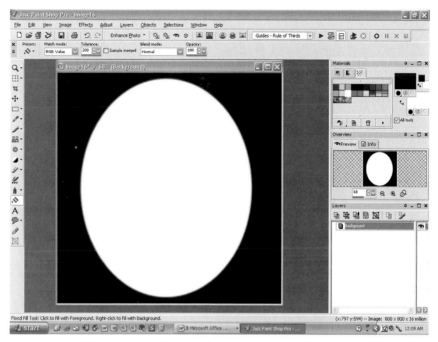

Figure 4-25 *When the mask is applied to an image, the area in white will be visible.*

TIP

Click File, Preferences, General Program Preferences. Then click the Transparency and Shading tab to determine the way that Paint Shop Pro displays a transparent area on your screen.

---

10. Now that you've created the mask, you will probably want to save it for future use. Click the Layers menu and select Load/Save Mask; then click Save Mask To Disk. The Save Mask To Disk dialog box seen in Figure 4-26 will open.

11. Enter a descriptive name for the mask and click Save.

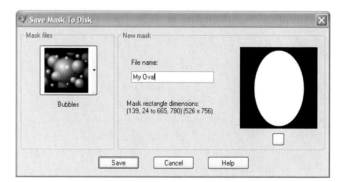

Figure 4-26 *Paint Shop Pro names mask files with a .pspmask extension to identify it as a mask.*

Now you can apply the mask whenever you want it. See Figure 4-27.

Figure 4-27 *The default blend mode for masks is Normal, but for some interesting special effects, experiment with the masked Group Blend Modes.*

What's Next?

In this chapter, you learned about some of Paint Shop Pro's most powerful tools, selections, layers, and masks. In Chapter 5, "Compositing," you'll have fun learning how to use the Paint Shop Pro tools you've mastered to create montages, combining multiple photographs together in a single image.

5

Compositing

Composite, combination, blend, mixture, montage, assortment, mosaic, medley. With Paint Shop Pro, all those terms refer to the ability to combine two or more images together to create a brand new image.

Up until this point, you've learned how to use the Paint Shop Pro tools to remove the "less than perfect" elements in your photographs. By using those same tools you use to correct and enhance, you can create artistic masterpieces of an entirely new level. This is where your creative talents can flow freely.

I hope you enjoy reading this chapter as much as I enjoyed writing it.

Widen an Image—Expand the Canvas Size

You've already learned a little about compositing when you worked with blends and masks in Chapter 4, and you learned that when you blend images, you should use photos of the same size or scale, one of which has an element that would look somewhat natural if placed in the second photo. Certainly, you could resize a photograph (Image, Resize), but that could create some scaling distortion when you combine the two images together.

In some photographs, you can expand the image by selecting a portion of the image and duplicating it into another area. In an earlier example, we took a photo of a beautiful sunset, and by placing it on a separate layer of a lake scene, we blended them together. In reality, the sunset photograph was too small to use effectively, so we expanded the image width without distorting it by using the following technique involving a floating selection.

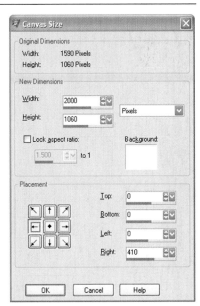

Figure 5-1 *Determine the canvas size and the current image placement.*

1. Open the picture you want to resize and resize the canvas (not the image). Click the Image menu and select Canvas Size. The dialog box in Figure 5-1 will open.

2. Enter the new canvas dimensions either in pixels, inches, centimeters, or millimeters.

3. Select a background color for the new area. The added area on the background layer fills with the color you select. On other layers, the added area appears as a transparency.

4. Determine the placement for the original image in relation to the new size. For our example, we want the original image placed to the left, but if we were doing this to add a picture frame, we would probably want to center it.

5. Using the Shape selection tool and a rectangle shape, similar to what you see in Figure 5-2, drag a selection over the part of the photo you want to duplicate on the edge of the photo.

Figure 5-2 *Select the portion of the image you want to copy. (Original image by James Hutchinson)*

6. Create a new raster layer.

7. Click Edit, Copy.

8. Click the new raster layer to make it active; then click Edit, Paste as New Selection. Your mouse pointer will have a copy of the selected data attached to it.

9. Move the mouse pointer, making sure you are on the new raster layer, drag to the new blank area of the image and click. When you click the mouse button, the new area gets pasted down (see Figure 5-3).

The pasted-in section will probably need transitional cleaning up, such as softening the edges. You'll find the Eraser tool very helpful, and if you merge the layers, you can use the Clone tool, as well as the Smudge and Soften tools, to make the new section look more natural, like the one you see in Figure 5-4.

Figure 5-3 *Use the Retouch tools to eliminate any sharp edges.*

Figure 5-4 *Expanding the image can look completely natural.*

Clone Two Images—A Dream Come True

In Chapter 2, you learned how to use the Clone Brush to remove unwanted elements and how to fill in "dead" areas with duplicate areas in the image. What if you want to place a portion of one image into another one? Again, the Clone Brush will come to the rescue.

The example you'll see probably isn't a photographer's dream, but it was fun to work with. One image is a mama seal, and the other image is a baby seal. In our example, we're going to make mama dream about the baby.

Open both photos and click Window, Arrange Vertically or Arrange Horizontally, so one lines up next to or above the other. With the window active that you want to paint the new area on, add a new raster layer.

Select the Clone Brush tool and set your desired options, which in the example you see in Figure 5-5 included the brush size at 125. Since we want this to resemble a dream, we lowered the opacity to 50. Begin by right-clicking the area you want to duplicate (the baby seal). Then on the new raster layer of the other image, use your left mouse button to paint in the cloned area. Continue painting until you have covered the area you want to duplicate.

Figure 5-5 *Lowering the opacity makes the cloned area appear more translucent.*

Why was it necessary to place the new cloned area on a separate layer? If you notice, when you started clone painting, Paint Shop Pro created another layer, called a *Promoted Selection layer*. By placing the copied area on its own layer, you can easily move it around the image. If you clone to a Background layer, Paint Shop Pro doesn't create a Promoted Selection layer, and you cannot easily move your newly cloned area.

Select the Move tool, which makes your mouse pointer appear as a four-headed arrow, and placing the Move tool in the middle of your cloned area, drag it to the new location. Because you are moving the Promoted Selection layer, only the new area moves, not the rest of the image. Finally, we used the paint brush to paint a thought line to the new baby seal and merged the image together. Figure 5-6 shows the results. Awww...look at the mama's tear. She misses her baby. Like I said, not a great photography example, but lots of fun to do.

Figure 5-6 *Retaining the different shade of blue around the baby gives the impression of a soft blanket.*

Background Eraser—Create a Gradient Background

In Chapter 4, you saw how to use the Eraser tool to erase part of a layer, which allowed the underlying layer or background color to show through. Paint Shop Pro has another Eraser tool, the Background Eraser, which operates just like the regular Eraser tool but includes additional options that determine which pixels get erased.

Different than the regular Eraser tool, the Background Eraser tool works more from the center of the brush and works to erase around a specific area, which can give you softer erased edges. For example, if you have a photograph of a bird and you want just the bird without the trees and other items in the background, then the Background Eraser tool is what you want to use.

 The Background Eraser is the eleventh tool on the toolbar and shares space with the regular Eraser tool. When you select the Background Eraser tool, the Tool Options palette displays the typical brush tool options, plus the following options:

- **Tolerance:** Determines how closely pixels must match the sampled pixel. The range is 0 to 200. At lower settings, only pixels with very similar colors are erased, while at higher settings, more pixels are erased. If the Auto tolerance box is checked, this option becomes unavailable, and the Background Eraser determines the tolerance based on the pixels in the Eraser path, changing as the tool moves over different parts of the layer.

- **Sampling:** Determines how the Eraser tool determines what pixels to erase. Choices are Once, Continuous, BackSwatch, and ForeSwatch. *Once* samples at the center of the brush where you first click, and it erases all matching pixels for the duration of the stroke. *Continuous* samples at the center of the brush at every step and erases all matching pixels. *BackSwatch* erases all pixels that match the current background color on the Materials palette rather than sampling from the image. *ForeSwatch* erases all pixels that match the current foreground color on the Materials palette rather than sampling from the image.

- **Limits:** Determines whether erased pixels must be adjacent to each other. Choices are Contiguous, Discontiguous, and Find Edges. Find Edges restricts the erasing according to edge information.

- **Sample merged:** Select this to sample data from all layers merged together, although only pixels in the current layer are erased.

- **Ignore lightness:** Mark this check box when the colors in the object that you want to isolate are strongly saturated and the background is unsaturated, or vice versa. Note: This option may be hidden; click the Tool Options arrow at the right to display it.

Now that you know what the Background Eraser can do, let's put it to some use. For our example, we'll use a photo of a mountain bike rider. We're going to erase the background, leaving only the rider.

Oddly enough, the Background Eraser tool works only on raster layers and does not work on the background layer. If your image is not on a raster layer, Paint Shop Pro displays a dialog box prompting you to promote it to a full layer.

TIP

Since the center of the Background Eraser tool is the key to using this feature, it works best if you can easily see the center. To make the center easier to spot, turn on the precise cursor option. Click File, Preferences, General Program Preferences. Click the Display and Caching tab and select Use precise cursors.

Click the Background Eraser tool, which turns the mouse pointer into a circle with centering sights; then select an eraser size. If you have a large area to erase, you might want to start with a larger size, such as 50 or 100, and you will probably need to change the brush size frequently.

Click and drag the mouse pointer over the area you want to erase. However, instead of using the brush edge, as you would with the regular Eraser tool, don't worry about anything but the center of the brush where the crosshairs are located. As you drag across the area, Paint Shop Pro replaces the erased area with a transparency (see Figure 5-7). In some areas, you will probably want to zoom in and use the standard Eraser tool to remove pixel remnants.

TIP

To restore an area, drag the right mouse button over the erased area.

Figure 5-7 *Alternate between the standard Eraser and Background Eraser tools by pressing the spacebar.*

To complete our image once the background area is erased, we add a new raster layer, which we flood-fill with a rainbow gradient pattern, and then we move the mountain bike rider to the top layer. See Figure 5-8.

Figure 5-8 *Add a different image as a background or create one of your own, being sure to place the erased layer on top.*

Here's another example. In Figure 5-9, we started with an image of a bee on a flower (left), but we're going to place the bee on a different flower (middle). By erasing the background of everything but the bee, we then copied and pasted the bee in as a new layer, giving the final image (right).

Figure 5-9 *Isolating the bee was tedious but successful. (Original photos by James Hutchinson)*

Masking—The Sky Is the Limit

Sometimes it's difficult to find the perfect photo opportunity. You see a beautiful sky, but the background isn't worth taking a picture, or you see a pretty scene, but the sky is grey and dismal that day. In Chapter 4, you learned how you can use Paint Shop Pro masks to hide or reveal portions of an image.

Using the same concept, masking, you can take that beautiful image with the ugly sky and replace the sky with one much more to your liking.

Figure 5-10 illustrates a beautiful mountain range in southern Colorado, but the sky was dull and cloudless that day. We'll take the part of the sky from the top image and place it into the bottom image with the mountain range.

Figure 5-10 *Use layers and masking to replace the sky.*
(Photo by James Hutchinson)

Follow these steps to replace part of an image with an area from a second image:

1. Open the two photos you want to use and select the sky area of the image you want to copy. Don't worry if you select too much because you can mask out the unwanted area. Just be sure you have enough to cover the area in the second image.

2. Copy the selected area using Edit, Copy or by pressing Ctrl+C

3. Click the other image to activate it and then paste the selection in as a new layer (Edit, Paste as new layer or press Ctrl+E). If necessary, use the Move tool to position the layer as desired.

4. Create the Mask layer by selecting Layers, New Mask Layer, Show All. As you can see in the Layers palette, this creates a Mask layer grouped with the new raster layer. Notice that the Mask layer is now the active layer.

5. Lower the opacity of the Group Raster to about 40% so you can see through the clouds. You'll need to see the layer underneath so you know what to unmask.

6. Select the Paint Brush tool, which is the seventh tool down on the toolbar and occupies space with the Air Brush and the Warp Brush.

7. In the Materials palette, set the Foreground/Stroke style to Black and the Background/Fill style to White. Remember that masks work by hiding all pixels painted black and showing pixels painted white.

8. Making sure you are still on the Mask layer, paint on the unwanted image area, which allows the layer under it to show through (see Figure 5-11). Use slow, careful strokes and adjust the brush size as needed. If you make a mistake and uncover too much, paint over the area you didn't want to uncover with the right mouse button down.

Figure 5-11 *Take your time uncovering the hidden areas. Zoom in and out as needed.*

9. When you have finished painting the mask, increase the opacity back to 100 so you can see the bright blue sky appear. Figure 5-12 shows the image after replacing the sky, merging, and a little cropping.

Figure 5-12 *The brighter sky even makes the day appear much sunnier.*

Gradient Masks—Fading Away

You can achieve really nice image blends through the use of gradient masks. A gradient mask is a greyscale gradient that has been turned into a mask. The black areas of the mask cause complete transparency, while the greys cause varying degrees of transparency, and white causes no change to the image's pixel opaqueness. This allows two or more images in a layered image to blend together very well. You can apply the gradient mask to create an image that fades to transparent.

Figure 5-13 shows three different images: a sunset, the Blue Angels, and a seagull. Using a gradient mask, we will combine all three images, creating a single spectacular image that gradually fades from right to left.

Figure 5-13 *In the next step, we will combine these three different images into a single composite image. (Photos by Tim Koers)*

Begin by opening the images you want to blend together, which in our example are the three different images. We'll use the sunset as the background layer and blend the other images into it.

We'll need to copy the Blue Angels photo and paste it as a new layer in the sunset photo; then we'll decrease the opacity of the Blue Angels photo to about 50% so we can see the sunset through it. As you can see in Figure 5-14, the Blue Angels are too low in the horizon, so we'll use the Move tool to move the Blue Angels layer up.

Figure 5-14 *Use the Move tool to move the Blue Angels layer up so they won't look like they are flying out of the water.*

On the Blue Angels layer, we won't want the sky since we already have two skies in the other two images. We could use the background eraser, but in this example, it was easier to use the Magic Wand set with a high tolerance to select all the blue sky and then delete it by pressing the Delete key (see Figure 5-15). After moving the image and deleting the background, we reset the layer opacity back to 100.

Now we'll add the third layer, the one with the seagull. Again, we'll use the Copy and Paste as New Layer command to add it to the sunset image, on top of the Blue Angels layer. We will then create a mask so the other images can show through the seagull layer.

Figure 5-15 *The Magic Wand selection tool was perfect for this example.*

In preparation for the mask, in the Materials palette, set the Foreground Color to black and the Background Color to white. Next, make sure the Background and Fill Properties color is white and the style is Solid. To create the gradient, set the Foreground and Stroke Properties to Gradient; then click inside the box and set the gradient settings. We need the Black-White gradient pattern, a 90 degree angle, and the Linear style. Also, since we want to create a gradient mask that will gradually fade the image from left (opaque) to right (transparent), we need the white area on the left and the black on the right. Click the Invert box, which switches the gradient path.

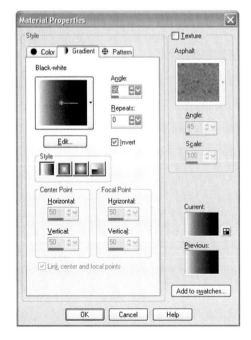

We are now ready to actually create the mask and fill it with our gradient. Create a new Mask Layer (Layers, New Mask Layer, Show All). Select the Flood Fill tool, setting the Blend mode to Normal, Match mode to RGB Value, Tolerance to 200, and Opacity to 100, and disable Sample merged.

Make sure that you are still on the Mask layer and click once inside the image. The sunset layer and the jets should now show through more solidly on the right, gradually fading to the left (see Figure 5-16).

Figure 5-16 *If desired, further fine-tune the image with retouch brushes or other Paint Shop Pro features.*

You can get very creative with the masks, including changing the style of gradient from linear to radial or sunburst, or you can simply change the angle of the linear gradient to better fit the image's objects.

Layers and Masks—Create a Digital Collage

A digital collage is a process by which photos are cleverly blended together rather than cut out and arranged. Digital collages are more aesthetic and pleasing to the eye because the images are very carefully blended into one another without harsh edges that come from cutting out subjects or edges of photos.

Collages are great for pulling together diverse images of varying sizes and backgrounds. It takes a bit more effort, but removing the background of some images and overlapping others can add life and fun to even the driest of subjects. You can create some lively, interesting layouts with this technique.

In Figure 5-17, you see a collage comprised of many different types of flowers, complete with a picture frame around the entire image. You'll learn about picture frames in Chapter 8, "Scrapbooking."

Figure 5-17 *Create a bright and cheerful collage using the Paint Shop Pro tools.*

To create this image, we'll use Paint Shop Pro layers, masks, selection tools, eraser, and many other tools.

Create a new image, large enough to hold all the images you will be using, 16 million colors, and a background that will complement your photos. It's fine to make the new image a little bigger than you need it. You can always crop it later.

The concept is that you will place each photograph on a separate layer of the collage background, position it where you want it, and set the opacity and blend to control how much of each layer shows through.

A collage works best if there are no obvious edges around the components, and we've found it easiest to set up the individual image before we copy it to the new background as a new layer.

Open all the images you want to use in your collage. It's obviously a good idea to make sure they're not too big, as you will be combining them into one big image. So now would be the time to resize or crop them if they're large images.

In some images, you'll want to apply a mask to hide parts of a layer or create soft edges around a layer, while in others you may want to select only portions of the image. It's a good idea to have some of both.

If you want to start with images by removing the background, select one of the images you want. Click Layers, Promote Background Layers because you want the uncovered area to be transparent.

Now, take your Freehand Selection tool set at Freehand and Feather at 20, and freehand select around the object you want to add to the collage. Don't worry about having a very steady hand. Feathering is very forgiving! Invert your selection (Selections, Invert) and press the Delete button on your keyboard. Deselect the object by pressing Ctrl+D. You should now have the object fading into the checkerboard background, showing that it is fading into transparent.

Copy the image and paste it as a new layer onto the large collage background. Move it where you want it.

Some masks give a rather hard edge, but others have a softer blend. The softer blend masks work best for collages. For those images you want to mask, promote the background layers and then click Layers, Load/Save Mask, Load Mask from Disk. Select a mask with a soft edge, such as the Edge Burst, and apply it to the image. After applying the mask, merge the layers (flatten); then Copy and Paste as New Layer into the main collage background.

You will need to perform one of these two options for each image. After getting all the images into the main collage, you will probably need to rearrange the layer orders until you are happy with the collection. If you still have any obvious edges showing (which is a no-no for a well-made collage), take your Eraser tool set at a very low opacity, such as 6–10 and 0 hardness, and on that image's layer, erase the hard edges. This will show whatever is underneath, which could be the background or perhaps part of an image on a lower layer (see Figure 5-18).

Figure 5-18 *For a nice effect, let some edges overlap into the mat area.*

Panoramas—Seeing the Whole Picture

Often, you might want to take a picture of a wide scene, so you have to back up to get everything you want into the photograph. The problem is that as you back away, you lose detail in the final photograph. One way to still get the entire scene without losing detail is to take a series of photographs with overlapping subject matter and then stitch the photographs together using Paint Shop Pro layers. This technique is called a *panorama*.

To create the panorama effect, you will need several photographs of the scene. The easiest way is to take a photograph and then step to the right (or left). Line up your next photograph, making sure that you have a portion of the previous photograph in the current photograph. Take another step to the right and take a third photograph, making sure that you have a portion of the second photograph in the third photograph. Repeat the process until you have encompassed the scene. So, basically you are taking a photograph and moving to the right, taking another photograph and moving to the right. You end up with a series of photographs that overlap at the right and left edges.

When shooting for a panorama, keep these tips in mind:

- Create overlap in each frame; a third or more of each picture should overlap with the previous frame.

- Keep your subjects somewhat distant. Anything close to the camera could be distorted or may not line up properly in the final image.

- Keep the camera level with the horizon in every image. If your camera tilts up a little in some pictures, but down in others, you'll end up with distortion in the final panorama.

- For the best results, mount the camera on a tripod.

- Consider your lighting conditions. If it is toward early morning or mid-evening, the horizon will be lighter than the rest of the scene. As you move away from the horizon, the scene will get darker.

The general principle in assembling a panorama is that you create an image with a transparent canvas large enough to display the panorama and then copy each photograph onto a separate layer. After you create the layers with the individual photographs, you align them and crop the overall image so that no transparency is showing.

Let's take a look at an example. In Figure 5-19 you see five images. We'll use these five images to create a panorama.

Figure 5-19 *Make tonal adjustments before you combine these pictures into the panorama.*

It might be necessary to make some color adjustments to each layer, but I have found that it's easiest to make most color or tonal adjustments on the individual photograph before you place them in the master layer. For example, the fourth image needed the water color adjusted so it would match the rest of the images.

Next, we need a new background image. Make a note of the image's height and add together the widths of all the images you are using and create a new transparent background that is wide enough for all the images. In this example, I created a new layer 1800 wide by 400 tall. It's better to make it wider and taller than you need it so you can freely move the images into place. You can crop the size to fit later.

Copy each of the individual images into the blank image as a new layer. It's not required you do them in order, but it's easier. You can work from left to right or right to left. It doesn't matter.

TIP

Editing the images is easier if you name each layer according to its placement in the panorama.

Zoom in on the new image, and using the Mover tool, move each image in place on top of the other so they overlap in exactly the same spot. It helps to reduce the opacity of the upper image to see the overlap better. After you position the image, increase your opacity back to 100% (see Figure 5-20).

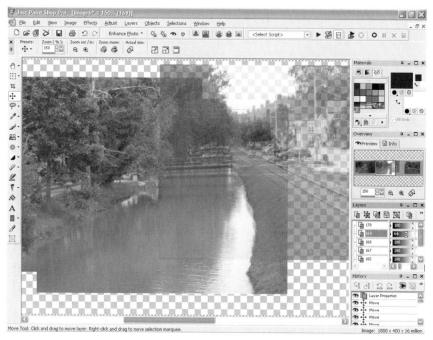

Figure 5-20 *Move each image into place.*

Most likely, you'll have some seam lines appearing. Take advantage of the fact that the layers overlap each other and use the Eraser tool at a fairly low opacity (20–40) to erase parts of the seamed edges. This technique helps merge the photographs together.

Finally, since the images probably didn't line up at the tops and bottoms evenly, crop the panorama so there are no transparent areas.

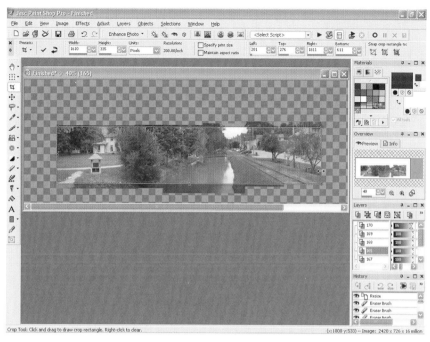

Figure 5-21 *Erase the rough edges and crop the image.*

Take a look at the final panorama:

Panoramas aren't limited to horizontal images. You can capture your images vertically and create great panoramas as well. Take a look at Figure 5-22, which shows four images of the interior in the Salamanca Cathedral.

In Figure 5-23, you see the images combined to create a beautiful vertical panorama.

Figure 5-22 *Create vertical panoramas using the same techniques as a horizontal one.*

Figure 5-23 *Create panoramas to see any large area. (Photos by Antonio Soberon)*

What's Next?

In this chapter, you learned the Paint Shop Pro skills needed to combine all or parts of images to create new composite images. In Chapter 6, "Special Effects," you'll discover many special effects that you can apply when working with images.

6

Special Effects

Filters are important correction and creativity tools. Many cameras, especially those used by professional photographers, have a plethora of filters available. Sometimes these filters fit in front of a lens and sometimes inside the camera lens. The function of a filter is to change the way the camera lens sees the subject. Some filters have a tint and can block certain colors; others can blur the image or even add distortion and special effects.

With digital image manipulation, you don't have to take your shots using those expensive and sometimes cumbersome filters. You can add the effect later using Paint Shop Pro.

In Paint Shop Pro, the terms *effects* and *filters* basically serve the same purpose, and you'll hear the words used interchangeably. The wonderful folks at Jasc Software consider items under the Effects menu as effects and items under the Adjust menu as filters, but this is not a hard and fast rule, as often you hear a lot of effects referred to as filters. Complicate this rule by the fact that items from the Adjust menu appear within the Effect Browser, which you'll learn about later in this chapter, and you have total chaos. Confused? That's certainly understandable. For clarity, try thinking about all of them as *filters* and the names given under the Effects menu as a result of a filter.

You've already worked with some filters when you adjusted saturation, contrast, color balance, and noise. Most of those filters did corrections to your photographs in maintaining color and sharpness. The filters we'll look at in this chapter have more to do with distorting your images into unique works of art. Some you may use a lot and others rarely. What we'll do in this chapter is take a brief look at the many deformation effects available with Paint Shop Pro and see how they can easily give your images extra touches of character.

Working with Blur

Most good photographic images demand clarity. Sharpening and Unsharp Mask help clarify your images as well as removing the noise with the Salt and Pepper filter, the DCNR filter, and JPEG Artifact Removal tools, just to name a few. Sometimes, though, instead of clarifying your image you want to blur or soften all or part of the photograph. In Chapter 4, you discovered

139

one of the blur filters, the Soft Focus filter. Other blur filters, which actually add noise to your image, include Average, Blur, Blur More, Gaussian, Radial, and Motion Blur.

Blur filters compare pixels to other nearby pixels and average their values, which in turn reduces the contrast between them. Most of the blur filters focus primarily on high-contrast areas, and all blur filters work only on greyscale and 16 million color images.

Blur and Blur More

You might use the Blur and Blur More filters to reduce graininess in your image. These filters remove noise by applying smooth transitions and decreasing the contrast in the image. As you might expect, the Blur More effect applies the Blur effect with more intensity.

You apply the Blur and Blur More filters by clicking the Adjust menu, selecting Blur, and choosing Blur or Blur More. Neither filter provides you with any options; they simply apply a preset amount of blur to the image.

Figure 6-1 shows a portion of an image with no blur, Blur, and Blur More applied. You can easily see the blur around the animal fur and in the rock grain.

> ## TIP
>
> Control the blur area by applying the filters to only selected areas of the image.

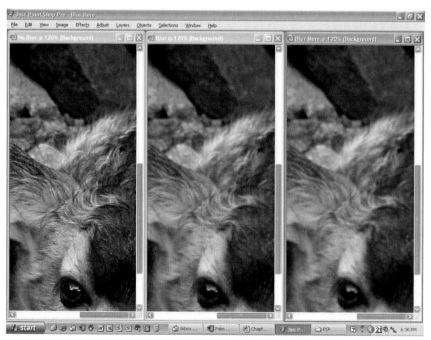

Figure 6-1 *Decrease image contrast with the Blur and Blur More filters.*

Average Blur

The Average Blur filter is really helpful at removing dithering that often occurs when you increase the color depth of an image. By reducing the contrast between pixels, you get less waffling and a smoother, more consistent appearance.

When you use the Average Blur filter, Paint Shop Pro prompts you for an amount, measured in aperture. Aperture options run from 3 to 29, in odd numbers only. The higher the aperture, the more blur that Paint Shop Pro applies. Access the Average Blur filter by clicking the Adjust menu, selecting Blur, and then choosing Average Blur.

Gaussian Blur

Another type of blur is Gaussian Blur, which originates from German mathematician and astronomer Karl Friedrich Gauss. Mr. Gauss had many mathematical theories, some of which are what Paint Shop Pro applies when you use Gaussian Blur. Gaussian Blur is very similar to the Average Blur, but Gaussian Blur is a little stronger and gives more realistic results. It works by controlling the amount of blurring applied to any given pixel or edge by an adjustable amount, making the blurring appear dense in the center and soft and feathery around the edges.

Like other blurring effects, you can apply the blur to an entire image or just a selected portion of it. Most of the time, you won't want to apply the blur to the entire photograph but only to a portion of it, which changes the depth of field.

You'll have best results if you place the area you want to modify on its own layer and then add the Gaussian Blur to the layered image. Follow these steps:

1. Promote the background to a Raster layer (Layers, Promote background layer).
2. Select the area you want to blur. In the example we use here, we'll select the fawn, using the Freehand Selection tool with Smart Edge and, to give a softer edge, feathering set at 2.
3. Move the selected area to its own layer by clicking Selections, Promote Selection to Layer.
4. Click Selections, Select None or press Ctrl+D to remove the selection lines.
5. Now you can apply the blur. Again, making sure you are on the Raster layer, click the Adjust menu, select Blur, and then select Gaussian Blur. You'll see a Gaussian Blur dialog box like the one in Figure 6-2.

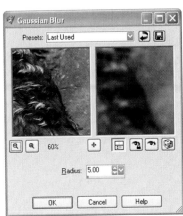

Figure 6-2 *Set the amount of blur you want.*

> **TIP**
>
> Don't forget that you can click the Reset button to reset all options to their default.

6. Set the blur radius you want and click OK. Values range from 0 to 100, with 100 being totally blurred.

Figure 6-3 shows the image before and after adding a 5 radius Gaussian blur.

Figure 6-3 *Paint Shop Pro applied the blur only to the Raster layer and not the fawn on the upper layer. (Original photo by James Hutchinson)*

Motion Blur

Today's cameras have built-in features that reduce the chance of getting motion blur during a shot; however there will be times when you want a motion blur to add to the visual impact an object has on the image. Paint Shop Pro includes a Motion Blur filter, which simulates taking a picture of a moving object using a fixed exposure time. This filter works best when used inside a selection.

Motion effects are placed in a directional manner to achieve the illusion of motion. You can adjust not only the intensity of the blur but also the direction in which the blur effect is applied.

Take a look at the beautiful car shown in Figure 6-4. It's a nice car, sitting on a nice quiet street, lacking even a hint of motion. How boring is that? Let's add a little action to it, giving the impression of movement.

Figure 6-4 *Put your car in motion with the Motion Blur filter. (Original photo by Tim Koers)*

We want to add the blur from the middle to the back of the car, trailing off about an inch or so. Because we want to isolate the motion blur area, we have to make a selection first.

Using the Freehand Selection tool, then in the Tool Options palette, set the Selection Type to Freehand, Feather to 0, and enable Antialias. Select a rough selection around the area you want to blur. See Figure 6-5 for our selected area.

Figure 6-5 *Keeping the selection area rough prevents the blur from looking too stiff.*

Now you can apply the blur filter. Click the Adjust menu and select Blur. Next, select Motion Blur, which displays the dialog box you see in Figure 6-6.

The blur angle is a circular value ranging from 0 to 359 degrees. The strength value runs from 1 to 100, with 100 being a total blur. For our example, we want the blur angle at 270, which sets the motion blur direction toward the back of the car, and we will use a strength of 25. We do not want a full Motion Blur, as it would be too much for what we are trying to achieve. Click OK when you select your settings.

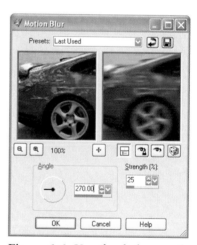

Figure 6-6 *Use the dial control or enter in an Angle value to set the blur direction.*

TIP

To add additional motion, apply a second Motion Blur, but feather the selection size first.

Notice that the blur applied only to our selected area. Since we don't need the selection any more, click Selections, select None, or press Ctrl+D.

Figure 6-7 shows our car with motion emanating from the rear of the vehicle.

Figure 6-7 *Vroom, vroom!*

Radial Blur

One other type of blur you can achieve with Paint Shop Pro is a Radial Blur. Radial Blur simulates blurring like spinning a camera in circles or zooming in quickly with a slow shutter speed. The Radial Blur filter can also give your image a twirling look to it.

Like many of the blur filters, you probably won't use the Radial Blur often, but with the right photograph, it produces a stunning effect like the one you see in Figure 6-8.

Paint Shop Pro's Radial Blur filter provides three different blur types: Twirl, Zoom, and Spin. Using the Zoom type blurs pixels away from the center of the image, and the Twirl blur type blurs pixels in a spiraling manner.

The third type, Spin, blurs pixels circularly around the image center. Figure 6-9 shows the same image with a Spin effect. Notice the circular motion.

Figure 6-8 *Add a twirl effect with Radial Blur. (Original photo by James Hutchinson)*

Figure 6-9 *Spin type radial blur makes the trees appear as if they are in the middle of a tornado.*

The following steps walk you through applying the Radial Blur filter to your image:

1. Click the Adjust menu, select Blur, and then select Radial Blur. You see a dialog box like the one in Figure 6-10.

2. Select a Blur type: Twirl, Zoom, or Spin.

3. In the Blur section, choose a Strength value. Measured in percentages from 1 to 100, lower values lessen the effect, while higher values intensify the effect. If you choose the Twirl option, you can also set the Twirl degrees value from −90 to 90, which determines the tilt of the twirl.

4. Click the Elliptical check box if you have a rectangular image and want the radius squeezed to fit the image, which produces elliptical-shaped blurring, as opposed to circular.

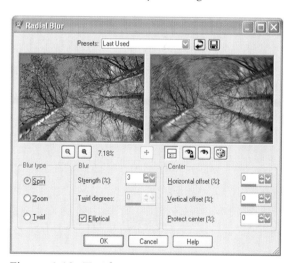

Figure 6-10 *Twirl, zoom, or spin your image.*

5. The Center section selects settings that affect the center of the image. The horizontal offset sets the horizontal center point of the blur, whereas the vertical offset sets the vertical center point of the blur. Values for both center points range from −100 to 100. The last option, Protect Center, determines how much to diminish blurring at the image center. With values from 1 to 100, higher values increase the radius of the nonblurred center area.

6. Click OK after making your selection.

Experiment with the blur settings. You could even use blur to create some awesome backgrounds that you could use in other images.

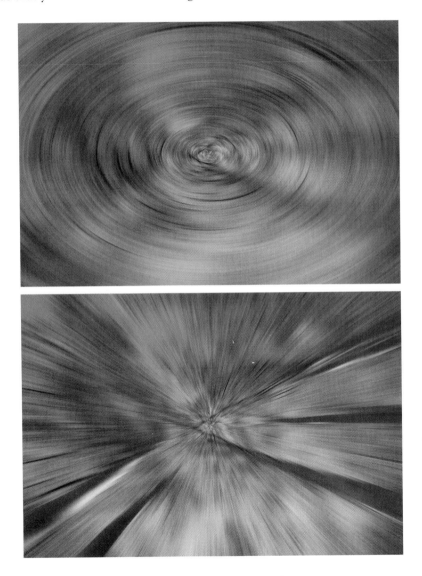

Effects and Filters

Paint Shop Pro includes many different creative and sometimes mystical filter effects, designed to radically change the nature of your images. Some are subtle and barely detectable, while others make the image jump right out at you. As a photographer, you probably won't use these effects much, but in special situations you may find them helpful, if not downright amusing.

Effects work on selections or the individual layers of an image, so you can apply a different effect for each layer, or you can apply multiple effects to a single layer. Like most filters you've already encountered, effects work only on raster images and only if the image is full (16 million) color or in certain greyscale settings. Paint Shop Pro includes over 80 different effects in 10 different categories:

- 3-D effects
- Art Media effects
- Artistic effects
- Distortion effects
- Edge effects
- Geometric effects
- Illumination effects
- Image effects
- Reflection effects
- Texture effects

We won't be able to look at each and every one of the effects, but we'll review each category and the type of effect the categories manage. Some effects, such as all of the Edge category effects, simply apply without any dialog box or options. Others require input from you.

NOTE

Thanks to James Hutchinson, Gary French, and Tim Koers for their images used in illustrating these effects.

The dialog box you see in Figure 6-11 is one of the easier effects dialog boxes. Only a single option appears in this Artistic Aged Newspaper dialog box.

Other dialog boxes provide you with lots of options to make the effect develop the way you want it. For example, take a look at Figure 6-12. This is the dialog box for the Artistic Balls and Bubbles. You can see there are four tabs for you to set options, and each tab has multiple selections. All these options may seem complex, but they provide you with lots of flexibility in applying the effect.

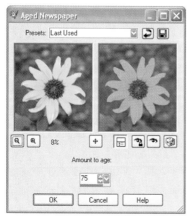

Figure 6-11 *Select the number of years you want your image to appear aged.*

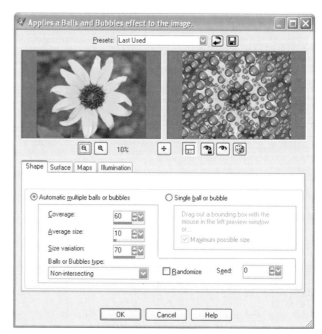

Figure 6-12 *Click the Help button for a detailed explanation of the dialog box options.*

3D Effects

The 3D category includes six special effects designed to give your selection or image a sense of depth and dimension. Three of the effects, Chisel, Drop Shadow, and Outer Bevel, can only be used with a selection, not an entire layer. You could apply them to an entire layer by selecting the entire layer first. The other three effects, Buttonize, Cutout, and Inner Bevel, can be used on layers or selections.

Buttonize

Inner Bevels

Art Media Effects

The six Art Media effects are an artist's dream. You can use them to make your image look as if it were hand-painted or drawn. Choices include Black Pencil, Brush Strokes, Charcoal, Colored Chalk, Colored Pencil, and Pencil.

Black Pencil

Colored Pencil

Artistic Effects

The Artistic Effects are my favorite category, as well as one of the largest, with 16 possible effects designed to provide a variety of different results to your image:

- Aged Newspaper and Sepia Toning both apply a yellowed aging look to your image.

- Balls and Bubbles let you create reflective transparent bubbles over your image.

- Chrome gives your image a metallic appearance.

- Colored Edges locates and enhances the edges in your photo.

- Colored Foil and Enamel gives the image a shiny, melded-together appearance.

- Contours presents an outline of your photograph.

- Glowing Edges applies to the image edges and makes them look like they are under a black light.

- Neon Glow, similar to Glowing Edges, applies a glow to the image edges and applies a speckled pattern along with the enhanced colored edges.

- Halftone provides gradations of light as though the photograph were taken through a fine screen.

Aged Newspaper

Chrome

Hot Wax

Balls and Bubbles

Glowing Edge

Neon Glow

- Hot Wax Coating makes your image look as if a layer of melted wax were poured over the top of it.

- Magnifying Lens simulates placing a magnifying lens on a portion of the image.

- Posterize blends, smoothes, and compresses the image color to give a soft appearance.

- Solarize simulates the look of double-exposed photographic paper that accentuates the contrast areas.

- Topography provides a graphic representation of the image surface features.

Distortion Effects

Just as their name implies, the Distortion Effects distort your image. Another large category of effects, this one contains 13 choices, many of which can completely turn your image into an unrecognizable but artistic form. Select from Curlicues, Displacement Map, Lens Distortion, Pinch, Pixelate, Polar Coordinates, Punch, Ripple, Spiky Halo, Twirl, Warp, Wave, and Wind.

Displacement Map

Ripple

Lens Distortion

Polar Coordinates

Edge Effects

None of the Edge effects offer options. Paint Shop Pro simply applies the effect that you can use to clarify your image and put emphasis on your image edges. Select from Dilate, Enhance, Enhance More, Erode, Find All, Find Horizontal, Find Vertical, and Trace Contour.

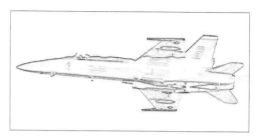

Find Horizontal

Find All

Geometric Effects

Don't worry...you didn't have to pass your high school geometry class to use the Geometric effects. This category includes eight options to transform your images into geometric shapes, including circles, cylinders, pentagons, and spheres.

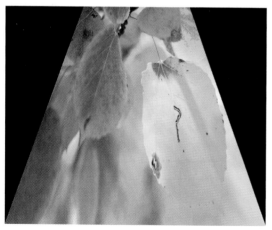

Vertical Perspective

Circle

Illumination Effects

The Illumination effects category has only two choices: Lights and Sunburst, both of which add lighting to your image or selection area.

Lights

Sunburst

Image Effects

Think of the Image effects category as the "Everything Else" category. There are three options available: Offset, Page Curl, and Seamless Tiling.

Page Curl

Seamless Tiling

Reflection Effects

From twisting your image into a kaleidoscope to using the Feedback (sort of the old mirror reflecting a mirror reflecting a mirror routine), the four Reflection effects project your current image into appearing as if you have multiple images. Choices also include Pattern and Rotating Mirror.

Kaleidoscope

Feedback

Texture Effects

Enhance the essence of your image by using one of the 15 Texture effects. Most of these effects make your image appear as if it were "top coated." Another of the larger categories, you can pick from 15 different Texture effects, such as Blinds, Emboss, Fine Leather, Fur, Mosaic–Antique, Mosaic–Glass, Polished Stone, Rough Leather, Sandstone, Sculpture, Soft Plastic, Straw Wall, Texture, Tiles, and Weave.

Blinds

Sculptured

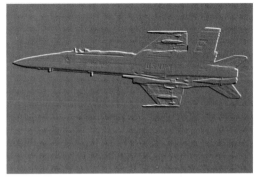

Emboss

Texture

Effect Browser

The easiest way to see what an effect applies to your image is with the Effect Browser. The Effect Browser displays a thumbnail of your open image layer with a sample of each effect with its Default and other Preset settings. The Effect Browser is the first option under the Effects menu. The Effect Browser (Figure 6-13) takes a moment to load, but you'll find it well worth the wait.

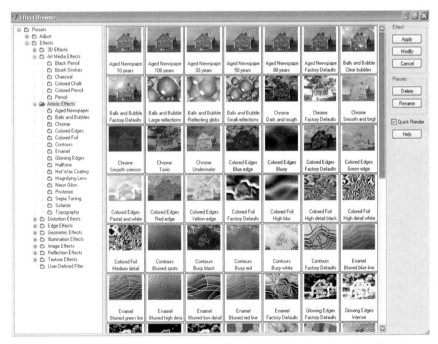

Figure 6-13 *The Effect Browser can also show thumbnails of each Adjust filter.*

On the left side, you see a tree view of all the different categories of Adjustments and Effects. Click the plus sign next to any category to expand that category or click the minus sign to collapse a category. When you locate and click the effect you want to use, click Apply, and Paint Shop Pro automatically applies that preset option to your image. If the preset filter is close but not quite what you want, click the effect thumbnail image and then click the Modify button. Paint Shop Pro will display the dialog box appropriate to the effect you selected.

User Defined Filters

All image editing is a result of math. Paint Shop Pro makes mathematical calculations for almost every command you issue, and filters are no exception. If you are a math wizard and really want a challenge, you can create your own effect filters. Paint Shop Pro includes a User Defined Filter box where you can enter your own values. Click the Effects menu and select User Defined Filter. A dialog box like the one you see in Figure 6-14 appears.

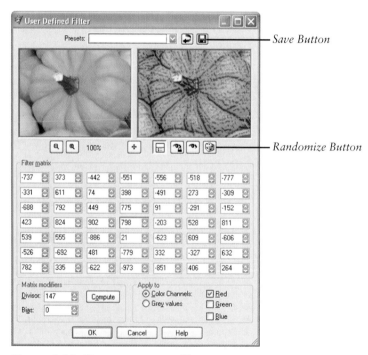

Figure 6-14 *Create your own filters.*

The Filter matrix allows you to enter the coefficients needed to process pixels for your needed effect. The Matrix modifier contains a Divisor number that Paint Shop Pro uses to divide the Filter matrix values. It also contains a Bias number that can shift each color value by a specified amount. Sound difficult? It is. While you *could* calculate and enter a value for every factor in the User Defined Filter box, there's an easier way.

Click the Randomize button, which randomly changes all the values. Keep clicking until you find a look you like. If you only want this look one time and don't plan on using it ever again, just click OK, and Paint Shop Pro will apply the filter to your image or selection.

If, however, you think you might use this filter again, you can save the settings as a preset option. Click the Save button and enter a name for the custom filter in the resulting Save Present dialog box. The next time you want the same filter, you select it from the Presets list (see Figure 6-15).

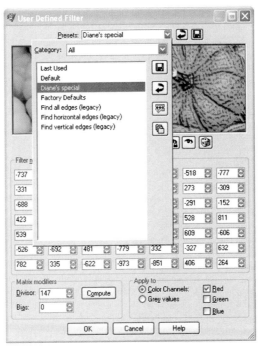

Figure 6-15 *Save your custom filters for future use.*

Working with Plug-Ins

If the over 100 filters supplied with Paint Shop Pro aren't enough, you can add other plug-in filters. Plug-in filters, by themselves, can't do anything, but combine them with Paint Shop Pro, and you can create an even wider variety of functions and effects. The concept of plug-in filters originated long ago with Adobe Photoshop, and the success of the feature has many different software companies constantly trying to develop better and more unique filters.

Some are quite pricey, whereas others are free. Typically, you won't find filters available in your local software store, but they abound on the Internet, and in many cases, you can get a trial copy to evaluate.

Most third-party filters are compatible with Paint Shop Pro and typically have .8bf as the filename extension, such as swirleypop.8bf or bubblejets.8bf. The .8bf extension is not, however, a requirement in Paint Shop Pro.

> ## NOTE
>
> Most Adobe Photoshop plug-ins are compatible with Paint Shop Pro.

Look around on the Internet, and we think you'll be quite pleased with what you find. Whether you choose Flaming Pear's SuperBladePro, Corel's KPT Collection, Alien Skin's Eye Candy, or one of the hundreds of others, you'll find unique special effects in each application. Here are a few places you can begin your search:

- **www.jasc.com**: From the makers of Paint Shop Pro, you can purchase an awe-inspiring plug-in called *Virtual Painter*, which can give your photographs a hand-painted appearance.

- **www.alienskin.com**: The creator of the award-winning Eye Candy filters provides a wide variety of photorealistic textures, such as snake and lizard skin, while their Xenofex 2 collection simulates natural phenomena such as lightning and clouds or even filters that can transform your photos into jigsaw puzzles or constellations.

- **www.andromeda.com**: Andromeda software provides several excellent filter collections, several of which are aimed at photographic correction and adjustments.

- **www.flamingpear.com**: The Flaming Pear family of filters includes the powerful SuperBladePro and a number of other unusual filters, such as ones that create images of planets or the illusion of flooding.

- **www.corel.com**: The folks who bring you WordPerfect now own KPT Collection, one of the first third-party filter sets, originally called *Kai's Power Tools* (KPT3).

- **www.thepluginsite.com**: This popular site offers free and commercial plug-ins, including its own Colorwasher and Focal Blade. The best part of this Web site is that it provides reviews of a variety of third-party filters and a master index to them.

- **www.autofx.com**: Auto FX software carries a variety of plug-in packages with some really unique effects, including edges, wrinkle, tape, and gels (see Figure 6-16).

- **www.humansoftware.com**: There are lots of great plug-ins available here, including a wide variety of frames and textures; these are great for working with photographs.

- **www.avbros.com**: AV Bros. has some fantastic page curl and puzzle filters. Even if you don't need extra filters, take a look at their Web site and see some of their examples.

Figure 6-16 *A photograph of calla lilies after applying the AutoFx Edge Brush filter.*

Installing Plug-in Filters

Each filter manufacturer provides its own method and directions to install its filters. When you install the filters, make a note of their file location because you need to tell Paint Shop Pro where you keep those filters on your computer. Paint Shop Pro stores instructions to file locations in its Preferences area. Follow these steps to install plug-ins:

1. Click the File menu and select Preferences.

2. From the Preferences submenu, click File Locations. You'll see a File Locations dialog box like the one in Figure 6-17.

3. Click Plug-ins from the File types section. A list of plug-in file locations will appear.

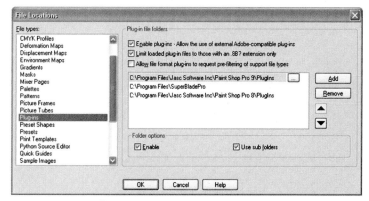

Figure 6-17 *Tell Paint Shop Pro where to locate your plug-in filters.*

4. Click Add to display the Browse for Folder dialog box.

5. Locate and click the folder where the filters are located; then click OK twice.

Any new plug-ins are listed under the Effects menu, Plugins.

Image Imagery

While not truly distortion effects or filters, two other items you might find interesting are the Mirror and Flip commands. Flip turns the image upside down on its head, and the Mirror command reverses the picture left to right as if looking in a mirror. Not many photographs would be appropriate for a Flip command, but many images could benefit from the Mirror command. The peony seen in Figure 6-18 illustrates a flipped image, and Figure 6-19 shows a mirrored image.

Both commands are located on the Image menu and can be applied to a layer or a selection. If your image has multiple layers and you want to mirror all of the layers, make the layers part of a layer group first.

Figure 6-18 *Flip your images top to bottom.*

Figure 6-19 *Mirror flips your images left to right. (Original photo by James Hutchinson)*

Morphing

While we're on the topic of distortion, let's take a brief look at a couple of other distortion tools included with Paint Shop Pro: the Mesh Warp tool and the Warp Brush. Like many of the effects, you probably won't use these tools much, but let's see how they work.

Mesh Warp Tool

The Mesh Warp tool warps the current layer or interior of a selection to a mesh frame, which can give the image dimension and depth.

 Categorized as one of the Deform tools, the Mesh Warp tool is the second tool down on the Tools toolbar, and it shares space with the Deform, Straighten, and Perspective Correction tools that you've already discovered.

When you select the Mesh Warp tool, Paint Shop Pro places a grid over the image. You can modify the grid size through the Mesh horizontal and Mesh vertical options on the Tool Options palette. The values indicate the number of mesh lines within the frame, not including the border lines.

At each grid intersection, you see a small node box that acts as a handle to drag and deform sections of the image. Use these nodes in one of several ways:

- Click and drag a node to move it.
- Press Shift while dragging a node to move the entire row or column.
- Press Ctrl while dragging a node to deform the row or column into a smooth curve.

Because of the power involved in using the Mesh Warp, you may see some lag time between when you move a node and when you see the results. If needed, you can change the grid size as you work. Entering new Mesh values reconfigures the grid and returns it to the original position, but the image retains any deformations you have already made.

Take a look at Figure 6-20. By moving the nodes on the warp grid, the image now has a hill, and the grass appears to be blowing slightly.

When you finish with Mesh Warp, double-click the image or click the Apply button.

Figure 6-20 *Stretch and twist with the Mesh Warp. (Original photo by James Hutchinson)*

Warp Brush

One of the most powerful paint brushes, the Warp Brush tool is akin to finger painting with your mouse. Applied in the same manner as a regular paint brush, the Warp Brush bends and warps the pixels under the brush.

Where can you use the Warp Brush? Well, some photography editors use the Warp Brush to increase eye size, giving the subject a wide-eyed appearance. Other uses might be to reduce and straighten other facial details. Still others just use the Warp Brush as a stress reliever by distorting an image of someone they are angry at!

 The Warp Brush shares space on the Tools toolbar with the regular Paint Brush and the Air Brush. When you select the Warp Brush, the Tool Options palette displays brush settings such as size, hardness, and strength.

The Warp Brush can apply the warp in any of several different modes. Push smears the pixels in the direction you brush; Expand smears the pixels away from the center of the brush; and Contract smears the pixels into the center of the brush. You can also twirl the pixels clockwise or counterclockwise around the center of the brush, and the Noise mode smears the pixels randomly. Iron Out and Unwarp both remove a warp.

Because of the power involved in using the Warp Brush, you may see some lag time between when you brush and when you see the results. Use the Warp Brush slowly and give the computer a chance to catch up with your brush. In Figure 6-21, the Warp Brush was used to lengthen and twist the flower petals.

Figure 6-21 *Go ahead...play a little. The Warp Brush is fun!*

What's Next?

In this chapter, you discovered more of the fun side of Paint Shop Pro. You'll find yourself spending hours trying out the different effects on your favorite photographs. But...back to work. In the next chapter, we are going to delve into the color fine-tuning functions available with Paint Shop Pro. We'll take an extensive look at color depth, curves, channels, and histograms.

7

More About Color

Color is cool. Color is hot. Photographers know that color is a powerful tool that can grab the eye, lead our attention to specific areas of an image, and, through some unknown process, generate feelings that run the emotional color gamut from ardor to anger.

Conversely, *bad* color can ruin an image. It's a fact of life that a well-composed image that might look sensational in black-and-white can be utterly ruined simply by presenting it in color with inappropriate hues or saturation. Bad color can override every other aspect of a photograph, turning wheat into chaff. But what, exactly, is bad color?

The most interesting thing about color is that the concepts of "good" and "bad" can vary by the image, the photographer's intent, and the purpose of the finished photograph. The weird colors of a cross-processed image are very bad if they show up in your vacation pictures, but wonderfully evocative in a fashion shoot. A photo that has a vivid red cast may look terrible as a straight portrait but interesting when part of a glamour shot taken by the glowing embers of a fireplace. A picture of a human with even the tiniest bit of a blue tinge looks ghastly, but it might add the desired degree of chill to a snowy winter scenic.

Strictly speaking, you don't have to understand how color works to use it to make corrections or generate striking effects. It's entirely possible to use trial-and-error experimentation to arrive at the results you want. However, just as you don't need an electrical engineering degree to operate a toaster, it's good to know a little something about electricity before you go poking around inside with a fork.

This chapter provides an in-depth look at the color theories that photographers work with every day and which become even more useful when you begin working with Paint Shop Pro. You'll learn more about the most frequently used color models and the differences between the way color is viewed in the real world, captured by a film or digital camera, displayed on your monitor, and output by your printer.

Wonderful World of Color

Human perception of color is a strange and wonderful thing, created in our brains from the variation of the wavelengths of light that reach our eyes. We typically see an object as a color, such as a blue sky, green grass, or a pink ribbon. But, in a sense, color is an optical illusion.

If you remained awake during high school science class, you'll recall that the retina of the eye contains rod cells (which are used for detail and black-and-white vision when there is not much light) and three types of cone cells, which respond to different wavelengths of light. Different wavelengths reflect different light that we see and perceive as color.

But color is really what we see as a result of the three factors interacting: light, the object, and the observer. As rays of light hit the object, the object absorbs some light and reflects some light. All the colors we could see (if our eyes were constructed that way) would reside in that continuous color spectrum, like the one shown in Figure 7-1. However, we can't directly sense each of those individual colors. Instead, each of the three kinds of cone cells in our eyes "sees" a different set of frequencies, which happen to correspond to what we call red, green, and blue (RGB). Our brains process this RGB information and translate it into a distinct color that we perceive.

Figure 7-1 *Human eyes are able to perceive thousands of colors in the visible spectrum of light.*

Color films use a minimum of three different layers of photosensitive emulsion, each sensitive to red, green, and blue light. Digital cameras have three sets of color sensors, and scanners use three light sources, three arrays of sensors, or filters to capture red, green, and blue information. Finally, when digital information is seen on computer monitors, the same three colors complete the circle by displaying the color information for our eyes to view again.

This process is significant for an important reason. *None* of the systems used to capture or view color are sensitive to red, green, and blue light in exactly the same way. Some are particularly sensitive to green light; indeed, digital cameras are designed with twice as many green-sensitive sensors as red or blue. Most systems don't respond to all the colors in a perfectly linear way either, so that a hue that is twice as intense may register slightly less or a bit more intense.

And it gets worse. The models used to represent those colors in the computer also treat colors in different ways. That's why an image you see in real life may not look exactly the same in a color slide, a color print, a scanned image, on your screen, or when reproduced by a color printer or printing press. Simply converting an image from RGB to CMYK (more on that later) can change the colors significantly. The concept of the range and type of colors that can be captured, manipulated, and reproduced by a given device or system—its color gamut—is an important one for photographers working in Paint Shop Pro.

Color Models

Artificial color systems, which include computer scanners, monitors, printers, and other peripherals, attempt to reproduce, or model, the colors that we see, using various sets of components of color. If the model is a good one, all the colors we are capable of detecting are defined by the parameters of the model. The colors within the definition of each model are termed its *color space*. Because nearly all color spaces use three different parameters, such as colors (red, green, and blue, for example) or qualities (such as hue, saturation, and brightness), we can plot them as x, y, and z coordinates to produce a three-dimensional shape that represents the color gamut of the model.

The international standard for specifying color was defined in 1931 by the Commission Internationale L'Eclairage (CIE); it is a scientific color model that can be used to define all the colors that humans can see. However, computer color systems are based on one of three or four other color models, which are more practical because they are derived from the actual hardware systems used to reproduce those colors.

None of these systems can generate all the colors in the full range of human perception, but they are the models with which we must work. Your best bet is to learn something about all color working spaces, since image editors like Paint Shop Pro support several different color models.

Of the three most common models, the one based on the hue-lightness-saturation (HLS) of colors is the most natural for human eyes to perceive color because it deals with a continuous range of colors that may vary in brightness or richness. You use this type of model when you adjust colors with the Hue/Saturation dialog boxes.

Additive color is commonly used in computer display monitors, while subtractive color is used for output devices such as printers. Since you need to understand how color works with these peripherals, we'll explain the additive and subtractive models first.

The Additive Color Model Known as RGB

Computer monitors produce color by aiming three electronic guns at sets of red, green, and blue phosphors (compounds that give off photons when struck by beams of electrons) coated on the screen of your display. LCD and LED monitors use sets of red, green, and blue pixels to represent each picture element of an image that are switched on or off, as required. If none of the colors are displayed, we see a black pixel. If all three glow in equal proportions, we see a neutral color—say, grey or white, depending on the intensity. We call this color model the *RGB model*.

Such a color system uses the additive color model—so-called because the colors are added together, as you can see in Figure 7-2. A huge selection of colors can be produced by varying the combinations of light. In addition to pure red, green, and blue, we can also produce cyan (green and blue together), magenta (red and blue), yellow (red and green), and all the colors in between. As with greyscale data, the number of bits used to store color information determines the number of different tones that can be reproduced.

Figure 7-2 shows one way of thinking about additive color, in a two-dimensional color space. The largest circles represent beams of light in red, green, and blue. Where the beams overlap, they produce other colors. For example, red and green combine to produce yellow. Red and blue add up to magenta, and green and blue produce cyan. The center portion, in which all three colors overlap, is white. If the idea that overlapping produces *no* color rather than some combined color seems confusing, remember that the illumination is being added together, and combining all three of the component colors of light produces a neutral white with equal amounts of each.

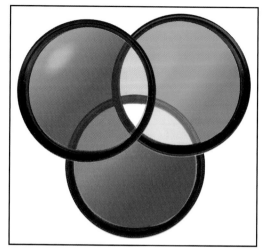

Figure 7-2 *The additive color system uses beams of light in red, green, and blue hues.*

However, if you look at the figure, you'll see that it shows overlapping circles that are each more or less the same intensity of a single color (allowing some artistic license for the 3D "shading" effect added to keep the individual circles distinct). For that reason, this two-dimensional model doesn't account for the lightness or darkness of a color, in other words, the amount of white or black. That added dimension is dealt with by, literally, adding a dimension, as you can see in the mock 3D model shown in Figure 7-3.

The figure shows red, green, and blue colors positioned at opposite corners of the cube, with their complementary colors arranged between them. White and black are located opposite one another, as well. Any shade that can be produced by adding red, green, and blue together can be represented by a position within the cube.

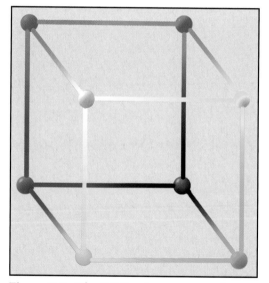

Figure 7-3 *The RGB color space can be better represented by a three-dimensional cube, simplified to corners and edges in this illustration.*

No display device available today produces pure red, green, or blue light. Only lasers, which output at one single frequency of light, generate absolutely pure colors, and they aren't used for display devices. We see images through the glow of phosphors, LEDs, or LCD pixels, and the ability of these to generate absolutely pure colors is limited. Color representations on a display differ from brand to brand and even from one display to another within the same brand.

Moreover, the characteristics of a given display can change as the monitor ages and the color-producing elements wear out. Some phosphors, particularly blue ones, change in intensity as they age, at a different rate than other phosphors. So, identical signals rarely produce identical images on displays, regardless of how closely the devices are matched in type, age, and other factors.

In practice, most displays show far fewer colors than the total of which they are theoretically capable. Actually, the number of different colors a display can show at one time is limited to the number of individual pixels. At 1024×768 resolution, there are only 786,432 different pixels. Even if each one were a different color, you'd view, at most, only around three-quarters of a million colors at once.

In Paint Shop Pro, when using the RGB model, you can adjust each color independently of the other by clicking the Adjust menu and selecting Color Balance. You then pick the last menu option, Red/Green/Blue, which displays the dialog box you see in Figure 7-4, where you can enter and preview each color adjustment.

Adjusting the amount of red, green, and blue in your image makes color corrections by changing the overall color cast. Reducing blue adds yellow, reducing green adds magenta, and reducing red adds cyan to the image. A value of 0% indicates the original value. If you want to add more of a color, you should use a positive number, but if you want to remove some of a color, use a negative number.

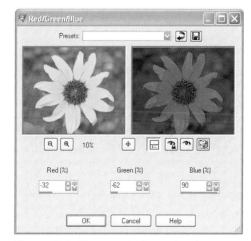

Figure 7-4 *You can independently adjust the red, green, and blue in your image.*

You can either increase its opposite color on the color wheel or reduce the amount of adjacent colors on the color wheel. For example, to color correct an image containing too much yellow, either increase the amount of blue or decrease the amount of red and green.

The Subtractive Color Model Known as CMYK

There is a second way of producing color that is familiar to computer users—one that is put to work whenever we output our Paint Shop Pro images as hard copies using a color printer. This kind of color also has a color model that represents a particular color gamut. The reason a different kind of color model is necessary is simple: When we represent colors in hardcopy form, the light source we view by comes not from the image itself, as it does with a computer display. Instead, hard copies are viewed by light that strikes the paper or other substrate and then is filtered by the image on the paper; then it is reflected back to our eyes.

This light starts out with (more or less) equal quantities of red, green, and blue light and looks white to our eyes. The pigments the light passes through before bouncing off the substrate absorb part of this light, subtracting it from the spectrum. The components of light that remain will reach our eyes and are interpreted as color. Because various parts of the illumination are subtracted from white to produce color, this color model is known as the *subtractive system*.

The three primary subtractive colors are cyan, magenta, and yellow, and the model is sometimes known as the *CMY model*. Usually, however, black is included in the mix, for reasons that will become clear shortly. When black is added, this color system becomes the CMYK model (black is represented by its terminal character, *K*, rather than *B* to avoid confusion with the additive primary blue). Figure 7-5 shows the subtractive color model in a fanciful representation, retaining the color filter motif we described in the additive color system. (You couldn't overlap filters to produce the colors shown, although you could print with inks to create them.)

In subtractive output devices such as color printers or printing presses, cyan, magenta, yellow, and, usually, black pigments (for detail) are used to represent a gamut of colors. It's

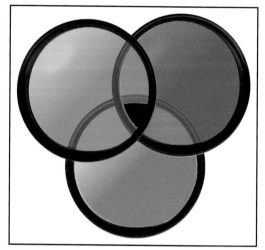

Figure 7-5 *The subtractive color system uses cyan, magenta, and yellow colors.*

obvious why additive colors won't work for hard copies: it is possible to produce red, green, and blue pigments, of course, and we could print red, green, and blue colors that way (that's exactly what is done for spot color). However, there would be no way to produce any of the other colors with the additive primaries. Red pigment reflects only red light; green pigment reflects only green. When they overlap, the red pigment absorbs the green, and the green absorbs the red, so no light is reflected, and we see black.

Cyan pigment, on the other hand, is supposed to absorb only red light. In theory, it reflects both blue and green, producing the blue-green shade we see as cyan. Yellow pigment absorbs only blue light, reflecting red and green, while magenta pigment absorbs only green, reflecting red and blue. When we overlap two of the subtractive primaries, some of at least one color still reflects. Magenta (red-blue) and yellow (red-green) together produce red because the magenta pigment absorbs green, and the yellow pigment absorbs blue. Their common color, red, is the only one remaining. Of course, each of the subtractive primaries can be present in various intensities or percentages, from 0 to 100%. The remainder is represented by white, which reflects all colors in equal amounts.

So, in our example above, if the magenta pigment were only 50% present and the yellow represented at 100%, only half of the green would be absorbed, while 100% of the blue would be soaked up. Our red would appear to be an intermediate color, orange. By varying the percentages of the subtractive primaries, we can produce a full range of colors. At least in theory we could.

You'll recall that RGB displays aren't perfect because the colors aren't pure. So, too, it is impossible to design pigments that reflect absolutely pure colors. Equal amounts of cyan, magenta, and yellow pigment *should* produce black. More often, what you'll get is a muddy brown. When daily newspapers first began their changeover to color printing in the 1970s, many of them used this three-color system, with mixed results.

However, better results can be obtained by adding black as a fourth color. Black can fill in areas that are supposed to be black and add detail to other areas of an image. While the fourth color does complicate the process a bit, the actual cost in applications like offset printing is minimal. Black ink is used to print text anyway, so there is no additional press run for black. Moreover, black ink is cheaper than critical process color inks, so it's possible to save money by using black instead of laying on three subtractive primaries extra thick. A typical image separated into its component colors for printing is shown in Figure 7-6. (You'll learn more about printing in Chapter 10, "Resolutions, Resizing, and Printing".)

Figure 7-6 *Full-color images are separated into cyan, magenta, yellow, and black components for printing. (Original photo by David Busch)*

The output systems you use to print hard copies of color images use the subtractive color system in one way or another. Some output devices, such as inkjet printers, color laser systems, and thermal wax transfer printers, are unable to print varying percentages of each of the primary colors, so they must simulate other colors by dithering. A few printers, such as a thermal dye sublimation printer, can vary the amount of pigment laid down over a broader range. These printers can print a full range of tones, up to the 16.8 million colors possible with 24-bit systems.

The subtractive color system can also be represented in three dimensions, as you see in Figure 7-7. In this illustration, the positions of the red, green, and blue colors have been replaced by cyan, magenta, and yellow, and the other hues rearranged accordingly. In fact, if you mentally rotate and reverse this figure, you'll see that it is otherwise identical to the one in Figure 7-3; RGB and CMYK are in this sense two sides of the same coin. However, don't make the mistake of thinking their color spaces are identical. There are colors that can be displayed in RGB that can't be printed using CMYK.

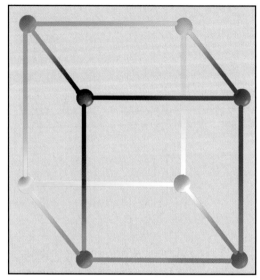

Figure 7-7 *The subtractive color model can also be represented by a 3D cube.*

HSL Color Models

The hue-saturation-lightness color model, also known as *HSL*, is a convenient way to manage color for some operations. In this model, individual colors are represented as they are in a rainbow, as a continuous spectrum and arranged in a circle.

Hue is the color reflected from an object, such as red, yellow, or orange. Saturation represents the vividness of the color, which is actually from the amount of grey in the color, from 0 (entirely grey) to 255 (fully saturated color). Lightness represents the perceived amount or intensity of light in the color. Lightness ranges from 0, which is no light, or black, to 255, which is total lightness, or white.

Paint Shop Pro provides a tool that adjusts these three elements individually. For example, if you want to adjust the saturation of a color without modifying its hue or brightness, HSB mode, click the Adjust menu, select Hue and Saturation, and click Hue/Saturation/Lightness (see Figure 7-8). The color rings represent the colors in the image, where the outer ring represents the original values and the inner ring represents the adjusted values.

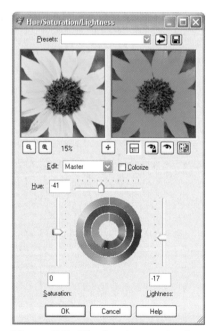

Figure 7-8 *The hue/saturation/ brightness color model starts with a color circle.*

You should know that the Hue value is not on the typical hue scale of 0 to 255. Instead, the value is the number of degrees of rotation around the 360 color wheel from the pixel's original color. A positive value indicates a clockwise rotation, and a negative value indicates a counterclockwise rotation. For example, when the Hue value is at 180, blue becomes yellow and green becomes magenta.

To adjust the values, drag the Hue, Saturation, and Lightness sliders. Hue values range from -180 to 180, and the Saturation and Lightness values range from -100 to 100. A value of zero means no change.

By selecting an option from the Edit drop-down list, you can edit the master color ring, or you can choose a specific color range to adjust. Additionally, checking the Colorize box turns the image into a two-color image.

Splitting Channels

You've seen how images work with the three color models. Each type of color information is stored in a channels, or planes, of colors. Both RGB and HSL use three channels: red, green, and blue or hue, saturation, and lightness. The CMYK model uses four channels: cyan, magenta, yellow, and black.

Paint Shop Pro provides a feature, called *Split Channels*, where you can separate the image into RGB, HSL, or CMYK color channels. Although you cannot create or edit an image using the CMYK model, you can still split the image to the four channels.

Using the Split Channel command creates a new greyscale image for each color channel, leaving the original image unchanged. For example, you can split an image into separate RGB greyscale images named "Red," "Green," and "Blue." Each greyscale image represents the percentage and location of a color (such as red) or, if splitting an HSL image, the characteristic (such as lightness) within the image. You access the Split Channel command through the Image menu.

Paint Shop Pro and Color Models

With all the previous information, how does Paint Shop Pro handle these models? It works with all three, so you can work onscreen and select colors using either the RGB or HSL color model, but you can output images using the CMYK model. The default screen model is RGB, but on the File, General Preferences, Palettes tab, you can select the one easiest for you.

Capturing Color Images

Today, we have several options for capturing images for manipulation in Paint Shop Pro. Color scanners have been around the longest, for around 50 years, in fact. The first ones we saw many years ago cost more than a million dollars when you included the computer equipment needed to drive them, and they were intended only for professional graphics applications at service bureaus and large publications. Today, color scanners, like the one shown in Figure 7-9, can cost less than $100.

Figure 7-9 *Modern color scanners can cost $100 or less.*

Color scanners are nothing more than a system for capturing the proper amount of each of the primary colors of light in a given image. So, these scanners use three different light sources—one each of red, green, and blue—to scan a color image. To do so, some older scanners actually made three passes over the image—once for each color. More recent scanners use multiple light sources, or "rotate" their illumination, using red/green/blue light in succession to capture an image in a single pass.

The amount of light reflected by the artwork for each color varies according to the color of the pigments in the original. Cyan pigment, for example, absorbs red light and reflects blue and green. So, when a cyan area is illuminated by the red fluorescent light in a scanner, relatively little light is reflected. Most of the light produced by the blue and green fluorescents is reflected. Your scanner software records that area of the original as cyan. A similar process captures the other colors in your subject during the scan. Even if you don't use a scanner yourself, you may work with scanned images that are captured by your photofinisher when converting your color slides or prints to digital form for distribution online or as a PhotoCD.

Digital cameras cut out the middle step by creating color images directly. Where scanners use a linear array that grabs an image one line at a time, digital cameras use a two-dimensional array that grabs a complete bitmap in one instant. Today, digital cameras with 3.3 to 8 megapixels (or more) of resolution can capture images that are virtually indistinguishable from those grabbed on film when reproduced or enlarged.

Color Correction

Sometimes, a horrid-looking image may have nothing more wrong with it than the balance of colors used to represent the image. Other times, the balance may be okay, but you'd like to make the colors look horrid in order to produce a desired special effect in your image.

Color balance is the relationship between the three colors used to produce your image, most often red, green, and blue. You need to worry only about three different factors.

- **Amount of Red, Green, and Blue.** If you have too much red, the image will appear too red. If you have too much green, it will look too green. Extra blue will make an image look as if it just came out of the deep freeze. Other color casts are produced by too much of two of the primary colors when compared to the remaining hue. That is, too much red and green produce a yellowish cast; red and blue tilt things toward magenta; and blue and green create a cyan bias. Figure 7-10 shows the same image with red, green, and blue color casts.

Figure 7-10 *Left to right you'll find reddish, greenish, and bluish color casts. (Original photograph by David Busch)*

- **Saturation**. That is, how much of the hue is composed of the pure color itself, and how much is diluted by a neutral color, such as white or black. Figure 7-11 shows the image with low, normal, and high saturation.

Figure 7-11 *The image has low saturation (left), normal saturation (middle), and high color saturation (right).*

- **Brightness/Contrast**. Brightness and contrast refer to the relative lightness/darkness of each color channel and the number of different tones available. If, say, there are only 12 different red tones in an image, ranging from very light to very dark, with only a few tones in between, then the red portion of the image can be said to have a high contrast. The brightness is determined by whether the available tones are clustered at the denser or lighter areas of the image. Many professionals use something called *histograms* to represent these relationships, but you don't need to bother with those for now. You'll learn more about histograms later in this chapter. Figure 7-12 shows the image with the contrast and brightness set low, normal, and high.

Figure 7-12 *Brightness and contrast have been set low at left, normal in the middle, and high at right.*

You may wonder what causes bad color in the first place. Indeed, knowing the sources of bad color can help you avoid the need for much color correction. Unfortunately, there are many culprits, whether you're using color negative film or slides, a scanner, or a digital camera. Here are the major sources of bad color.

Problem: Wrong Light Source

Reason: All color films are standardized, or balanced, for a particular "color" of light, and digital cameras default to a particular "white balance." Both are measured using a scale called *color temperature.* Color temperatures are assigned by heating a mythical "black body radiator" and recording the spectrum of light it emitted at a given temperature in degrees Kelvin. So, daylight at noon has a color temperature in the 5500 to 6000 degree range. Indoor illumination is around 3400 degree. Hotter temperatures produce bluer images (think blue-white hot), while cooler temperatures produce redder images (think of a dull-red glowing ember). Because of human nature, though, bluer images are called "cool," and redder images are called "warm," even though their color temperatures are actually reversed.

If a photograph is exposed indoors under warm illumination using film balanced for cooler daylight, the image will appear much too reddish. If you were using a slide film, you'd get reddish slides. The photo processing lab can add some blue while making prints from "daylight balanced" color negatives exposed under this warm light, though, giving you reasonably well-balanced prints. Some professional films are balanced for interior (tungsten) illumination. If one of these is exposed under daylight, it will appear too blue. Again, prints made from tungsten-balanced color negatives can be corrected at the lab.

At the same time, your digital camera expects to see illumination of a certain color temperature by default. Under bright lighting conditions, it may assume the light source is daylight and balance the picture accordingly. In dimmer light, the camera's electronics may assume that the illumination is tungsten and color balance for that. This may be what happens when your digital camera's white balance control is set to Auto. Figure 7-13 shows an image exposed under tungsten illumination with a daylight white balance.

Solution: You can often make corrections for this type of defect digitally in Paint Shop Pro. However, to avoid the need entirely, use the correct film or use a filter over the camera lens to compensate for the incorrect light source. You may not need to bother with color negative films because they can be corrected during the printing step, but you will certainly want to do something in the case of slide films, because what you shoot is what you get.

Figure 7-13 *Exposing daylight film under tungsten illumination or taking a digital picture with a daylight white balance setting produces a reddish image.*

> **NOTE**
> The light a filter removes must be compensated for by increasing the exposure in the camera.

With a digital camera, set the white balance manually using your camera's controls. Your camera probably has a setting that allows you to point the lens at a white object and let it use that as its white point. Or, your camera may have some built-in white-balance settings for tungsten, fluorescents, daylight, and other sources.

Problem: Fluorescent Light Source

Reason: The chief difference between tungsten and daylight sources is nothing more than the proportion of red and blue light. The spectrum of colors is continuous but is biased toward one end or the other. However, some types of fluorescent lights produce illumination that has a severe deficit in certain colors, such as only particular shades of red. If you looked at the spectrum or rainbow of colors encompassed by such a light source, it would have black bands in it, representing particular wavelengths of light. You can't compensate for this deficiency by adding all tones of red, either digitally or with a filter that is not designed specifically for that type of fluorescent light. Figure 7-14 shows an image that was exposed under fluorescent lights using a tungsten light balance.

Solution: Your camera retailer can provide you with color filters recommended for particular kinds of fluorescent lamps. These filters are designed to add only the amounts and types of colors needed. Since it's difficult to correct for fluorescent lights digitally, you'll want to investigate this option if you shoot many pictures under fluorescents and are getting "greenish" results.

Figure 7-14 *Some fluorescent lights can produce a greenish image.*

Problem: Incorrect Photofinishing

Reason: Here's one that digital photographers don't have to worry about. Equipment that makes prints from color negatives is highly automated and usually can differentiate between indoor and outdoor pictures or those that have a large amount of one color. Sometimes, the sensors are fooled, and you end up with off-color prints or those that are too light or too dark. The processing of color slides won't usually have any effect on the color balance or density of the transparencies, so you'll usually be concerned only about the color balance of prints.

Solution: Change finishers if it happens often. Ask that your prints be reprinted. If you'd rather not bother, you can often make corrections digitally after you've scanned the prints.

Problem: Mistreatment of Original Film

Reason: Your digital film cards won't deteriorate if you expose them to harsh environments briefly, but the same is not true for film. If you regularly store a camera in the hot glove compartment of your car or take a year or more to finish a roll of film, you can end up with color prints that are off color, sometimes by quite a bit. If your prints have a nasty purple cast or even some rainbow-hued flares in them, your negatives probably suffered this indignity. X-rays can also damage film by fogging it.

Solution: Usually, film that has been "fogged" by X-rays, heat, or latent image keeping effects cannot be corrected. If it hurts when you do that, don't do that. Figure 7-15 shows an image faded by heat and light.

Problem: Mixed Light Sources

Reason: You bounced your flash off a surface, such as a colored wall or ceiling, and the pictures picked up the color of that surface. Or, you took an indoor picture with plenty of tungsten light, but the subject was near a window and is partially illuminated by daylight.

Figure 7-15 *Leave your camera in the trunk for too long, and you may end up with a fogged image like this one.*

Solution: Avoid these situations. If some of your image is illuminated by the colored bounce flash or daylight streaming in through a window and other portions by another light source, you'll find it very difficult to make corrections. Investigate turning that picture into an "arty" shot by using one of Paint Shop Pro's special effects.

Problem: Faded Colors

Reason: The dyes in color prints and slides are not stable and will change when exposed to strong light or heat for long periods (one to five years) or with no further impetus even if kept in the dark for much longer periods (five to twenty years and up).

Solution: In the case of color prints, you can sometimes make a new print from the original negative if you can find the negative, and it was kept in a cool, dark place. Faded color prints and original slides can often be corrected digitally after scanning, because the color changes tend to take place faster in one color layer than another. You may be able to "add" missing colors by reducing the amount of the other colors in the photograph.

Problem: Unexpected Blue Cast in Flash Photographs

Reason: Certain fabrics, particularly whites, reflect a huge amount of ultraviolet light, making that neutral white garment turn a horrid blue. Because our eyes can't perceive ultraviolet light (except in the form of a brighter, whiter wash) but film can, we don't see this bluish cast as dramatically as the film does. Wedding photographers in particular have to cope with this.

Solution: Warming filters can cope with this, but you can often fix the problem in Paint Shop Pro by adding a little red to your photo. Human faces tend to accommodate a bit of extra warmth, as you can see in Figure 7-16.

There are other reasons why you can end up with poorly balanced images, but this section has covered the ones you can do something about. Now let's look at four different ways to color correct these images.

Figure 7-16 *Extra ultraviolet reflection from white fabrics can produce bluish pictures like the one at the top. Fortunately, Paint Shop Pro can correct for this error.*

Image Correction Made Easy

Entire books have been written on sophisticated color correction techniques, but there are several traditional ways to correct color in images and some newer, easier alternatives. You can select the method you're most comfortable with: hands-on, seat-of-the-pants corrections, or the simple, automated alternatives provided by Paint Shop Pro.

Just keep in mind that, as you try to improve the color balance, brightness/contrast, and other attributes of photographs, none of the following methods can add detail or color that isn't there. All techniques work well with photographs that have, say, all the colors somewhere, but with too much of one hue or another. The extra color can be removed, leaving a well-balanced picture behind. Or, you can beef up the other colors, so they are in balance once again. Paint Shop Pro can do that by changing some pixels that are relatively close to the color you want to increase to that exact color.

But remember that removing one color or changing some colors to another color doesn't add any color to your image; either way, you're taking color out. So, if you have a photograph that is hopelessly and overpoweringly green, you're out of luck. When you remove all the green, there may be no color left behind. Or, you can add magenta until your subject's face turns purple, and all you'll end up with is a darker photo. You must start with a reasonable image; color correction is better suited for fine-tuning than major overhaul.

Using Color Balance Controls

The first way we'll color correct an image is by using the color balance controls that virtually every image editing program has. This section lays down some principles you can use to create wild color effects, even if you decide to perform normal color corrections by one of the other methods.

In Paint Shop Pro, you'll find the color balance controls under Adjust, Color Balance, Color Balance (see Figure 7-17). Note that Paint Shop Pro lets you set color balance separately for shadows, midtones, and highlights. What we're interested in at this point are the color sliders.

These let you adjust the proportions of a particular color from -100 to 100 percent. You can either add one color or subtract its two component colors. For example, moving the Cyan/Red slider to +20 (sliding it toward the red end) has the exact same effect as moving the Magenta/Green and Yellow/Red sliders both to the -20 position (toward the left).

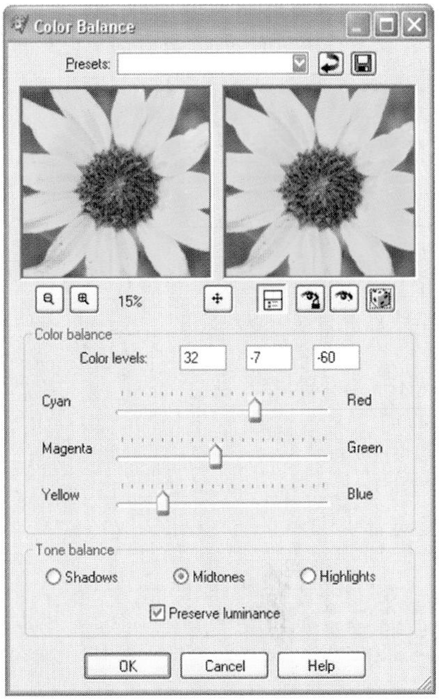

Which should you choose? If you want to add pure red (or green or blue), you can move the relevant control to the right. If your needs lean a little more toward one of

Figure 7-17 *Paint Shop Pro's Color Balance controls let you increase or decrease any color.*

the component colors than the other, move those sliders to the left instead. The following example will show what I mean.

Figure 7-18 shows a scenic photo of a mountain view. Unfortunately, the original print was over 20 years old and took on a strong reddish cast as it faded. We could have removed this red tone by simply sliding the Cyan/Red control towards the Cyan, which is the opposite, or complementary, color of red. Because Paint Shop Pro lets you preview the results, it would have been just a matter of subtracting red (adding cyan) until the picture "looked" right. In this case, a value of -36 applied only to the middle tones of the photo (those other than the highlights or shadows) would have been about perfect. In most cases, that's all you'll need to do to get the result shown in Figure 7-19.

So you can see that it is possible to remove red in one of two ways:

■ Add cyan (thereby subtracting red)

■ Add green and blue (thereby subtracting magenta and yellow)

Figure 7-18 *This photo has a distinct reddish cast. (Original photograph by David Busch)*

Figure 7-19 *Adding cyan removes the cast.*

It's a little confusing without looking at the color wheel, but the basic rules are simple. Reduce a color cast by:

- Adding the color opposite it on the color wheel

- Subtracting the color itself

- Subtracting equal amounts of the adjacent colors on the color wheel

- Adding equal amounts of the other two colors on its color wheel triangle

The biggest challenge is deciding in exactly which direction you need to add/subtract color. Magenta may look a lot like red, and it's difficult to tell cyan from green. You may need some correction of both red and magenta or be working with a slightly cyanish-green.

If you keep the color wheel in mind, you won't find it difficult to know how to add or subtract one color from an image, whether you are working with red, green, blue (RGB) or cyan, magenta, yellow, black (CMYK) color models.

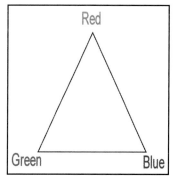 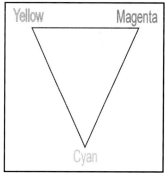

Here is an illustration designed to help you remember what the opposites of each color are. We have taken two triangles, the first to represent the RGB color model and the second to represent the CMYK color model.

Combine them together to get a composite diagram that illustrates each color's opposite. As you can see, the opposite of red is cyan, the opposite of blue is yellow, and the opposite of green is magenta. Of course, then the opposite of cyan is red, and so forth.

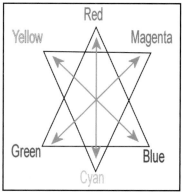

Uncovering Exposure Controls

Paint Shop Pro's Highlight/Midtone/Shadow dialog box does what the Brightness/Contrast controls should have done in the first place. As you'll recall, the Brightness/Contrast sliders darken/lighten and adjust the contrast of *all* the pixels in an image (or selected area of an image). So, when you have a dark area that needs a bit of brightening, adjusting the Brightness slider provides a lighter tone in the darker area but also makes highlighted areas that were probably just fine look brighter, too.

The Highlight/Midtone/Shadow command offers separate lightening/darkening controls for dark areas, light areas, and midtone areas. It's a great tool for making adjustments in images that need fixing in one area or the other or different amounts of compensation in each area.

Figure 7-20 is an example of such a photo, a rural church that is heavily backlit. By selecting Adjust, Brightness and Contrast, Highlight/Midtone/Shadow, the dialog box shown in Figure 7-21 appears.

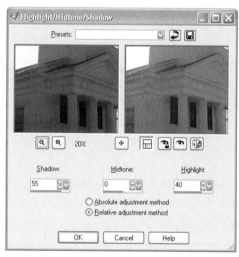

Figure 7-21 *Adjust each control independently of the others.*

Figure 7-20 *This sort of backlit photo is perfect for Paint Shop Pro's Highlight/Midtone/Shadow command. (Original photograph by David Busch)*

The Highlight/Midtone/Shadow box offers two adjustment methods: Absolute and Relative. If using the Relative adjustment method, the controls adjust the lightness relative to their original state, where positive values lighten the region, and negative values darken it.

If you use the Absolute method, the controls are used to set the absolute positions of the 25% histogram point (Shadows), the 50% histogram point (Midtones), and the 75% histogram point (Highlights). Typical values are about 35 for Shadow, 50 for Midtone, and 65 for Highlight, but they will vary, depending on the particular image you have. Increasing the value will lighten the region, and decreasing the value will darken it. (You'll learn more about histograms later in this chapter.)

For this (exaggerated) example, we'll brighten the shadows even more (to 55 percent) and darken the highlights (to 40 percent), creating the version shown in Figure 7-22.

Figure 7-22 *For this example, the highlights have been darkened and the shadows lightened, both independently of each other.*

Adjusting Lightness Levels

Another way to adjust image brightness and contrast, as well as gamma, is with the Levels command. Adjusting the gamma changes the brightness values of middle grey tones. You can apply the adjustments directly to the image or to an Adjustment layer.

TIP

Select an area prior to choosing the Levels command to limit the correction to a specific area.

Click the Adjust menu and select Brightness and Contrast, Levels (see Figure 7-23).

You can adjust the RGB channels together or independently by selecting an option in the Channel drop-down list. Notice the two sliders, Input and Output, and notice that both have a black diamond on the left and a clear diamond on the right. The Input level slider also has a grey diamond, which is for the Gamma.

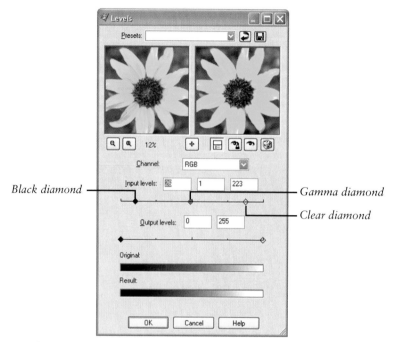

Black diamond

Gamma diamond

Clear diamond

Figure 7-23 *Change the individual channel brightness levels with this dialog box.*

The Input level bar indicates the image's brightness values, and you can increase the contrast by dragging the black diamond to the right to darken the dark values or to the clear diamond to the left to lighten the lighter values. To change the value of medium grey, drag the grey Gamma diamond left or right; the range of the gamma value is 0 to 7.99, with 1 being in the middle.

Just the opposite is the Output level, which you use to decrease the contrast. To lighten the darkest pixels, drag the black diamond to the right. To darken the lightest pixels, drag the clear diamond to the left.

Turning Curves

To take the brightness/contrast adjustments to the next level, you can use the Curves command, which lets you adjust the individual brightness values by using a graphic plot of your image's brightness values.

Based on a scale of 0 to 255, you can change all pixels that have a brightness value of 128 to a value of 150, for example. You can apply the Curves command directly to the image, to an Adjustment layer, or to a selected area.

Open the Curves dialog box you see in Figure 7-24 by clicking Adjust, Brightness and Contrast, Curves.

Similar to the Levels command, you can adjust the RGB channels together or independently by selecting an option in the Channel drop-down list. Either select RGB to edit the red, green, and blue channels together or pick from the individual channels of Red, Green, or Blue.

From the graphic chart, you add points to the values' line by placing your cursor over the dotted red line until the cursor changes to an arrowhead and displays "+ADD"; then click the line. You adjust the curve by dragging on the points, pulling up to increase brightness and pulling down to decrease the image brightness. If you want to remove a point, simply drag it off the graph.

Figure 7-24 *Manage your own Curve settings or select one of Paint Shop Pro's Presets.*

Recalling Histograms

You've already discovered several Paint Shop Pro tools to adjust color, contrast, and brightness, but one way to view the image tonal values is the histogram, which provides a useful graphical representation of the red, green, blue, greyscale, hue, saturation, and lightness values in your image. Casual users may not want to use the histogram, but for image-editing professionals, the histogram is a powerful tool for understanding and correcting images.

A histogram consists of a series of up to 256 different vertical lines in a graph, arranged horizontally with the black tones represented on the left side of the graph, the white tones at the right side, and the middle tones located (you guessed it) in the middle of the graph. The taller each of the lines is, the more tones that are present at that brightness level. A typical histogram has one or more peaks, and the black-and-white tones often don't extend to the theoretical limits possible for the image (0 for pure black at the left side and 255 for pure white at the right side).

As a general example, if you are working with an overexposed photo, you might see most of the tones concentrated at the right side of the histogram, whereas an underexposed photograph might have most tones concentrated on the left side. With such an image, you could analyze the image weaknesses using the histogram and then use the other Paint Shop Pro adjustment tools to correct the problem.

Paint Shop Pro includes a Histogram Palette, which you can display or hide as needed by pressing the F7 key or selecting View, Palettes, Histogram.

TIP

Select an area to limit the histogram to the selection area.

The Histogram graph, like the one you see in Figure 7-25, represents how many pixels are at each value in the selected channel. The vertical axis is the number of pixels from zero to the highest number. The horizontal axis represents the 0 to 255 value for each channel. Use the check boxes to turn on or off the display of the various channels.

Histogram Palette ——

Statistical information ——

Channel selections ——

Figure 7-25 *The curves of the histogram tell a story about the photo's tonal values.*

Here's how a histogram works:

- If a line spikes, there are lots of pixels in that value range.
- If a line is relatively flat and close to the horizontal axis, there aren't many pixels in that value range.

- If the graph is spread out, the image is probably pretty balanced and can be easily corrected if needed.

- If the lines are compressed into a narrow area, the image probably doesn't contain enough detail to be easily corrected.

- If the greyscale is mostly on the left, the image is probably too dark, and if the greyscale is mostly on the right, the image is probably too light.

- If the greyscale lines aren't spread out much, you might want to increase the contrast.

A couple of other available options on the Histogram Palette include the Sample merged box, which if checked graphs all layers in the image, and the Selection only box, which when marked graphs only the active selection.

The numeric display at the right of the palette probably looks like a lot of mumbo jumbo at first glance, but as you become experienced using the Histogram Palette, you'll find this information increasingly valuable. It is displaying statistical information regarding the various channels and the image pixels:

- **Value(s):** Value shows the count or quantity (from 0 to 255) of the point over which the cursor is positioned in the graph.

- **% in Range:** This statistic displays the percent of image pixels that are the value of the selected point or range. The number in parentheses is the number of pixels that are the selected value. For example, if the Percentile reads 70, then those pixels are brighter than 70 percent of all the pixels in the image.

- **% Above:** The percent of image pixels that are above the value of the selected point or range.

- **% Below:** This represents the percentage of image pixels that are below the value of the selected point or range.

- **Mean:** This represents the average intensity value of all the pixels in the image. If the number is very low, that will confirm that the image is rather dark; a high number means that the image is, on average, very bright.

- **Median:** The median is the middle number in the range of intensity values; half the individual values are higher than the median, while half are lower.

You can't actually change levels from the Histogram Palette, but you view the results of the changes as you make them by using the other Paint Shop Pro commands.

Working with Black, White, and Greyscale

If this chapter is entitled "More About Color," why are we now going to talk about black, white, and greyscale? Well, black is full color and white is no color...that's color related, isn't it?

When it comes to converting color images to black-and-white images, you have several choices. The method you select depends on the look you want for your image and the image itself. Some photographs lend themselves better to one way over another. Let's try three different methods using the two different images you see here:

The first method is to use Paint Shop Pro's greyscale conversion feature. When you convert an image to greyscale, Paint Shop Pro changes the color depth to 8-bit and uses a palette that contains white, black, and 254 shades of grey. The Greyscale function is under the Image menu and offers no options—it simply converts the photo by replacing each pixel in the image with a grey that matches its lightness value.

Figure 7-26 illustrates our two images after using the Image, Greyscale command.

Figure 7-26 *Images converted to greyscale have a tendency to look a little flat.*

The second method involves simply removing the color saturation by using the Hue/Saturation/Lightness tool in the original image. Click the Adjust menu, select Hue and Saturation, and then select Hue/Saturation/Lightness. Set the Saturation to a negative 100, which removes all color from the image. Then click OK.

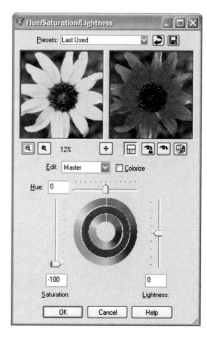

Using this method produces the images as you see them in Figure 7-27.

Figure 7-27 *Using this method brings out the detail in the flower but leaves the lake scene still looking a little dull.*

The third method takes a little more work on your part but can produce some very interesting results. It uses the Channel Mixer command, which you access through the Adjust menu, Color Balance, Channel Mixer.

First, you need to change the image to a monochrome, which looks like a greyscale but has a color depth of 16 million colors. To do this, check the Monochrome check box. The Output Channel drop-down list displays Grey. When you adjust the color channels in the next step, you change the amount of each channel that is used to create the monochrome image.

Black-and-white is a personal preference, and everyone is different, so you need to experiment with the Grey Output channel setting until your image takes on the look you want. For Figure 7-28, we adjusted the Red channel to 112, the Green to 35, and the Blue to 19. By adjusting these figures, you are reducing the amount of the color by a percentage. For example, if you are editing the Red channel and set the Red value to 50%, you reduce the amount of red in the image to 50% of its original amount. You'll probably also need to lighten or darken the color channel by setting a Constant value. We used a setting of -58.

So, as you can see, there's usually no right or wrong method when converting images to black-and-white. It depends on your taste and the image itself.

Figure 7-28 *This method produced a dramatic effect on the flower but created a stunning lake scene.*

Colorizing Old Photographs

Remember the old Three Stooges movies, which were filmed in black-and-white? (My favorite character was Curly.) Recently, some of the Three Stooges movies became available on DVD, which allowed the viewer to watch the original black-and-white version or a new digitally colorized version. Even the famous *Wizard of Oz* was originally in black-and-white, but later Ted Turner colorized it, which upset film purists that anyone would tamper with these old movies.

In the previous section, you learned how to convert color images to black-and-white, but what about all those black-and-white images you have that you'd prefer to see in color? Using the same basic principals used to colorize the Three Stooges and the folks in the land of Oz, you too can add color to your old photographs. But unlike Ted Turner, you won't get any grief from the critics.

The following steps help you colorize black-and-white (which, by the way, are actually greyscale) photographs like the one you see in Figure 7-29. Obviously, the steps you use will depend on the image you are using.

Figure 7-29 *Begin with a black-and-white or greyscale image.*

1. So we don't cause a problem with your original image, make a duplicate on which you will work (Window, Duplicate). Go ahead and close the original image.

2. If your image has scratches or needs other repairs, use the Scratch Removal, Clone brush, or other tools and do any needed touch-ups.

3. Increase the image color depth by clicking Image, Increase Color Depth, 16 million colors (24-bit).

4. Duplicate the Background layer. You will do your work on the duplicate layer.

5. Begin by changing the overall image color cast to flesh tones. Click Adjust, Hue and Saturation, Colorize, which displays the Colorize dialog box you see in Figure 7-30.

6. For Caucasian flesh skin tones, set the hue to 5 and the saturation to 75; then click OK. You may need to adjust the saturation to better fit the skin tone you need. If your image has multiple subjects with multiple skins, select the most common one here; then after applying the tone, select the subjects with different skin tones and apply the tone as needed to the selected areas only.

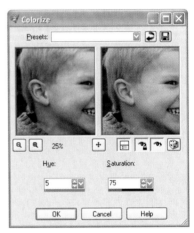

Figure 7-30 *Select a skin tone that looks close to natural.*

TIP

From the www.courseptr.com/downloads Web site, you can download a graphic illustrating other skin tones. Locate the skin tones image, as well as other images used in this book, by entering Paint Shop Pro or Diane Koers in the search box.

---

7. You may want to brighten the skin tones a little, so try setting the Brightness to 3 and the Contrast to 15 (Adjust, Brightness and Contrast, Brightness and Contrast).

8. Now you need to begin adjusting the individual image elements such as hair, eyes, clothing, and background.

TIP

Make your hues and saturations just a little darker than you think you want because we are going to decrease the opacity later, which makes them blend in better but also lightens everything.

---

9. Use the Freehand Selection tool to select the hair. You may need to add and replace parts of the selected area until you have only the hair selected (see Figure 7-31).

Figure 7-31 *The Freehand Selection tool set to Smart Edge is great for selecting the hair.*

10. Again, using the Colorize dialog box, adjust the hue and saturation until the hair color is representative of your subject's hair. For the blond hair, we used a hue of 18 and saturation of 115.

TIP

Press Ctrl+D to deselect any selections so you can start selecting fresh.

---

11. Next, using the Freehand Selection tool in Freehand Selection type, select the subject's eyes and colorize them. You can do one eye at a time or, using the Add mode, select them both and do them at the same time. For the blue eyes, I set the hue to 141 and saturation to 86.
12. If your subject has distinctive eyebrows, you might want to select each of them and apply a hue and saturation to make them look more natural. In our sample image, we didn't need to do so because the child's eyebrows are very light and almost nonexistent.
13. Most subjects could use a little facial colorizing, sort of a digitized make-up job. The best way to do this is by using the airbrush and lightly (very lightly) applying some color to the cheeks and lips. Set the airbrush size to a 6, hardness to 46, and opacity to a very light 4.

14. Set the foreground color to something rosy such as a Red 255, Green 83, and Blue 120. Click the foreground Material Properties box and select the colors like you see in Figure 7-32.

15. Lightly brush the cheekbones and lip areas with the airbrush. Make sure there is no distinct line of color, just highlights.

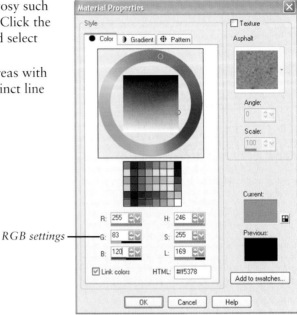

RGB settings

Figure 7-32 *Enter the setting in the RGB boxes or select a color from the color wheel.*

TIP

Using the airbrush set to an opacity of 13 and a color of white, you can dab the teeth to make them look whiter.

---

16. Now we need to colorize the individual's clothing. Select an article of clothing and colorize the hue and saturation until the clothing becomes what you want. In our image, we wanted the boy's sweater to be a teal blue, so we used a hue of 136 and saturation of 45.

17. After you have colorized the clothing, you'll want to colorize the background as well. Again, using your Freehand Selection tool, select the background area and colorize it as needed. Depending on the background elements, you may need to do this in several steps. For the brick background in our image, we set the hue to 18 and the saturation to 67.

18. When you've finished colorizing your image, decrease the opacity of the top layer so it better blends with your bottom greyscale image. For our example, we decreased the opacity to 64. We left the layer blend at Normal, but you may want to experiment with some of the different blend modes such as Lighten.

19. Merge the layers together by clicking Layers, Merge, Merge All.
20. Finally, you may want to sharpen your image, soften any edges, or remove any unwanted noise.

Figure 7-33 shows our final image.

Figure 7-33 *Happy colorizing!*

What's Next?

Well, this was certainly an intensive chapter and may have covered more about color than you wanted to know, but since a big chunk of a photograph relates to color, it's good to know how and why it works as it does. In the next chapter, we'll take a look at some of the fun side of Paint Shop Pro, scrapbooking, where you'll work with text, picture frames, borders, and other tools to show off your gorgeous photographs.

Light: While the Christmas cactus can adapt to low light more abundant blooms are produced on plants that have been exposed to high light intensity. Keep your plants in a sunny location indoors. Christmas cactus needs shading from the sun between May and September.

Soil: Well-drained soil is a must for Christmas cactus.

Water: Water thoroughly when the top half of the soil in the pot feels dry to the touch. When fall arrives, water the plant only well enough to prevent wilting. During the month of October, give the plant no water. Cautiously resume watering in November.

Fertilizing: As tender growth appears in the spring, apply a weak solution of liquid houseplant fertilizer at 2 to 3 weeks.

Temperature: Prefers warm temperatures, although evening temperatures of 50 to 55 degrees can be used to initiate flower bud formation From October on, keep the plant where it is cool at night. Keep away from drafts from heat vents, fireplaces or other sources

Scientific name:
Schlumbergera bridesii

Origin:
A group of epiphytic cacti native to the South American jungles

Christmas cactus

8

Digital Scrapbooking

We've been told that a picture is worth a thousand words, and Paint Shop Pro has certainly proved that statement to be true over and over again. But sometimes you just *have* to spell it out and want to tell a story about those pictures. Whether you create traditional or digital scrapbooks, you can combine the story and the photographs you've so painstakingly taken and then corrected and enhanced. Scrapbooking, which has been around as long as there have been photos, is the practice of combining photos, memorabilia, and stories in a scrapbook style album.

Digital scrapbooking is the newest, hottest trend in the scrapbooking world. With digital scrapbooking, you can merge your passion for preserving precious memories with your love for working on the computer. Whether you add to or replace altogether your traditional scrapbook supplies and tools, you can use your computer, digital graphics, and Paint Shop Pro in this exploding art form.

There's a lot to learn, so just take it a little at a time and don't expect perfection right away! Every layout you create will turn out better than the one before. And if you are really unhappy with the first layouts you do, you can always go back and redo them and change the bad parts later. That's something that's much harder to do with traditional scrapbooking!

Before we begin, you need to know there's no right or wrong scrapbook page. Each page is unique according to your subject, your personal taste, and the story you want to tell. Some scrapbook pages will be very simple, and others can be quite elaborate. Therefore, all we can do in this section is to provide you with the basics. The rest is up to your imagination. In this chapter, you'll learn more about the tools you need to create backgrounds, mats, embellishments, text, and other items you might want to appear on a scrapbook page.

Why Digital Scrapbooking?

Scrapbooking has really come a long way from the days when your grandmother used to do it! With traditional scrapbooking, you end up with paper scattered throughout your house and ink and glue all over your hands, and you make many trips, spending hundreds of dollars (or more) buying expensive paper and supplies. And what about the times you spend hours working on a layout, only to decide that you really wish you'd used a different color scheme or design? Sigh…you probably had to start all over again.

Digital scrapbooking provides you with complete freedom of design because you aren't limited to the supplies you have on hand. You'll find it affordable, convenient, efficient, and flexible.

Affordability

It is easy to see why digital scrapbooking is versatile and economical. As a digital scrapbooker, you don't have to purchase anything to start your scrapbook because you already have your computer and Paint Shop Pro.

For traditional scrapbooking, you often buy a lot of different items because you aren't sure which things are going to work for the look you want achieve. You end up spending a lot of money and then not even using half of what you buy.

However, with digital scrapbooking, once you have your backgrounds and graphics, which you can create yourself or purchase from other scrapbookers, you can use them over and over again, totally unlike the stickers or background papers you buy. You'll never run out of letters and other items.

You also always have just the right colors of whatever you need when you use Paint Shop Pro because you can change the color of anything instantly. You can design a layout and then print out as many times as you need it in just minutes, so you can make identical scrapbooks for everyone in your family if you want to! With digital scrapbooking, your only consumables are your paper and ink if you plan to print your layouts.

Convenience

There are very few full-time scrapbookers. Most scrapbookers work on their creations in their spare time. With traditional scrapbooking, unless you are fortunate enough to have a room devoted exclusively to scrapbooking, you end up with papers and supplies strewn all about a room or the dining room table. You find yourself constantly having to take out the supplies, work for a while, and then put them all back.

Whenever you have a free five minutes, you can work on your digital scrapbooking project without dragging out any supplies. This gives you a chance to tweak your layout, save it, and then come back to it whenever you have another few free minutes. No mess to drag out and put away.

Efficiency

When you work with digital scrapbooking, you never have to compromise your layout because you don't have the right color of materials. You can use Paint Shop Pro to create your own exact perfect color. With over 16 million colors to choose from, one of them is bound to be right for your layout.

Flexibility

Digital scrapbooking allows you to be very creative and adventuresome when working with your designs. With traditional scrapbooking, you take your scissors and glue and manipulate your photograph into the shape and size you want. But once you've cut the image, you're stuck with the new smaller size and shape. Not so with digital scrapbooking. Since you don't use the original photographs in the layout page, you can let your creative side flow with virtually no risk to your precious photographs.

If you don't like something you did, or you make a mistake, use the Undo or Delete command and try something else.

Scrapbooking Components

So, besides your computer and Paint Shop Pro, what do you need to begin scrapbooking? Most scrapbook pages use several types of elements, including backgrounds, text, photographs, mats, and embellishments. With the exception of the photographs, you can create all of these elements with Paint Shop Pro, but if you don't feel that ambitious, you can use elements created by other digital scrapbook artists, many of which are free or available for a small charge.

Figure 8-1 shows a sample, very simple scrapbook page. Let's take a look at each type of element:

Figure 8-1 *Not all scrapbook pages have to contain every element.*

When you begin planning your scrapbook page, you need to consider whether you will print it yourself, have a professional printer print it, or just keep it only for Web viewing. If you plan on printing it and placing it in a scrapbook album, plan your page size accordingly. Some scrapbookers print at an 8" × 8", 12" × 12", or 8.5" × 11" size.

Create a new Paint Shop Pro canvas with a white background at the size you intend to use. While you can enlarge or reduce the canvas at anytime, there's a possibility that resizing could distort your entire layout. Use a resolution of 180 to 200 dpi. Scrapbook pages tend to get quite large, especially if you use a very high resolution and a large page size. Make sure you have *plenty* of hard disk storage space or the ability to write to CDs before you begin. I've seen individual scrapbook pages anywhere from 10MB in size up to 150MB in size!

Photographs

Scrapbook pages don't *have* to have photographs, although most of them do. When planning your scrapbook page layout, determine which photographs you intend to use. Some pages contain multiple images, some contain a single image, and some contain a single image but also include smaller cutouts based on the original image, like the one you see in Figure 8-2.

Figure 8-2 *Select the photographs that best tell your story.*

Here are a few tips to keep in mind when working with your photographs:

- Choose a few pictures of a single event. Pick out the best photos. Get rid of the blurry photos and the photos that do not help tell the story or don't show any one's face clearly.

- You should have 3–5 photos of the event. A general rule of thumb in design is to use an odd number of images if you use multiple images (although this is not a requirement, just a tip).

- Try to select the one great photo that should be the focal point of the page.

Backgrounds

A scrapbook page background plays a crucial part in the overall layout of your page. It's the largest element you use, and typically the other components are modeled, color wise, after the background. Backgrounds can be solid, textured, gradients, patterned, or created from photos. Again, the choices are limitless, but let's take a brief look at how to create the backgrounds you see in Figure 8-3.

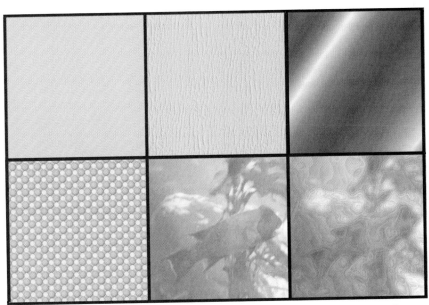

Figure 8-3 *Starting at the top left: solid, textured, gradient, patterned, photograph, and photograph with effect applied.*

The following steps show you how to create each of the effects listed:

- **Solid Color:** Use the Fill tool to fill a raster layer with a color of your choice.

- **Textured:** Use the Fill tool to fill a raster layer with color; then click Effects, Texture, and Texture. Select the desired texture from the Texture dialog box.

- **Gradient:** Click the Foreground/Stroke color palette; click the Gradient tab and then select the desired gradient and gradient options. Use the Fill tool to fill a raster layer with the gradient.

- **Patterned**: Click the Foreground/Stroke color palette; click the Pattern tab and then select the desired pattern and pattern options. Use the Fill tool to fill a raster layer with the pattern.
- **Photograph**: Open the photograph you want to use and then copy the photograph as a new layer in the scrapbook page document.
- **Photograph with Effect**: Open the photograph you want to use and then copy the photograph as a new layer in the scrapbook page document. Next, apply the desired effect to the image layer.

TIP

If you are using a photograph for a background, you may want to reduce the layer opacity.

Titles

Another optional feature is a title for your page. Scrapbook page titles can help describe the moment or occasion. Typically, you create any text, including titles, on a vector layer, which you'll learn about shortly. Figure 8-4 shows a scrapbook page with a title. You can use a single font or mix them up. You can run the title across the page, vertically along the side, or have it repeat along all four sides. The choice is yours.

You'll learn later in this chapter how to manage text items such as titles and journaling.

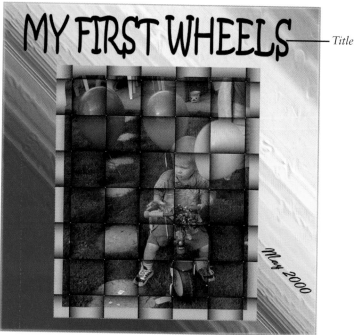

Figure 8-4 *Titles help tell part of your story.*

Journaling

Another type of text element is journaling. Journaling refers to text on a scrapbook page giving details about the photographs. The art of telling a story in print is what separates scrapbooks from photo albums. It is probably the most important part of memory albums. Your scrapbook page won't be complete until you tell the story behind the photos.

Some journaling consists of quotes or sayings to enhance the page (see Figure 8-5). Personal journaling lets you connect the page viewer with the actual event. Personal journaling records more than just titles, dates, and names. You can describe your reactions to what was happening, tell what the subject was doing and why, share how you feel when you look at the photos, or point out what you notice now that you didn't when the photo was taken. Recollections may seem trivial at the time—the weather, what you ate, a travel situation, something funny that happened, for example—but these details will prove fascinating to those who read your scrapbook pages years from now.

Journaling

Figure 8-5 *Use journaling to bring the viewer into the image event.*

One journaling trick is to pull your five senses into your writing. Sight, touch, sound, smell, and taste—using your senses to describe things when you journal creates an interesting read as you peak the interest of your viewers and invite them to join in your world.

Mats

Use matting to make your photos, journaling, and memorabilia stand out on the page. You can coordinate matting colors and textures with your photographs and memorabilia. For example, use a solid color mat to blend in with the layout or a patterned mat to make it stand out. Figure 8-6 shows two scrapbook pages, one with mats and one without mats.

Figure 8-6 *Use mats to enhance the other elements on your scrapbook page.*

You create a mat by drawing a rectangle on its own layer, making it a coordinating color and slightly larger than the image that you are matting. The rectangle can be on a raster or vector layer, but you'll have much more control over the rectangle size and placement if you place it on a vector layer. You'll learn how to create and work with vector images later in this chapter.

TIP

Create a mat by adding a picture frame to your image. Picture frames are reviewed later in this chapter.

Embellishments

Use embellishments or decorations to personalize and further enhance your scrapbook pages by highlighting photos, drawing attention to journaling, or helping to set a theme. Nearly anything can work as an embellishment. In scrapbook pages, you might see buttons, rivets, shapes, tags, blocks, lines, or Paint Shop Pro picture tubes. You can create the decorations yourself in Paint Shop Pro, or you can purchase them online.

Fonts

Fonts, the typefaces used in text, are one of the most important pieces of digital scrapbooking. The title and journaling you place must be readable but still be creative. There are thousands of fonts available, but the ones you have available depend on the different software programs you have on your system. Many fonts come with Windows, but others are often provided with various software. Many, many fonts are available on the Internet, often for free. Once you get a font, you must install it on your computer before you use it. Figure 8-7 displays some sample fonts that you could use in your scrapbook pages.

Figure 8-7 *All the fonts listed here came with Windows or were free off the Internet.*

TIP

To install fonts on your system, open your Control Panel, double-click the Fonts icon, and choose File, Install New Fonts. You then need to locate the new fonts you want installed, and your computer will do the rest.

In the nonscrappers world, such as in a letter or memo, mixing more than two fonts in a document is typically a "no-no," and you should *never* mix fonts in a single sentence. But in scrapbooking, you can place great emphasis on your statements by mixing your fonts. Go ahead...get creative.

Layers

In Chapter 4, you learned how you can use layers to enhance your photographs, particularly with Adjustment layers. You also created other raster layers so you could combine multiple photographs to make a single image, and you discovered Mask layers so that you could hide portions of your image.

The flexibility of digital scrapbooking comes from using layers. You create a layer for each element on your scrapbook page so that you can easily reposition, delete, angle, resize, or recolor the elements individually. In Figure 8-8 you see the scrapbook page consists of nine layers, with the text being on a vector layer and everything else on raster layers.

Figure 8-8 *Using layers makes element manipulation easier.*

Vector Graphics versus Raster Graphics

Computer graphics and their formats are probably the most complicated aspect of computer scrapbooking. Most computer graphics fall into one of two distinct categories: vector or raster. Understanding their basic differences will help you know what you can do with each of them since both formats have a place on our scrapbook pages.

Up to this point, you've worked primarily with raster objects, which use pixels to store image information. Every pixel has a color, and the pattern of all of the colored pixels creates the image we see. Raster images are always a rectangular or square shape, and every pixel within each graphic must have a color assigned to it. White is a color too, and if no other color is given to a pixel, it is assigned the color white. Because of this, raster images, such as a photograph, cannot have a transparent background.

The other type of Paint Shop Pro object, vector objects, are stored as separate items with information about each item's position, starting and ending points, width, color, and curve. Working with vector objects gives you more flexibility in moving and editing the individual objects because they are made up of a series of mathematical instructions that tell Paint Shop Pro how to create the image.

Now that we've gone over the basic structure of these two formats, let's look at their strengths, as well as why and where you should use both for scrapbooking.

Digital photographs are always raster graphics. In fact, a traditional photograph is very similar to a raster graphic. If you enlarge a regular photograph large enough, you can see the pixels that make up the picture.

Other than digital photos, the best format choice for the other graphics you use for scrapbooking will generally be vector-based graphics.

Vector graphics can, and generally do, have transparent backgrounds. This is a wonderful feature of this format and gives you the flexibility to layer graphics on top of backgrounds, photos, other graphics, and text, too. You can't do this with raster graphics because they are always a rectangle or square shape of pixels with every pixel having a color assigned to it.

A great feature of vector-based graphics is their ability to be resized as large or small as you like. Vector images don't rely on a set number of pixels, like in raster graphics, to draw the image. Instead, they use instructions that tell the software program how to draw the image and how big to make it. So, regardless of size, vector images always print as sharp, high-resolution images. This gives you unlimited flexibility when creating scrapbook pages because you don't have to worry about the image becoming blurry or rough. You have complete freedom to use the graphic at whatever size you like.

Another important difference in the way raster versus vector images work has to do with their ability to rotate images. Vector graphics are easily rotated at any angle because there are no pixels in the image to deal with. With Paint Shop Pro, you can rotate a vector graphic any amount you like, and the image still retains its high-resolution sharpness.

Adding Vector Shapes

An image can contain both raster objects and vector objects; however, vector objects and raster objects cannot be mixed on a layer. Vector objects must be on a vector layer. If you try to create a vector object on a raster layer, Paint Shop Pro automatically creates a vector layer for you. If the current layer is already a vector layer, Paint Shop Pro adds the new object to the current layer. Paint Shop Pro files can have many vector layers, and each layer can have many objects.

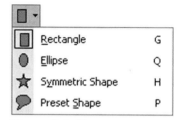

Figure 8-9 *You can create these shapes as vector or raster images, but for most scrapbooking elements, you'll create them as vector images.*

You don't have to be a superlative artist to draw shapes and other items with Paint Shop Pro because it includes many common preset shapes, including rectangles, triangles, stars, and ellipses, and fun shapes such as flowers, gears, starfish, and callouts.

On the Tools toolbar, the third tool from the bottom contains the various shape items (see Figure 8-9). The first three tools, Rectangle, Ellipse, and Symmetric Shape, work in a similar fashion to one another. The last tool on the option, the Preset Shape, provides additional shapes and options.

Drawing Common Shapes

A few common shapes include rectangles, squares, ellipses, circles, polygons, and stars. Paint Shop Pro has included quick access separate tools for these commonly used shapes.

   The Rectangle tool draws rectangles or squares, the Ellipse tool draws ellipses or circles, and the Symmetric tool draws polygons and stars. Any of those shapes can have square corners or rounded corners.

The Tool Options Palette is where you select the specific shape, whether you want to draw the object as a vector (you do), and depending on which tool you select, whether the corner radius is square or round. Rectangular or square corner radius values run from 0 (square) to 1000 (rounded), and symmetrical star shape radius values are from 0 to 100. On the symmetrical shapes, you can also select the number of sides you want the star or polygon to have.

Figure 8-10 shows samples of the first three tools, along with various options.

To draw the shapes, select the tool you want to use, set any options on the Tool Palette, and then click and drag in your document to create the shape. When you are satisfied with the shape, click the Apply check mark on the Tool Palette. Don't worry if it's not quite what or where you want it. You'll discover shortly how you can edit a vector object.

TIP

Create a shape as a photograph mat and place the layer behind the image.

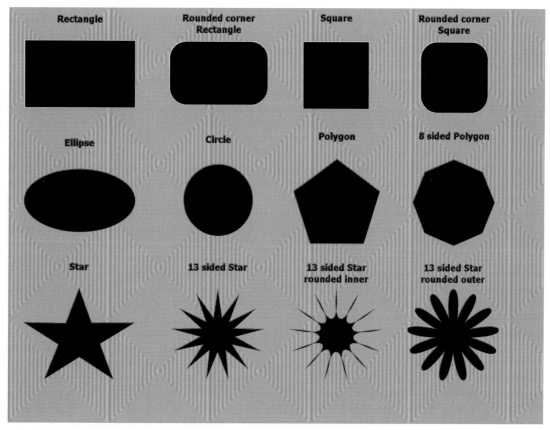

Figure 8-10 *Create lots of different shapes with each tool by setting different options.*

Creating Preset Shapes

Another way to draw the rectangles, ellipses, and symmetric shapes is through the Preset Shapes tool. You also get additional shapes such as inkblots, talk balloons, flowers, gears, and starfish.

By selecting a preset shape, you get a few more options than are available with the regular drawing tools. Also, keep these facts in mind when you're drawing a preset shape:

■ If you click and drag from the top of the canvas toward the bottom, the image shape will be drawn from corner to corner.

■ If you click and drag from the bottom of the canvas toward the top, the image shape will be drawn upside down.

■ If you click and drag using the right mouse button instead of the left button, the image will be drawn from the midpoint to the outer edges.

The following steps show you how to work with the Preset Shape tool:

1. Click the Preset Shape tool. The mouse pointer appears as a black cross with a square and circle on it.

2. From the Tool Options Palette, click the Shape list arrows and select the desired shape.

3. The Retain style check box will maintain the shape and appearance as you see it in the drop-down box. Uncheck this option to use your own line style, corners, or colors. For example, if the arrow is all black in the preset shapes and you'd prefer it to be red or a gradient pattern, you would uncheck the Retain style check box.

4. Click the Line Style arrow; then select a line style, choosing from solid, dotted, dashed, and others.

5. Click the line width up or down arrow to select a border line width. The number you select is indicated in pixels, and the values range from 0 pixels, which is no border, to 255 pixels.

6. If you are using one of the thicker line widths and a shape other than a rounded or elliptical shape, you can choose the types of corners you want your shape to take. The corners are called the *join*, indicating how you want the corners joined together. Join choices include mitered corners, round corners, and beveled corners.

7. Click a color, gradient, or pattern from the Materials Palette.

8. Click and drag in the image window. An outline of a shape will appear, and the shape will appear with your selected options when you release the mouse button (see Figure 8-11).

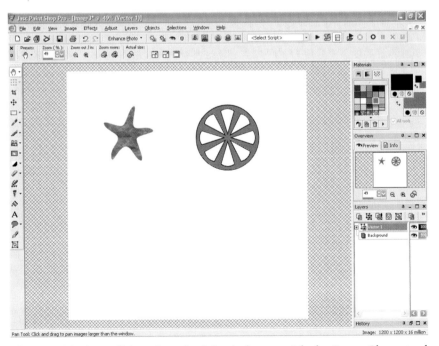

Figure 8-11 *A starfish and a wheel, both drawn with the Preset Shape tool.*

Drawing Vector Lines

Although the Paint Brush tool gives you freedom in drawing by emulating a real paintbrush, the Pen tool is more like a drafting tool, drawing straighter, more distinctive lines. You can use the Pen tool to draw polygons and other similar objects, as well as drawing freehand.

Drawing Lines

You can easily create straight lines, thick lines, thin lines, and even lines with arrows by using the Pen tool and the Line Segments option.

 Click the Pen tool, which turns the mouse pointer into a black arrowhead with a plus below it. Then from the Tool Options Palette, click the line style and the line thickness you want to use. From the Materials Palette, select the color you want for your line. If you want to draw polygons or lines that are connected, you need to have the Connect Segments option selected. Click and drag on the canvas to draw your line.

TIP

To constrain your lines and make them perfectly straight or at 45-degree angles, hold down the Shift key while you're drawing the line.

The Pen tool, like many other features in Paint Shop Pro, requires you to let it know when you've completed drawing a particular shape by clicking the Apply button.

 If you don't see a line drawn on your screen, Paint Shop Pro may have entered Edit mode. Make sure the Draw mode is selected by clicking the Draw button on the Tool Options Palette.

Drawing Freehand

Another option with the Pen tool is for freehand drawing. Drawing freehand with the Pen tool is similar to using the Paint Brush tool, except that the Pen tool lines appear slightly more crisp and sharp than with the Paint Brush tool.

 Click the Pen tool and any desired options for your line, but additionally click the Freehand mode, which is the last tool on the Tool Options Palette under the Mode section. Click and draw freely on your canvas, clicking the Apply button when you are finished. Figure 8-12 illustrates three straight lines, an angled straight line, and a freehand line, all drawn with the Pen tool.

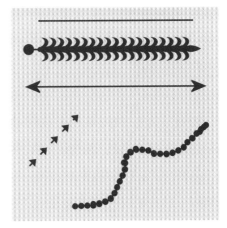

Figure 8-12 *Each line in this drawing uses a different line style.*

Modifying Vector Objects

Before you can modify a vector object, the object(s) must be selected. Only objects on the active layer can be selected at any one time, meaning that you cannot select objects that exist on different layers at the same time.

Paint Shop Pro provides a tool called the *Object Selector* for working with vector objects. The Object Selector is available only when the current active layer is a vector layer.

Use the Object Selector, the last tool on the toolbar, to choose which objects you want to modify. When you activate the Object Selector tool, the mouse pointer turns into a white cross with a boxed arrowhead beside it. When you click on the object you want, selection handles and a box appear around the object. Figure 8-13 shows a selected vector object.

If the object is filled in the center, you can click anywhere on the object to select it. However, if the object has no fill, you have to smile, hold your mouth just right, and click on the outline of the image.

Figure 8-13 *Selected vector objects are surrounded with a dotted-line box and sizing handles.*

TIP

Hold down the Shift key and click to select additional objects (the mouse pointer will display a plus sign), or hold down the Ctrl key and click to deselect objects (the mouse pointer will display a minus sign).

To deselect all objects, choose Selections, Select None or press Ctrl+D.

Here are two additional methods you can use when selecting vector objects. Both methods require you have the Object Selector tool active. One method is to draw a boundary box around the objects you want to select. Paint Shop Pro selects all objects that are *completely* surrounded by the boundary box. The second method uses the Layer Palette. Click the object name from the vector Layer Palette. If you don't see the object name, click the plus sign next to the vector layer.

TIP

Press the Delete key to delete a selected vector object.

Moving a Vector Object

If an object is not in the position you require, move it easily by using your mouse. Moving vector objects is a little different than moving raster objects. With raster objects, you use the Mover tool, but with vector objects, you don't use the Mover tool; instead, you simply use your mouse after selecting the object with the Object Selector tool.

Select the object you want to move and then position the mouse in the center of the object over the move circle. Notice that the mouse pointer turns into a black, four-headed arrow. Click and drag the object to the new position. As you move the object, you see an outline of the object, which indicates the new location. Release the mouse button to complete the move.

TIP

Freely rotate any selected vector object to any angle by using the rotation handle in the middle of the object to turn it.

Resizing a Vector Object

Changing the size of a vector object is a simple process. You can change the object size from a corner in an equal conformed amount, or you can change only the width or height of the object.

You use your mouse and the selection box handles to change the size of a vector object. Begin by selecting the object you want to resize; then place the mouse pointer over one of the handles. If you point to a corner sizing handle, the mouse pointer turns into a four-headed arrow, but if you point to a side or top handle, the mouse pointer becomes a double-headed arrow.

- Use the handle on either side of the object to resize the width of the object.
- Use the handle at the top or bottom of the object to resize the height of the object.
- Use any corner handle to resize both width and height at the same time.

Click and drag a handle. As you drag, an outline of the object indicates the new size, but when you release the mouse button, the object takes on the new size (see Figure 8-14).

TIP

Use the right mouse button with a corner handle to maintain height to width proportions.

Figure 8-14 *As you drag the handle, Paint Shop Pro indicates the new object size.*

Making Objects the Same Size

If you have multiple objects and want them to be the same size, Paint Shop Pro includes a tool to resize them quickly. You can make the objects the same height, the same width, or both the same height and width.

The secret to working with most multiple object features is the order of selection. The object you select *first* is considered the "base" object—the one the others will adjust to. This applies to alignment, spacing, and resizing features. The following steps show you how to make objects the same size:

1. Select the object you want the other objects to imitate in size.
2. Hold down the Shift key and click on the objects you want to resize.
3. Click a button from the Make same size buttons on the Tools Options Palette. Choices include making the selected objects the same width, making the selected objects the same height, or making the selected objects the same width and height.

Figure 8-15 illustrates some vector objects before and after making them the same size. Notice that the circle did not resize because it was not included in the selection. The rectangle and the flower resized to conform to the star in the middle.

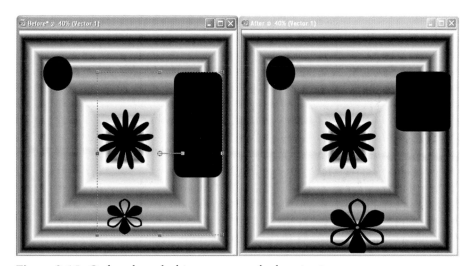

Figure 8-15 *Only selected objects are matched up in size.*

Altering Vector Properties

Even after you create a vector object, you can easily change its line style, color, style, thickness, and other properties.

 Select the object you want to modify and then click the Properties button, which is the last button on the Tool Options Palette. The Vector Properties dialog box similar to the one in Figure 8-16 opens. Make any desired changes and click OK.

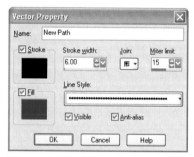

Figure 8-16 *If you have multiple objects selected, all objects take on the property change.*

Working with Text

You use the Text tool to create text in Paint Shop Pro. Similar to the other tools you've used so far, when you select the Text tool you will have additional options where you determine items such as font, size, style, stroke, alignment, kerning, and leading. Paint Shop Pro provides three types of text: vector, floating, or selection, but this section is devoted to vector text, which is what you should use when creating scrapbook pages.

Setting Text Options

Later in the chapter, you will see where you can change text options after you create the text object, but you will find it much easier to select the options prior to creating the actual text. Follow these steps:

1. Click the Text tool, which turns the mouse pointer into a cross with the letter A beside it. The Tools Options Palette will display options for working with text (see Figure 8-17).

Click here for more options

Figure 8-17 *Select your text option from the Tool Options Palette.*

2. Click the Font list drop-down box and select a font.

3. Click the Size drop-down box and select a font size. As a general rule of measurement, when printing, a 72-point font is 1-inch tall; however, when viewing text on a computer screen, the sizes vary, depending on the screen resolution.

4. Select a stroke width. When you have a stroke width of one or greater, your text will take the stroke color and form a line around the text characters. The stroke is the foreground color, and the background color is the fill color on the text.

5. Paint Shop Pro provides text enhancements such as bolding, underlining, italics, or strikethrough on any portion of your text. Click one or more of the four available text enhancements. Enhancements include the following:

   - **Bold**: Makes the text characters darker and thicker.

   - *Italics*: Makes the text characters slightly slanted.

   - <u>Underline</u>: Provides a line under each character and space.

   - ~~Strikethrough~~: Provides a line through the middle of each character and space.

6. Click an Alignment button, which determines how multiple lines of text line up with each other. Alignment choices include Left, where the left edges of each text line align together; Center, where each line centers to the one above it; and Right, where the right edges of each text line align together.

7. When working with text, you have the same materials options available as with other Paint Shop Pro objects. The stroke style is the color of the edge around the letters, while the fill style is the center or body of the letters. Select a color, gradient, or pattern for the stroke and fill of your text.

TIP

Selecting Null for the fill creates outlined text, but you cannot choose Null for both the stroke and fill.

Typing Vector Text

Now that you have set your options, you are ready to create the text. Paint Shop Pro provides a dialog box in which to type your text, but different than using a word processor, the text does not automatically wrap around to the next line. You need to tell Paint Shop Pro when you want the text to begin on a new line.

The following steps guide you through working with vector text:

1. With the Text tool selected, click the canvas approximately where you want the text to appear. Don't be concerned about the exact placement because you can easily move the text wherever you want it. When you click the canvas, Paint Shop Pro opens the Text Entry dialog box.

2. Type the text you want and press Enter if you have more text to add under the first line and type the additional text. Add as many lines of text as you would like.

3. Click the Apply button, which closes the Text Entry dialog box.

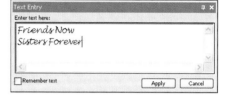

Figure 8-18 shows text applied to a vector layer.

Vector layer text

Figure 8-18 *Vector text is easily edited or moved.*

Editing Text

To resize, move, or delete vector text, use the same methods as described earlier in this chapter as referring to vector shapes. But...suppose that after you created your text, you see a problem—perhaps you misspelled a word, or you want a different font or style. Paint Shop Pro provides tools for you to edit your text objects easily.

Click the Object Selection tool and click the text object. Right mouse click while over the selected text and select Edit Text from the shortcut menu. The Text Entry dialog box re-opens with your text where you can edit the text, font, size, attributes, alignment, leading, or materials. The text in the preview box will reflect the changes, as does the text on the screen. Click Apply when finished.

> **TIP**
>
> To change options for only a portion of the text, before you make any changes, drag your mouse to highlight only the text you want to change.

Wrapping Text Around a Shape

You can easily create text that wraps around any vector object. Wrapping text to these shapes or lines can create fun and interesting effects on your scrapbook page. When you wrap the text, you can optionally hide the shaped object. There are two ways to create text on a path. You can either create the shape (or line) first and then create new text on the shape, or you can create the path and the text as separate objects and then fit the text to the shape. We'll use the first method.

To create new text and fit it to a path:

1. Create the vector shape or line.
2. Click the Text tool and select other options (font, size, alignment, and so on) as desired. Use the Materials Palette to set the text's Background/Fill property as well as its Foreground/Stroke property.
3. Move the cursor over the line or shape until the cursor changes to an A with a circle under it (like this ▦) and then click, which displays the Text Entry dialog box.
4. Enter the text and click OK. The text displays along the path of the shape.

Figure 8-19 illustrates text created along a curved line.

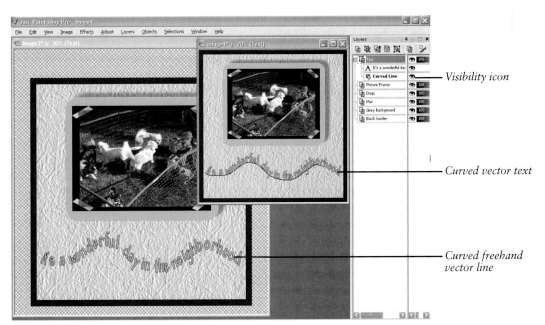

Figure 8-19 *Create vector text along any vector object.*

> **TIP**
>
> Click the visibility icon to hide the curved line or shaped object.

Converting Vector Layers to Raster

The main drawback to vector objects is that you cannot apply effects and filters to vector objects. Don't give up hope, though! Paint Shop Pro includes a feature to convert vector layers with all its objects to raster objects on a raster layer. From there, you can apply effects. Click the Layers menu and select Convert to Raster Layer. The vector layer and all its vector objects will become a raster layer with raster objects. The Layer Palette reflects the change to a raster layer.

> **NOTE**
>
> When you attempt to save the file in a format other than a Paint Shop Pro format, such as .gif, .jpeg, or .png, Paint Shop Pro automatically converts the entire image to a raster image.

Picture Frames

Another variation often used when creating scrapbook pages includes placing a picture frame around it. Paint Shop Pro contains a variety of picture frames, which are raster images, ranging from wood to metal, stone, and other decorative surfaces. Lots of additional frames are available over the Internet, many of them free.

Paint Shop Pro includes a Picture Frame dialog box that takes all the work out of adding a frame to your image.

Open the image on which you want a picture frame, click the Image menu, and select Picture Frame. You'll see the Picture Frame dialog box similar to the one in Figure 8-20.

> **NOTE**
>
> If your image is not 16 million colors or greyscale, accessing the Picture Frame will display a dialog box prompting you to increase your color depth.

Click the Picture Frame arrow and select the picture frame you'd like to try. You can preview your image in the frame as you select any desired frame options.

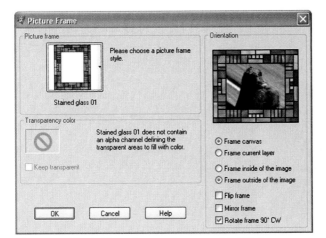

Figure 8-20 *Add a picture frame to highlight your image.*

Depending on the shape of the frame you selected, you may need to select a color to fill the transparent areas outside of the frame. Odd-shaped frames usually have a transparent area. Here are some other picture frame options:

- **Frame canvas:** The frame will fit around the canvas size. This gives the appearance of a picture frame around the entire image.

- **Frame current layer:** The frame will fit around the current layer, which in the case of scrapbooking may contain a photograph smaller than the overall canvas. This gives the appearance of only one photograph having a frame, not a frame around the entire image.

- **Frame inside of the image:** Paint Shop Pro will resize the frame to fit within the edges of the image. Part of the image is covered by the picture frame, and the dimensions of the image are not altered.

- **Frame outside of the image:** Paint Shop Pro will increase the canvas size to accommodate the frame. The original image is not covered, and the dimensions of the image are increased by the size of the frame.

Figures 8-21 and 8-22 illustrate scrapbook pages after applying a picture frame.

Figure 8-21 *Picture frames appear as their own layer entitled Picture Frame.*

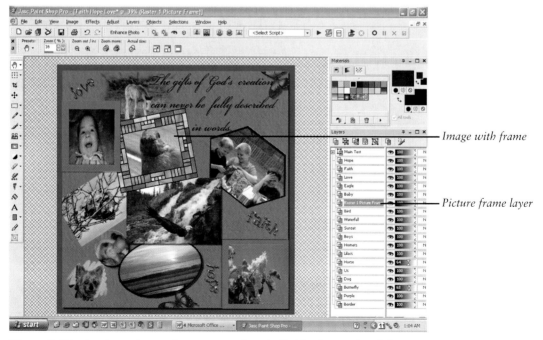

Figure 8-22 *Apply a picture frame around an individual scrapbook image.*

Picture Tubes

Earlier in this chapter, we talked about embellishments that add decoration to your scrapbook page. One kind of embellishment is the Paint Shop Pro picture tubes.

If you run down to Wal-Mart and look in the scrapbooking supplies section, you're bound to see lots of ink stamps. You know—the kind that creates an image that you can stamp on the paper over and over again. Well, Paint Shop Pro's picture tubes are similar to those stamps but even better. You can actually paint images with these tubes. In addition, whereas the stamps you find at the store can each produce only a single image, that's not necessarily the case with tubes. Some tubes might contain only a single image, but many tubes produce several variations of a single image or several different images with a common theme. Use them in combination with other images, and you can create quite a masterpiece.

For ease in editing the image after it is drawn on the screen, place each tube on its own layer. Picture tubes are raster images, so place them on a raster layer. Follow these steps:

1. Create your new raster layer; then click on the Picture Tube tool, which is the twelfth tool down the toolbar. The mouse pointer will look like a tube of paint.

2. Click on the preview arrow in the Tool Options Palette and select the tube you want to use. A selection of tubes similar to Figure 8-23 will display.

3. Similar to the Paint Brush tool, click on the canvas to place a single tube or drag across the canvas to achieve the look you want. Depending on the tube you select, another identical or related image will appear each time you click.

> ## TIP
>
> Draw your picture tubes in a straight line by clicking once at the beginning of the line. Then hold down the Shift key and click a second time at the end of the tube line. Paint Shop Pro draws a straight line using the tube between those two points.

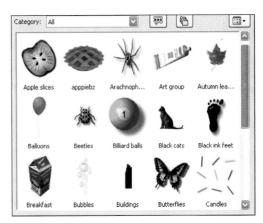

Figure 8-23 *Your selections will vary from the ones displayed in this figure.*

If you find that a picture tube is painting an image that is too large or too small, too far apart, or too close together, you can edit the settings. You must change the settings before you paint the image. There are two main settings you will use with your picture tubes—scaling and steps.

The Scale control can adjust the size of the tube from its originally created size of 100 down to 10 percent of its original size or up to 250 percent of its original size.

The Step control modifies the distance between the intervals in which the tubes appear. The larger the step, the more distance between the tubes.

Try drawing with the different tubes. Many of them are more exciting than they appear in the preview box. The Piano Keys, Metal Hose, Metal Springs, and Spiral Garland tubes are perfect examples of the actual tube looking tremendously different from the sample in the preview window.

Adding New Picture Tubes

Many picture tubes come with the Paint Shop Pro application, and even more are available on the CD. You can even find thousands of free picture tubes on the Internet. In most cases, Paint Shop Pro automatically reads the picture tubes, provided that you copy them to one of the locations specified in File, Preferences, File Locations.

When you download any picture tubes, you need to tell Paint Shop Pro where they are located. By default, the picture tubes that are supplied with Paint Shop Pro are located in the Picture Tubes folder where you installed the Paint Shop Pro program. Typically, this would be C:\PROGRAM FILES\JASC SOFTWARE INC\PAINT SHOP PRO 9\PICTURE TUBES. Tubes that you create or import are typically stored in a folder under your My Documents folder, such as C:\DOCUMENTS AND SETTINGS*YOUR NAME*\MY DOCUMENTS\MY PSP FILES\PICTURE TUBES.

> ### TIP
> You can specify additional file locations under File, Preferences, File Locations.

Sometimes, however, you might want to save your own files as picture tubes. A picture tube is really a drawing or a series of drawings that is created and saved in a special format. The images are created on a transparent background so that all you see is the image. Here are a few other stipulations required by Paint Shop Pro for picture tubes:

- The image must have a color depth of 24-bit (16 million colors).

- The image must be on a single raster layer.

- The background of the image must be transparent.

- If your file has multiple images on it, the items should be symmetrical in position, dividing the canvas space equally between the items. Paint Shop Pro saves picture tube files in a row and column pattern.

The following steps show you how to save your own file as a picture tube:

1. Create or open the file that contains the picture tube.
2. Click on File, Export, Picture Tube.
3. In the Export Picture Tube dialog box, specify the number of cells across and down in the image. In the example you see in Figure 8-24, the image consists of two cells across and two down.
4. Type a name for the tube and click OK. Paint Shop Pro saves picture tube files with a file extension of .psptube.

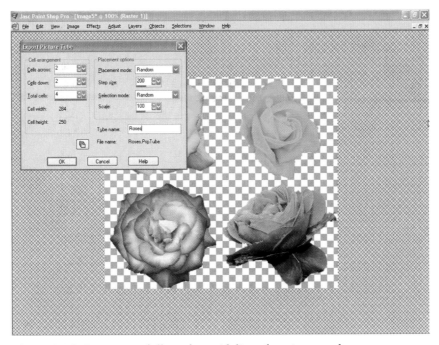

Figure 8-24 *Be sure to follow the guidelines for picture tubes.*

3D Images

One really imaginative trick you can use on your scrapbooking pages is to make your images look 3D. Great with action shots, you can make a runner jump out of the photograph or a fish propel itself out of the water. Take a look at the photographs in the scrapbook page seen in Figure 8-25.

Figure 8-25 *Add 3D images to your scrapbook pages.*

Follow these steps and you'll learn how to make your images look alive.

1. Open your original image and duplicate the layer. You will be working off the duplicate layer, so you could delete the background layer if you wanted to.
2. Create a bottom layer totally filled with black.
3. Create a top layer and draw a white raster rectangle on the layer large enough to cover the portion of the image you want inside. (Unclick the Create on Vector box before drawing.)

4. Select the rectangle and shear it to distort it, giving the paper the correct perspective. To shear it, select the Deform tool and drag the corner handles while holding down the Shift key.

5. Put the white paper layer under the picture and reduce the opacity of your picture so you can temporarily see the paper underneath the picture.

6. Cut away or erase parts of the picture that you don't want. In this example, I used both the Eraser tool and the Freehand Selection tool.

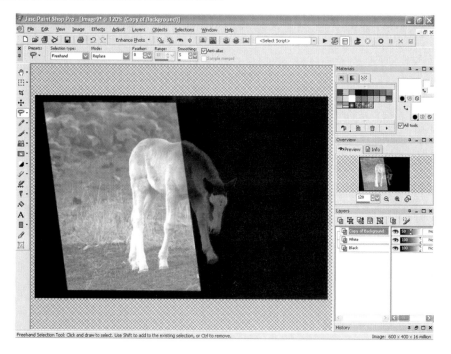

7. Make your picture solid again so you can see the true image to ensure that you have cut away everything you don't want.

8. Select the white layer and using the distortion tool, enlarge it on all four sides to give the appearance of a frame around your picture.

9. Select the black layer and fill it with dark grey or whatever color you want for the "outside" area. Make sure this layer is on the bottom.

10. Go back to the picture layer and add any desired drop shadow and crop it, if necessary.

What's Next?

Hasn't this been a fun chapter? You've discovered that scrapbooking digitally frees you from being confined to just working with memory albums and elements that you can find in your local scrapbook store. In the next chapter, we'll take a look at some of the time-saving Paint Shop Pro features, such as scripting and batch processing. We'll also take a look at how Paint Shop Pro handles working with RAW format image files from your digital camera.

9

Special Projects

I probably should have selected a different name for this chapter because the majority of this chapter is about saving time. For example, how you can save time with customized toolbars that display your favorite tools. Or saving time with a customized workspace displaying only the toolbars and palettes you want for a particular project. Or saving time by using scripts that are prerecorded steps and actions, especially those you use a lot. And finally, saving time with batch processing, for example, resizing a group of images at one time. With all the time you'll be saving, you can take the day off and go shoot more great photographs!

Finally, we'll take a look at working with your camera's RAW file format. That's not really a timesaver, but it sure produces a good-looking image. Besides, I didn't have anywhere else in the book to really put it!

Customizing Toolbars

You've probably realized by now how handy the toolbars are and that they save you time in searching through the sometimes puzzling menu commands. In Chapter 1, "Digital Imaging Basics," you discovered how to turn different toolbars on and off at your discretion. The toolbars contain the commonly used commands, but each user is different. For example, you may never use the Twain Acquire tool on the standard toolbar, so you don't want it on there. Perhaps you frequently use the menu command Layers, Promote Background Layer, which isn't on any toolbar. Paint Shop Pro provides an easy way to customize your toolbars, making them the way you like them, containing the tools you use most.

Modifying Existing Toolbars

You can remove or add tools from any toolbar, or you can create your own toolbars, which is especially handy for those repetitive projects. Let's take a look at customizing toolbars:

Click the View menu and select Customize. You'll see the Customize dialog box in Figure 9-1. Click the Commands tab that controls the menu options.

To remove an icon from any toolbar, drag the unwanted item off the toolbar anywhere into the Paint Shop Pro window. When you release the mouse button, the icon is removed.

If you want to add an icon to a toolbar, from the Commands tab, scroll through the categories list and select the category of the command (File, Edit, and so on). Then in the Commands list, select the feature you want to add and drag it to the toolbar. When your mouse pointer looks like the I-beam you see in Figure 9-2, release the mouse button, and you'll see that Paint Shop Pro added the feature to your toolbar.

Figure 9-1 *The Customize dialog box lets you modify any toolbar.*

If you need to move an icon to a different location, drag the icon into the space you want it and then release the mouse button. Again, use the mouse pointer I-beam as your guide.

I-beam pointer

Figure 9-2 *Locate the feature you want to add to a toolbar.*

Create Your Own Toolbars

You can take toolbar customization to the next level by creating your own toolbars. All these toolbars do take space on your screen, so many users like to combine all their favorite tools onto one custom toolbar and turn off the display of the standard toolbars. The following steps show you how to create your own customized toolbar:

1. Click the View menu and select Customize.
2. Click the Toolbars tab and then click the New button.
3. Enter a name for the new toolbar; for example, use your name (Diane's toolbar). A small toolbar with no tools appears in the middle of the Customize dialog box (see Figure 9-3). You'll need to move it so you can add tools to it.
4. Drag a blank area of the new toolbar onto your screen, which moves the toolbar off the Customize dialog box.
5. Click the Command tab and add the desired tools as you learned in the previous section.
6. Click Close when you are finished with the Customize dialog box.

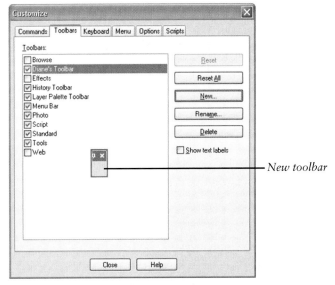

> ## TIP
> To delete a customized toolbar, click View, Customize; then on the Toolbars tab, select the toolbar you want to get rid of and click the Delete button.

— New toolbar

Figure 9-3 *Put your favorite and most frequently used tools on your own toolbar.*

Customizing Workspaces

Anytime you tackle a project, writing thank you notes, for example, you need a place to work. Let's suppose you use your desk, but before you can lay out the cards, stamps, envelopes, and so forth, you need to move the items away that you don't need right now.

Throughout this book, you've seen references to the Paint Shop Pro workspace, which is the screen area where you keep all your tools, palettes, and your current project, similar to the desk space where you place your cards, stamps, and envelopes.

Paint Shop Pro provides the option of changing the screen layout to meet the needs of your current project, allowing you to load those preferences quickly for the given project, saving you time. For example, if you are working on a project for client ABC Company, and you want Paint Shop Pro to display their images in the browser, plus display only the special toolbar you designed for working on their projects, you can save and subsequently load the workspace you called ABC. Then with a couple of mouse clicks, you can redisplay the settings you use everyday.

To save your workspace, first display the toolbars and palettes you want, along with any Paint Shop Pro browser preferences and any tool settings you know you'll use. You can also open any images you know you'll want with the project, and when you switch to the workspace, Paint Shop Pro will open those images for you automatically. Figure 9-4 shows a workspace we'll save and recall whenever needed.

Figure 9-4 *Set up your workspace and then save it for future use.*

Click the File menu, select Workspace, and select Save. You'll see a dialog box like the one in Figure 9-5.

Figure 9-5 *Optionally include open images in a workspace.*

Give the workspace a name you'll easily identify, and if you want the currently open images included in the workspace, click the Include Open Images check box. Click the Save button.

Anytime you want to use your special workspace or return to the Paint Shop Pro default workspace, select your option under the File menu, Workspace and Load. Also, under the Workspace menu, Paint Shop Pro lists the last three workspaces used. You can pick from any of those choices as well.

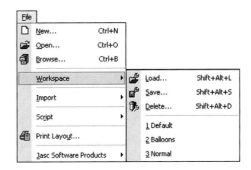

Scripting

Let's say you worked a long time and came up with a really cool but complicated effect. Sometime in the future, you'd like to use that effect again, but you dread having to repeat the procedure. By creating a script to record your actions, you can tell Paint Shop Pro to produce the steps for you without you doing all the work.

What is a script? Well, a script is a file containing instructions that produce a series of actions or effects. This is similar to how actors follow a script to produce the results a writer or director wants. The concept is to perform an action that produces a likeable result and record it. When you want to apply the same set of effects to another object or image, all you need to do is run the script you recorded.

Paint Shop Pro's productivity enhancing scripting engine, based on the Python programming language, allows you to record, pause, save, play, edit, or cancel scripts. You may have worked with other programs, such as Microsoft Word or Excel, that have a Macro command listed under their Tools menu. Paint Shop Pro's scripts work basically like the Microsoft Macro command, except that they use a different engine to automate your tasks.

Paint Shop Pro scripts fall into two categories: restricted and trusted. Because scripts are created with a programming language, this feature offers the possibility that someone will use this powerful tool to create malicious scripts. To prevent scripts from damaging other parts of the Paint Shop Pro application or even your operating system, you can place some scripts into a restricted execution mode. In restricted mode, scripts have restricted access to other parts of the Paint Shop Pro program and your computer operating system. The first time you save a script in Paint Shop Pro, the path defaults to the Restricted folder. After that, saving a script defaults to the last used folder.

Some scripts contain File menu commands that are not allowed when a script is run in restricted mode. You can either place the script in a trusted scripts folder or not use these commands. The following commands are not allowed when run from a restricted script: Save, Save As, Save Copy As, Close, Close All, Send, Exit, Export: GIF Optimizer, Export: PNG Optimizer, Export: JPEG Optimizer, Export: Image Mapper, Export: Image Slicer, Preferences: File Locations, Batch: Process, and Batch: Rename.

The Script Toolbar

Although all of the scripts commands are available through the File, Script menu, it is much easier to work with scripts using the Script toolbar. If the Script toolbar is not already displayed, click View, Toolbars, Script. The following list describes each tool on the Script toolbar that you see in Figure 9-6:

- **Select Script:** Displays a list of scripts stored in the Trusted and Restricted script folders or other folders, as specified in File Locations.

- **Run Selected Script:** Executes the script displayed in the Select Script box.

- **Edit Selected Script:** Opens the Script Editor box or opens a Windows Notepad window displaying the programming code. (See "Editing a Script," later in this chapter.)

- **Toggle Execution Mode:** This applies to scripts that include dialog boxes and turns interaction on or off between you and the script. When the button has a border around it, it is in Interactive mode, and the dialog boxes will open when the script is run, asking for your input. When Interactive mode is off, the script will run without asking you for options in the dialog boxes. Paint Shop Pro calls this *Silent mode.*

- **Run Script:** Works like the Run Selected Script option, but prompts you for the script location first. Use this for scripts you don't store in the Restricted or Trusted scripts folders or subfolders. If a script is not in the Trusted or Restricted folder, Paint Shop Pro treats it as a Restricted script.

- **Stop Script:** This button is active only when a script is running; you click this button to stop the running script.

- **Start Script Recording:** Click this button to begin recording actions for a script.

- **Pause Script Recording:** Click here to temporarily stop recording a script. Click the button again to restart the script recording.

- **Cancel Script Recording:** This button cancels the script recording actions.

- **Save Script Recording:** Consider this the Stop button on your recorder. When you click this button, Paint Shop Pro displays a dialog box prompting you for a script name.

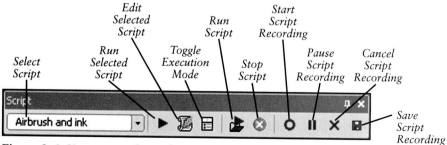

Figure 9-6 *You can easily perform script actions by using the Script toolbar.*

Selecting a Script

When you install Paint Shop Pro, over 50 prerecorded scripts are installed. Some of the out-of-the-box scripts include Art, Bevel/Selection, Black-and-White, Black-and-White Sketch/Pencil, Color Sketch, Full Image Drop Shadow, Photo Edges, Pointillist, Sepia Frame, Vignette, Watercolor, and many more.

Unless the script author places a script description when the script is saved, it's difficult to determine exactly what the scripts can do for you. Try selecting a script from the Select Script list and then click the Edit Selected Script button. If you're lucky, a dialog box like the one you see in Figure 9-7 appears, and you can read the script's basics. If you're not lucky…well, good luck in trying to understand the script language window. See "Editing a Script," later in this chapter.

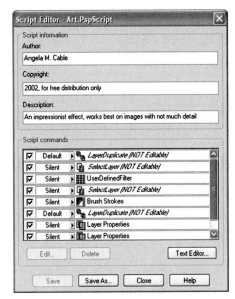

Figure 9-7 *The Script Editor dialog box can provide a description of the selected script.*

Running a Script

This is the easiest part of all. Regardless of which script you are using, you will need to have an image open before you can execute the script. After you select the script you want to run, click the Run Selected Script button in the Script toolbar. It may take a few moments for the script to run, so keep an eye on the status bar at the bottom of your screen to make sure it has finished. Depending on the script, you may see dialog boxes pop up, prompting you for options.

> **TIP**
>
> Clicking the Undo command reverses all steps taken during the script action, regardless of how complicated the steps were.

Recording a Script

The Script Recorder makes creating your own scripts quite simple. You can control all of the script actions from the Script toolbar buttons. Lay out a plan for your script before you begin recording because editing a script is not an easy task. You are better off rerecording a script rather than trying to edit it. To record and save a script, use the following procedure:

1. On the Scripts toolbar, click the Start Script Recording button. The Script Recorder tool works like a video recorder. Be aware that every action you take will now be recorded and added to the script until you click the Pause, Save Script, or Cancel Recording button.

TIP

Don't undo mistakes you make while recording a script or you will record both the mistake and the Undo action. Cancel the recording and start over again.

2. Perform the actions you want in the script. At any point while recording a script, you can pause the script recording by clicking the Pause button on the Script toolbar.

3. When you have finished recording, click Save Script recording, which opens the Save As dialog box you see in Figure 9-8.

4. Enter a name for the script; then click the Description button to display a Description dialog box where you can enter your name and a description of the script. Entering an author name or description is optional but recommended.

5. Click OK to close the Description box and Save to save the script.

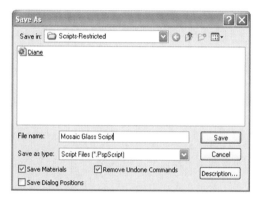

Figure 9-8 *Paint Shop Pro saves Scripts with a .PspScript file extension.*

The script now appears in the Script toolbar drop-down, assuming you saved it in a Scripts folder.

Editing a Script

Unless you have programming experience, you'll find it much easier to rerecord a script than to try and edit it. If you must delve into script editing though, make sure you're comfortable with the Python programming language. You can learn more about the Python programming language at http://www.python.org/moin/ BeginnersGuide_2fNonProgrammers. The tutorials on this Web page are recommended for users new to the Python language.

Figure 9-9 shows the commands used in the Mosaic Glass script that you saw saved in Figure 9-8.

Understanding the Python programming language is beyond the scope of this book, but we can take a peek at what is involved. Figure 9-10 illustrates the script text.

Figure 9-9 *Click the Text Editor button to see the script text.*

```
from JascApp import *

def ScriptProperties():
    return {
        'Author': u'Diane Koers',
        'Copyright': u'',
        'Description': u'Creates Squared Mosaic Glass Effect',
        'Host': u'Paint Shop Pro 9',
        'Host Version': u'9.00'
        }

def Do(Environment):
    # EnableOptimizedScriptUndo
    App.Do( Environment, 'EnableOptimizedScriptUndo', {
        'GeneralSettings': {
            'ExecutionMode': App.Constants.ExecutionMode.Default,
            'AutoActionMode': App.Constants.AutoActionMode.Match,
            'Version': ((9,0,0),1)
            }
        })

    # LayerDuplicate
    App.Do( Environment, 'LayerDuplicate', {
        'GeneralSettings': {
            'ExecutionMode': App.Constants.ExecutionMode.Default,
            'AutoActionMode': App.Constants.AutoActionMode.Match,
            'Version': ((9,0,0),1)
            }
        })

    # Layer Properties
    App.Do( Environment, 'LayerProperties', {
        'General': {
            'Opacity': None,
            'Name': None,
            'IsVisible': None,
            'IsTransparencyLocked': None,
            'LinkSet': None,
            'UseHighlight': None,
            'PaletteHighlightColor': None,
            'GroupLink': None,
            'BlendMode': App.Constants.BlendMode.Overlay
            },
```

```
            'BlendRanges': None,
            'Path': (0,0,[],False),
            'ArtMediaTexture': None,
            'BrightnessContrast': None,
            'ChannelMixer': None,
            'ColorBalance': None,
            'CurveParams': None,
            'HSL': None,
            'Threshold': None,
            'Levels': None,
            'Posterize': None,
            'Overlay': None,
            'GeneralSettings': {
                'ExecutionMode': App.Constants.ExecutionMode.Silent,
                'AutoActionMode': App.Constants.AutoActionMode.Default,
                'Version': ((9,0,0),1)
                }
            })

    # Texture
    App.Do( Environment, 'Texture', {
        'Ambience': 0,
        'Angle': 243,
        'Color': (255,255,255),
        'Depth': 50,
        'Elevation': 31,
        'Intensity': 50,
        'Shininess': 50,
        'Size': 400,
        'Smoothness': 40,
        'TextureName': u'Squares',
        'Category': u'',
        'GeneralSettings': {
            'ExecutionMode': App.Constants.ExecutionMode.Silent,
            'AutoActionMode': App.Constants.AutoActionMode.Match,
            'Version': ((9,0,0),1)
            }
        })
```

Figure 9-10 *Aren't you glad the Script Recorder can do the work for you?*

The Script Output Palette

While your script is executing, you can monitor it. Through a palette called the *Script Output Palette*, you can see the actions that occur when a script is running and the results of a script as it runs, which ensures you that all the steps in your script execute completely. If there is an error, the Script Output Palette warns you of which steps it could not complete due to a given condition.

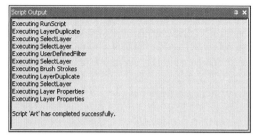

To display (or hide) the Script Output window (see Figure 9-11), press Shift+F3 or click the View menu, select Palettes, and then Script Output.

If the window becomes too cluttered, you can clear it out by clicking File, Script, Clear Output Window.

Figure 9-11 *The Script Output window helps you see the script commands as the script runs.*

TIP

You can copy text from the Script Output window to the Windows clipboard for pasting into other applications, such as a word processing application.

Batch Processing

Another time-saving feature included with Paint Shop Pro is batch processing. Like scripting, batch processing automates steps for you. Scripts, however, usually execute a number of steps to a single image at a time, where batch processing executes a single command to multiple images. There are two batch processing commands included with Paint Shop Pro. One command works with saving images, and the other command works with renaming images.

The first, which is actually named *batch process*, is great if you have a group of pictures you want to copy to another location or save as a different file format. The second batch process is the Batch Rename command, which assigns a different filename to a group of images. Let's take a look at the Batch Rename command first.

Batch Rename

Most digital cameras name their images by assigning a number to each image you take. Unfortunately, that's not very intuitive to the photographic contents. Suppose you have a large batch of vacation photos that your camera named DISC101, DISC102, DISC103, and so forth, but you'd rather they be named in a more descriptive manor such as Bryce Canyon Trip 1, Bryce Canyon Trip 2, Bryce Canyon Trip 3. Renaming these images one at a time can be very tedious, especially if you have lots of them.

Take a look at the list of files in Figure 9-12. This is a list of 144 images taken by several family members at a recent vacation on the beaches of Mississippi. We can use the Paint Shop Pro batch rename command to rename them all at once. The following steps walk you through using the batch rename command.

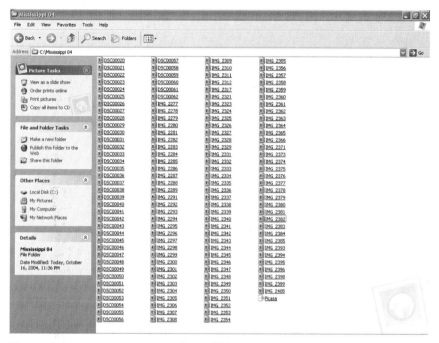

Figure 9-12 *Rename any number of files at one time by using the batch rename command.*

1. Click the File menu, select Batch, and then Rename. You'll see the Batch Rename dialog box.
2. Click the Browse button, which opens the Select Files dialog, and navigate to the folder containing the files you want to rename.
3. Click the files you want to rename. You can use Shift+Click to select a contiguous list of files or Ctrl+Click to select noncontiguous files (Figure 9-13). Optionally, use the Select All button to select all images in the open folder.
4. Click Select and Paint Shop Pro displays the files you chose in the Files to rename list.

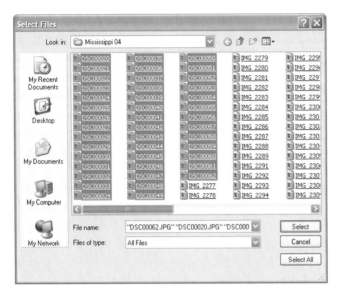

Figure 9-13 *Select the files you want to rename.*

5. Now you need to specify the naming convention that you want Paint Shop Pro to use. Click the Modify button, which opens the Filename Format dialog box. You have a number of naming options available, including adding the date to the filename, retaining the original filename as well as the new filename, and whether you want the current time added to the new filename.

6. In many cases, you'll want the Custom text and the Sequential options. In the Rename options area, click Custom Text and then click the Add button.

7. In the Custom Text text box, enter the name you want for the new images. For our example, I'm naming the images Mississippi 2004—. In the next step, I'll have Paint Shop Pro add a sequential number after the dash.

8. Add Sequence to the Included list, and in the resulting Starting Sequence text box, enter a number you want the images to begin with. In my example, I'm using 001. Figure 9-14 shows the dialog box after making my selections.

Custom Text text box ⎯⎯

Filename preview ⎯⎯

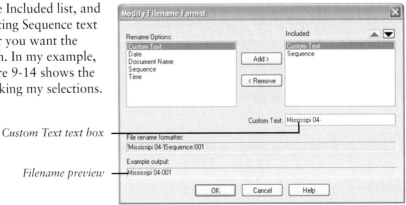

Figure 9-14 *Specify a name and sequence for your images.*

9. Click OK, which closes the Modify Filename Format dialog box and redisplays the Batch Rename dialog box.

10. Click the Start button. Paint Shop Pro executes the batch rename command. Figure 9-15 shows the list of files after Paint Shop Pro renamed them.

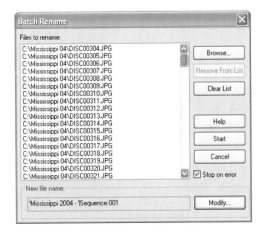

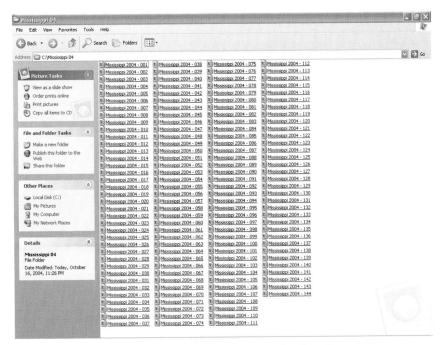

Figure 9-15 *After renaming, you can more easily identify your images.*

Batch Process Command

The Batch Process command works similarly to the Batch Rename command in that it executes a single command to multiple images. Using the Batch Process command, you perform any of four functions. All Batch Process features are related to saving files.

You can convert your group of files to a new format. Since most digital cameras automatically save your image in JPEG format, which uses compression, you might want to change the photos from a JPEG format to a TIFF format or even a PspImage format to prevent you from accidentally resaving the images in JPEG again, which can cause quality loss. When you convert images to a new format, the Batch Process command leaves the originals alone, and it creates duplicate images with the new format.

You can copy your group of files to a new location. Suppose that you want to practice adjusting color on a group of vacation photos. By copying them to a different location, you can work on the duplicates, leaving the originals intact. You *could* copy your images using the Windows Explorer, but using the Batch Process is easier, faster and allows you to copy images from multiple folders in one step. Besides, this book is about Paint Shop Pro, not Windows Explorer.

The next two options, Overwrite and Obey Script, are related to scripts. To use the Overwrite option, you must also specify a script in the Script text box. When executed, the command runs the script and resaves the image in its original location, overwriting the original file. The Obey Script command doesn't automatically save the image, it only runs the script. If you use the Obey Script option, you should make sure that the script contains a command to save the image. If the script doesn't contain a Save command, you're wasting your time running this option because Paint Shop Pro runs the script on the image and then tosses the entire process away.

Like the Batch Rename command, you access the Batch Process command through the File menu and the Batch submenu. When you select Process, you see the dialog box shown in Figure 9-16.

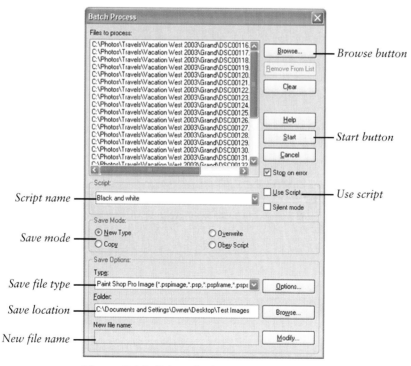

Figure 9-16 *Select the images you want to modify and the options you want to use.*

Depending on the options you select, some areas of the dialog box may be unavailable. Let's take a look at each area.

- **Files to process:** Click the Browse button to locate and select the images you want to modify. If you add images in error, click the Clear button.

TIP

In the Batch Process command, don't use the Select All button when browsing for images. Clicking the Select All button not only selects all the images in the folder you're browsing, but executes the Batch Process command.

- **Stop on error:** It's a good idea to have this box checked so that if you accidentally select a file that Paint Shop Pro cannot open and process, it stops and displays an error message notifying you of the problem.

- **Save Mode:** This is where you select the function you want Batch Process to run.

- **Script:** If you are using Overwrite mode or Obey Script mode, you can select the script you want Paint Shop Pro to run when processing the files. If you select Silent mode, no script dialog box options appear, and the script runs as recorded.

- **Type:** If you select the New Type mode from this drop-down list, you select the file type you want the images to take. If you do not select the New Type mode, this option is unavailable.

- **Folder:** Specify the folder where you want the Batch Process command to place the processed images. This option becomes available if you select New Type or Copy mode. If you don't specify a folder, Paint Shop Pro places the processed images in their original folder. You should select a different folder if you select Copy mode; otherwise, the command copies the image on top of itself, which is useless.

- **New file name:** This works just like the Batch Rename command. You need to specify the naming convention you want Paint Shop Pro to use for the new images by clicking the Modify button, which opens the Filename Format dialog box. You saw the Filename Format box earlier in Figure 9-14. If you leave the New file name box blank, Paint Shop Pro uses the original filename.

When you have selected all your options, click the Start button to begin the Batch Process. Paint Shop Pro displays a Current Step window similar to Figure 9-17. The Current Step window displays each filename and its status, and the Job Progress bar indicates the conversion progress. Click the Abort button to stop the process, or click the OK button when the process is complete.

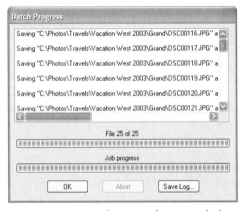

> ## TIP
> When converting to some file types, you may see other dialog boxes asking for other options.

Figure 9-17 *For future reference, click the Save Log button to save the progress window text to a file.*

Working with RAW Camera Files

In Chapter 1, you learned about the different file formats supported by Paint Shop Pro, including RAW file format. The RAW file format is an uncompressed, unprocessed data file, which acts as a digital negative by containing all the information gathered by the camera. The camera, instead of applying the information to the image, such as white balance, sharpening, contrast, and saturation, saves all the information into a separate area, called the *header*. When you open the image, Paint Shop Pro reads the header and displays an image of the RAW data.

So how is this different from other file formats? Well, for example, when using a JPEG format, a couple of things happen to the image before the camera even saves the image to your camera memory card. While the image information is at the RAW stage, which is after the sensor gathers the information from the photosites, the camera takes the white balance, sharpening, contrast, saturation, size, and quality settings you selected before you took the photograph, and it applies the data to the image. Finally, the camera compresses the information and saves it to your camera memory card. Remember that every single time you save a JPEG file, the lossy compression throws away some of the image information.

RAW File Pros and Cons

Let's take a look at some of the pros and cons of working with RAW image files. Some of the pros include that the RAW format offers lossless compression, so no image information is lost when the file is saved. What the camera saw and recorded is what you get. RAW formats provide the greatest flexibility in image editing. You select the white balance, contrast, saturation, and other factors after you download the image, instead of having the camera do it for you before you ever see the image. As newer and better technologies arise for processing RAW files, you always have the original RAW file to work with. Since a JPEG file is already processed, you cannot ever retrieve the original image data.

On the flip side of the RAW image coin, RAW images take longer to save. Although this time difference is usually a matter of milliseconds, if you are taking photos in rapid succession, you may notice some slowdown between shots. RAW file sizes are substantially larger than JPEG, so you can't fit as many images on a memory card. You'll need to carry extra memory cards if you shoot RAW images. One large problem is that no two camera manufacturers encode their RAW image information in the same way. That creates a problem for the image editing software, such as Paint Shop Pro, to keep up with all the different camera manufacturers and models. The nonstandard encoding problem may change in the future as a new standard is being introduced, but it remains to be seen whether the camera manufacturers will ever all agree to it.

One other thing to mention is that many amateur photographers (and some professionals) don't want to apply all the processing after the fact. It is extra work, and not everyone enjoys doing that! In many instances, the camera's JPEG image is more than sufficient.

Supported Cameras

As previously mentioned, no two camera manufactures manage RAW image data the same way. As a result, Paint Shop Pro doesn't presently support all camera models, although the list will continue to grow.

Table 9-1 lists the supported camera models at the time this book was published, but support for additional cameras models is provided through Paint Shop Pro's auto-update feature as they become available.

Table 9-1 Paint Shop Pro Supported RAW Camera Formats

Brand	Currently Supported Models
Canon	300D Rebel, D30, D60, 10D, 1D, 1Ds, 1D Mark II, Powershot G3 & G5
Fuji	S2 Pro, S7000
Kodak	760, 14N, 14c
Minolta	A1, A2
Nikon	D1, D1h, D100, D2h, D1X, D70
Olympus	5050, 5060, E1, E10, E20
Pentax	*ist

Opening a RAW File

Typically, when you download RAW files from your camera, Windows saves them with a camer-specific extension, such as CRW for a Canon format or NEF for a Nikon format. You open a RAW file using the same steps as opening any other file in Paint Shop Pro. Click the File menu and select Open, locate the file, and double-click it. The difference is that when opening a RAW file, Paint Shop Pro displays the Raw Camera Data dialog box seen in Figure 9-18, which prompts you for instructions on processing the image.

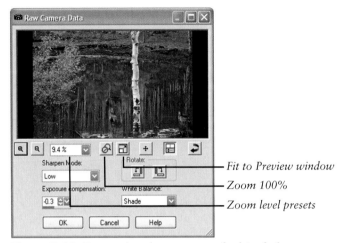

Figure 9-18 *Determine the amount of white balance, exposure compensation, and method of sharpening all before Paint Shop Pro opens the image file.*

The Raw Camera Data dialog box works the same as other Paint Shop Pro dialog boxes, but because you typically want to look at the image close when determining settings, they've provided additional viewing tools. Notice the standard Preview button, Reset defaults button, Zoom in and Zoom out buttons, as well as the Pan button, but you also have two additional viewing buttons, Zoom 100% and Fit to Preview window button and a Zoom Level Presets drop-down list. These viewing features help you see your image better while making adjustments.

Remember that like many other photo processing options, processing RAW camera data is a subjective issue. What one person thinks is perfect, another may find horrible. Take a look at the settings in the Raw Camera Data dialog box.

- **Sharpen**: Sharpen settings control contrast between pixels. Settings include Low, Normal, High, Standard, and Off. The Off setting applies no sharpening, Low applies the smallest amount of sharpening, and the level increases if you select Normal. Selecting High introduces the largest amount of sharpening but may also produce noise on the image. The Standard setting tells Paint Shop Pro to use the sharpening as specified by your camera.

- **Exposure**: The Exposure setting determines a certain amount of lightness in the image. Settings range from -2.0 to 2.0, where a lower number darkens the image.

- **White Balance**: White Balance settings control the color cast caused by lighting conditions. You determine the settings you want for your image. Options include As Shot, which applies the settings as determined by your camera, Incandescent, Fluorescent, Sunny, Cloudy, Shade, and Flash.

- **Rotate**: You can rotate the image in 90-degree increments to the left or right.

Make the selections you want for your image and click OK. The image opens in Paint Shop Pro, and you can further apply other photographic corrections and enhancements.

In Figure 9-19 you see an image as it was first saved in a JPEG format from the camera and a RAW image after processing in Paint Shop Pro. On this particular image, we used the following settings:

Exposure - .3

Sharpen = Low

White Balance = Shady

After opening the image, we then cropped it, applied Automatic Contrast, Clarify, Automatic Saturation, and applied the Unsharp Mask.

Figure 9-19 *The figure on the left is from the camera as it saved the image in JPEG format, while the figure on the right is the image after manipulating the RAW file in Paint Shop Pro.*

What's Next?

In this chapter, you discovered some excellent time-saving techniques, as well as how to work with RAW files, which don't save you any time, but certainly give you more flexibility in working with your images. In the next and final chapter, we're going to talk about what is usually the final step with your images—printing them. We'll look at resizing the images so they fit properly on a page. We'll learn about printing resolutions and how different printers work with images.

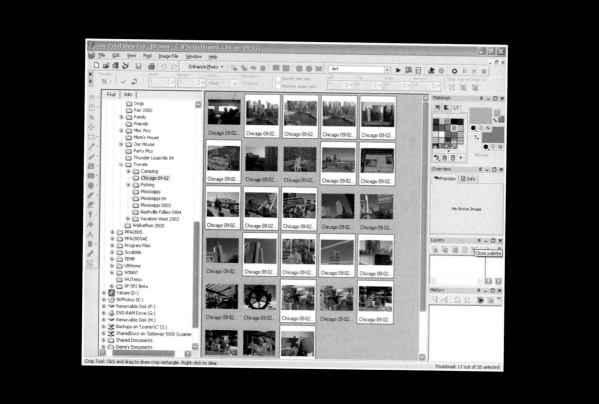

10

Resolutions, Resizing, and Printing

For many situations, the end result for your photographs will be to print them. Many of the images will remain on your hard drive or CD, but those special ones look their best when you print them. The computer monitor just can't let you touch and feel that image like a print.

If you plan on printing your photos, you should plan for it from the beginning. So many different factors affect the quality of your prints, including how they are managed in Paint Shop Pro.

Understanding Resolution

One of the most misunderstood topics in the digital realm is about resolution. A writer once said that trying to understand resolution is easier than spit-roasting jellyfish—but only marginally. Unfortunately, that's true.

In Chapter 2, we discovered that digital images are made up of pixels and that pixels (short for *picture elements*) are the small sections of color and light that make up a digital image like pieces of a mosaic. A digital image is really a grid of those pixels, and when the pixels are viewed together, the image is formed. When there are enough pixels and they are small enough so as not to be individually discernible, the digital image can achieve photo quality.

A digital image, as it is stored on a hard drive or a flash card, is simply an informational record of the image pixels and has no physical size. But when an image is displayed on a monitor or printed, it takes on physical form. At that point the image has spatial dimensions—width and height. The physical dimensions are the number of pixels a digital image is made up of and are expressed in pixel dimensions such as 1600 × 1200.

The resolution of a digital image is defined as the number of pixels per inch it contains, So when considering resolution, you need to determine what you intend to do with the image. Are you going to use it on a Web page? Are you going to print it? If so, what size? Fine detail is rendered by having an ample amount of pixels. Too few and the picture appears jagged or pixilated.

Let's take a look at the two principal types of resolution measurements and how they are used.

PPI

Ppi, which stands for *pixels per inch*, is a measurement of how many pixels can fit into an inch square of your image. If they are large pixels, obviously you won't get as many into an inch as you would if they were smaller. Think of it as how many peas you can fit into a sandwich bag versus how many apples you can fit into that same sandwich bag.

Ppi actually has a dual purpose. One place that uses ppi is your screen display, which is called *monitor resolution*. You learned how to set monitor resolution in Chapter 2 by adjusting Display Properties from your Windows desktop. Settings you select for the monitor resolution affect all programs that you run on your computer, including Web pages. The options you choose are based upon the graphics card installed in your computer, your overall monitor size, and how good your eyes are. When you are setting the pixel resolution in the Display Properties dialog box, remember that as you increase the number of pixels, you can display more information on your screen, but the information, including text and icons, gets smaller in size.

The use of PPI we are going to discuss in this chapter refers to how ppi is used in *image resolution* and how it relates to the photo dimensions. People often get confused about how many inches a digital image is. To understand digital image size, you simply have to understand that pixels are more tightly packed for printing than for display on a computer screen.

A combination of the image size and pixels determines how large you can print your image. Obviously, you can physically make your image any size you want, but that doesn't mean it will print well. Images that are printed too large for their pixel size lose their quality. We will show you later in this chapter how you can change your image size.

TIP

We're using the term PPI here, but besides pixels, Paint Shop Pro allows you to optionally measure your image in inches, centimeters, or millimeters.

Unlike conventional photographs where we refer to a 4 × 6-inch or 8 × 10-inch print, the overall size of a digital image is measured by its pixels. The image's final destination, whether to a good printer or to the screen, also factors into the image size. Check the actual dimensions, as well as the resolution of your image, to know how it will print.

For example, if you have an image that is 1200×1500 pixels, and the resolution is set at 300 PPI, the image will print a 4×5 inch size, but if the image resolution is set at 200 PPI, the image will print approximately 6×7 inches.

Required pixel dimensions can be calculated by multiplying the print size by the resolution, so an 8×10-inch print at 300 dpi requires an image size in pixels of 2400×3000. Or let's look at it from another perspective and divide the size by resolution. If we know the image size in pixels and we know the resolution, what size print can we get? If we know our image is 2400×3000 and the resolution is 300, we'll take 2400 and divide it by 300, then we'll take 3000 and divide it by 300, which gives us a print size of 8×10 inches. Got it?

DPI

DPI represents *dots per inch* and refers to your *printer resolution*. Printer resolution is independent of and unrelated to image resolution. DPI is the measure of how many dots of ink or toner a printer can place within an inch (or centimeter) on paper. The maximum value is determined by your printer and cannot be changed through Paint Shop Pro, although most printers provide settings where you can select low, medium, or high settings from within the printer's DPI range. DPI affects the quality of your printed image but does *not* affect the size of your printed image.

Most printers print the same number of dots horizontally and vertically, so basically a 600 dpi printer prints 600 tiny little dots across one inch of space and 600 dots vertically, creating a one-inch square. The lower the DPI, the less fine the detail it will print and the fewer shades of grey it will simulate.

Better printers have a higher DPI resolution. For photographs, you will probably want to print between 300 and 1000 DPI. Anything less than 300 DPI can produce spotty, pixilated images, and DPI over 1000 provides little extra benefit. In addition, the paper you use can have some bearing on the final outcome. We'll talk about paper types later in this chapter. With good printer resolution, you get better tones, especially in areas that have uniform color and density, such as a sky. Good printer resolution also provides a smoother transition from one color to another. In general, the more dots, the better and sharper the image will be.

Let's now take a look at Paint Shop Pro and how it handles image sizes.

Manipulating Image Size

If you need to manipulate your image size for printing, start big and work your way down the scale. When you shoot your image, use a high-resolution setting on your camera, which provides the largest number of pixels. That way, you will start with a larger physical image that you can scale down if needed without losing any image detail. The problem arises when your image is too small for the size you want to print. You can make your image larger, but there's no way for Paint Shop Pro to add details that aren't in the image to begin with which can result in the image losing crispness and often becoming fuzzy or pixilated.

Viewing Image Information

Paint Shop Pro includes a dialog box that tells you all about your image, including type, size (both physical and digital), color depth, resolution, number of layers, and all sorts of other information. You view the image information by clicking the Image menu and selecting Image Information. Optionally, you can press Shift+I. Both options display the dialog box you see in Figure 10-1.

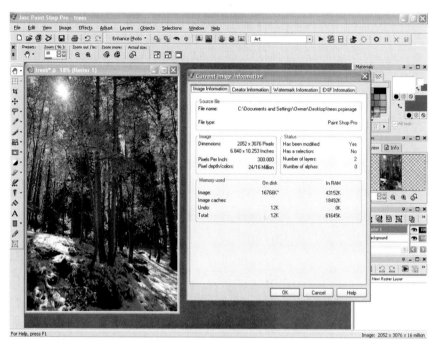

Figure 10-1 *The Image Information tab does not have any editable boxes but contains image information. (Original photo by James Hutchinson)*

Another piece of valuable information regarding your images is the EXIF information. The EXIF, which stands for *Exchangeable Image File Format*, includes information such as the date and time a photograph was taken, but more importantly, it displays the camera settings when the image was taken, including resolution, exposure, focal length, white balance settings, metering mode, and color space. Click the EXIF Information tab to view the EXIF information.

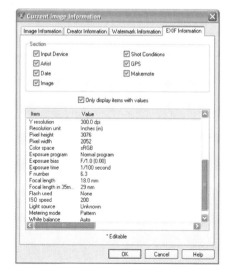

Resizing versus Resampling

Adjusting an image resolution's ppi, or its size in inches, has no effect on the actual pixels. This is called *resizing* or *scaling,* and it involves specifying the printing resolution if and when the image is printed. The image remains the same grid of pixels with the same pixel dimensions and pixel data.

However, if you change the image's size in pixels, changing the actual pixel dimensions, this is called *resampling*. Resampling changes the actual image file, which results in a different number of pixels and alters some pixel color and tonal data to maintain the same appearance over the altered amount of pixels.

The bottom line is that there are two different ways to make the same digital image print at different sizes. You can resize it, which changes the print resolution to yield the desired physical dimensions without changing the existing pixel dimensions, or you can resample it, which changes the existing pixel dimensions to yield the desired physical dimensions at a given output resolution.

Resampling changes the amount of pixels the image consists of, whereas resizing changes how many pixels are being printed per inch. Resampling affects the nature of the digital image itself; resizing affects only the printing of the image.

Table 10-1 illustrates an example of what happens to an image when you modify your image size:

Table 10.1 Resizing Results

	Dimensions in ppi	Print Size	Resolution ppi	Resize Type	Result
Original image	900 × 600	6×4	150	N/A	N/A
Increase size only to 200%	1800 × 1200	12×8	150	Resize	Increases print size, but decreases quality
Increase resolution only to 300 PPI	900 × 600	3×2	300	Resample	Decreases print size, but improves quality
Increase size to 200% & resolution to 300 PPI	1800 × 1200	6×4	300	Resize	Keeps print size the same but improves quality.
Decrease resolution only to 100PPI	900 × 600	9×6	100	Resample	Enlarges print and decreases quality
Decrease size only to 50%	450 × 300	3×2	300	Resize	Reduces print size and maintains quality

More pixels per inch creates smaller printed pixels and a smaller printed image, while fewer pixels per inch creates larger printed pixels and a larger printed image. As you can see, as the output resolution gets smaller, the print size gets larger. It sounds strange, and in a way it is, but that's how the image sizing process works.

Resizing an Image

As stated earlier, when you resize an image, you're changing the image physical dimensions. Paint Shop Pro provides a dialog box where you can change your image size.

Click the Image menu and select Resize or press Shift+S. You'll see a Resize dialog box like the one in Figure 10-2. The Pixel Dimension area is where you resize your image, and the Print Size area is where you resample your image.

When you make a change, you should make sure the Lock Aspect Radio is on. As you make changes to the image width, Paint Shop Pro also changes the height, maintaining image proportions. If you change the aspect ration, it can distort your image by making it larger or smaller in one dimension than the other. If you need specific heights and widths, try using the Crop tool after you resize the image.

In this example, at its original dimensions, the image is 2052 pixels × 3076 pixels, with a print size of 6.840 × 10.253 inches. If we resize the pixels to 3000 pixels × 4497 pixels, the image print size changes to 10.000 × 14.990. Notice we are *not* changing the resolution.

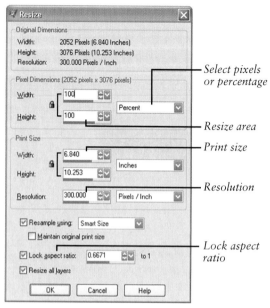

Select pixels or percentage

Resize area

Print size

Resolution

Lock aspect ratio

Figure 10-2 *Change pixel dimensions either by a percentage or by pixel amounts.*

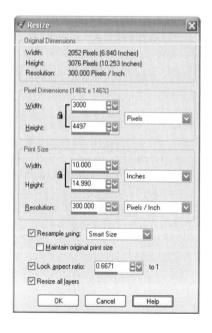

TIP

For best results, only resize your image once. If you resize it and aren't happy with it, use the Undo Resize command and try it again.

Resampling an Image Up

When you resample an image to a larger size, Paint Shop Pro must do some interpolation. Interpolation is the process of upsizing a photograph by adding pixels that were not there originally. Since every pixel must have a color, this process usually involves assigning a color to the newly created pixels based upon the colors of the pre-existing pixels surrounding the new ones. The result is a larger image in terms of resolution, but one that now has less clarity because you simply cannot produce something from nothing.

Paint Shop Pro has several resampling type methods to calculate the interpolation. All of them are based upon mathematical calculations:

- **Smart Size:** Smart size is the option you should use in most cases. It lets Paint Shop Pro determine, based upon current image information, which of the other four resampling types is best for your image.

- **Weighted Average:** When creating new pixels, this option looks at nearby pixels and then, by calculating a weighted average color value, uses that result to create the new pixels.

- **Bilinear:** The Bilinear method determines new pixels by using the two pixels nearest each existing pixel.

- **Bicubic:** Bicubic is similar to the Weighted Average calculation in that it does use a weighted average, but the Bicubic method uses a larger area of pixel samples to calculate the new pixel values. The Bicubic method generally takes a little more time, but it usually produces a more accurate sample.

- **Pixel Resize:** The Pixel Resize resampling type duplicates or removes pixels, as needed, to reach the desired image's width and height. This method works best with line drawings and other simple graphics.

Like the resizing options, you make your resampling choices through the Resize dialog box. Make sure the Resample using check box is selected and you have selected a resampling type (see Figure 10-3).

The Resolution and Print size areas are where you resample your image.

After you resample an image, you should run the Unsharp Mask filter.

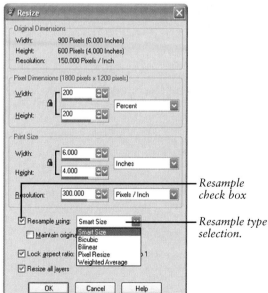

Resample check box

Resample type selection.

Figure 10-3 *Select a Resample type.*

> # TIP
>
> For best results, only resample your image once. If you resample it and aren't happy with it, use the Undo Resize command and try it again.

Printing Options

After all the work you did in manipulating your images in Paint Shop Pro, you want to make sure you get the best output. There are actually a number of different ways you can print your images. Some options include nonprinting sources such as e-mailing your images, posting them to a Web page, or simply storing them on a CD for personal viewing or distribution. But the type of output we will compare here is the actual physical print options of your color images from your printer.

NOTE

Besides printing your own prints, you can outsource your image printing to a professional printing service, whether a brick and mortar store or an online shop. Or you can take them to one of the kiosks at your local drugstore. Having images printed from an outside source is usually less work on your part but generally more expensive.

Ink Jet versus Laser Printers

The two main types of printers that most people use are ink jets and laser printers. The technology behind each is distinctly different from the other.

Ink Jet Printers

Ink jet printers are the slowest but most affordable type of printers. They work by shooting tiny sprays of colored wet dyes through microscopic holes in a print head onto pages, one row at a time. Price-wise, ink jet printers are very inexpensive to purchase, many under $100, but the real price of an ink jet printer comes in the replacement cartridges.

Ink jets printers usually come in two flavors: regular and photo-quality. If you're doing photo printing, most of the time you'll get better results with the photo-quality printer. They usually cost a little more but are designed specially for photographs and the high quality required in printing them. When shopping for an ink jet, pay attention to the resolution advertised by the manufacturer, but also take that resolution promise with a grain of salt.

On the other hand, while ink jet printers usually do a beautiful job on photographs, especially on glossy paper, you'll often find ink jet printers produce somewhat fuzzy, jagged text.

Some photo-quality ink jets include extra features, such as a dedicated USB port for connecting your digital camera directly to the printer, built-in media card slots that let you plug in a storage card and hit a button for instant prints, and a special menu for selecting prints. All those features mean you can bypass your computer. But if you use their instant printing features, you don't get the option of first correcting and enhancing your image in Paint Shop Pro. Where is the fun in that?

Laser Printers

Cost-wise, a black-and-white laser printer can be purchased today for under $100, but obviously a black-and-white printer won't work if you want a color print. So we look to color laser printers. Designed for high-volume printing, color laser printers are among the most expensive printers you can purchase. Current prices run from $1,200 to $3,000 (or more), depending on the features offered, but like most electronics, that price will probably continue to drop. Only a few years ago, the average color laser cost around $20,000! Per-page cost, however, is generally less than an ink jet.

Laser printers don't use a wet ink process; instead, they use a dry toner, similar to a copy machine. The principal behind the laser printer is to apply the toner to the paper through a controlled electrostatic charge. Laser printers print razor sharp text, color charts, and other two-dimensional graphics, and if you need to print images for a layout, they produce acceptable quality. But when it comes to color photographs, most color laser printers can't match an ink jet printer's quality.

Printer Inks

The consumables cost of a printer plays a huge factor in image printing. With an ink jet printer, a color photograph can cost between 6 and 18 cents to print. Many ink jet manufacturers include a single ink cartridge containing all three colors. If you print a lot of images with red in them, you'll obviously run out of red ink faster, and even though you have hardly used the green ink, you have to throw it away and replace the entire cartridge. Other manufacturers such as Canon, Epson, and HP sell models with individual cartridges for each color instead of one cartridge for all three colors. The downside is that while you save ink by replacing cartridges one at a time, the individual color cartridges cost a few dollars more, so per page, they end up costing about the same.

Another option is a do-it-yourself refill kit for ink cartridges. Some people think they are great, but most people find them messy, time-consuming, and feel that they produce a lower quality print. If your vendor offers higher capacity cartridges, you might want to take advantage of them as a better alternative. They cost more to purchase, but they contain twice the amount of ink, so they cost less per page.

On the other hand, color laser printers cost about 3 to 8 cents for a color page. Obviously, they are less expensive per page than ink jets, but the cost increases because color lasers have separate toner cartridges for each color, which can cost as much as $250 each. Even with their very high cost, however, in sufficient volume, the cost per page of a color laser's cartridges is still less than for color from an ink jet because the yields are much higher, ranging from 6,000 to 12,000 pages.

Either way, with ink jet or laser printers, whether you buy the manufacturer's brand of ink cartridge or toner or one from a third party, it comes down to being a matter of your preference. Some people prefer companies such as Canon, Epson, and HP because they formulate their printers, ink, and paper as a complete system, and they think that if you buy from a third party, you may not get the results you expect. Others find that the third-party producers are equally good and less pricey.

Paper Types

You'll find the quality and cost of your print also relies upon the type of paper you use. For best results, use photo quality paper, which is available in a number of sizes, such as 8.5 × 11 inches, 4 × 6 inches, 5 × 7 inches, and so forth. Photo paper costs more per page because the paper itself is more expensive. But hands down, using photo paper instead of regular paper, produces a far better print.

Photo paper is available in a variety of finishes, such as glossy or matte. Glossy finishes provide a reflective, vibrant look to your images, while matte paper is specially formulated so that light won't bounce off the photos, which reduces reflection and adds depth. Photo paper resists fading and is smear proof and water resistant, so your photos never lose their brilliance and can give your images a more professional photo lab type of look.

Most people have a variety of sizes at their disposal. The smaller, individual sizes are per inch and usually more expensive than the full page size papers. But if you just want to print a single picture of your new puppy or your son in his football uniform, you will probably want a single sheet of 3 × 5 or 4 × 6 inch paper. If, however, you plan on printing several copies to hand out to Aunt Martha, Cousin Jack, and Grandma Mary, you should consider using the larger 8.5 × 11 inch paper for speed and economic reasons, because Paint Shop Pro, as you will discover in the next section, makes it easy to print multiple images or multiple copies of an image on a single sheet. You can even print out a page of wallet sizes so that you can give one to each of your co-workers.

Two other paper aspects you should consider because they also affect print quality are the brightness and the weight. The paper brightness, sometimes referred to as *whiteness*, is the measure of how much light is reflected from the paper. How white it is depends on how evenly it reflects colors. For example, if the paper reflects more blue than red or yellow, it will have a cool hue to it, making it appear even brighter than white, sometimes creating an optical impression because cool white sheets tend to brighten colors. A bright white surface is perfect for high-resolution digital photos, as well as cherished family photos. You'll get realistic skin tones and true photo quality. Don't worry, though, you don't have to stand there and figure out the reflection value yourself. The paper manufacturers list the brightness levels on the packages. Most photo papers have a brightness level between 90 and 104.

Paper weight is measured in pounds or mil. The higher the mil or the heavier the weight, the thicker and sturdier the paper is, making it more durable for framing, albums, and frequent handling than the standard paper you use for printing documents or making copies. Standard copy paper is usually a 20 pound paper, and cardstock is around 110 pounds. You'll find a pretty good range in photo papers running from around 45 pounds to 88 pounds. Keep the paper weight in mind when determining the final use for your image.

Printing with Paint Shop Pro

Well, you've finally reached the summit. You've snapped, downloaded, corrected, enhanced, resized, and done all kinds of things to your photographs. Now, it's time to print them. Paint Shop Pro provides several different printing methods for doing just that, and it all boils down to what you want to print.

- If you want to print images on nonstandard size paper, such as 4 × 6 or 5 × 7, you will print through the standard Print menu.

- If you want to print multiple images or multiple copies of images on standard size paper, you will use the Paint Shop Pro Print Layout feature.

- If you want to print a contact sheet containing thumbnails of a group of pictures, you will use the Paint Shop Pro Browser to print.

We will now take a look at all three printing methods, beginning with printing thumbnail-size images.

Printing Thumbnails

In the first chapter, we took a look at the Paint Shop Pro Browser and how you could navigate among your folders and open, manage, or just view thumbnail sizes of your images visually rather than by filename. Another option in the Browser window is to print a contact sheet of images. You can print all the images in a folder or just the ones you select. You can only select images from a single folder; in other words, you cannot select some images from one folder and others from another folder.

Open the Paint Shop Pro Browser window by clicking File and then Browse (or just press Ctrl+B). In the Browser window, navigate to the folder containing the images you want to print. Use one of the following methods to select the files you want to print:

- Click once on a single thumbnail if you only want to print that image.

- Hold down the Ctrl key and click a nonsequential group of images. Selected images appear with a white border surrounding the thumbnail (see Figure 10-4).

- Click the first image that you want to select; then hold down the Shift key and click the last image you want to select in a sequential group of images. The selected images will have a white border around them.

After you select the files you want, click the File menu and select Print, press Ctrl+P, or just click the Print button on the standard toolbar. Because you access the Print option through the Browser menu, the Browser Print dialog box displays instead of a standard Print dialog box. The Browser Print dialog box (see Figure 10-5) contains options relevant to printing thumbnail images.

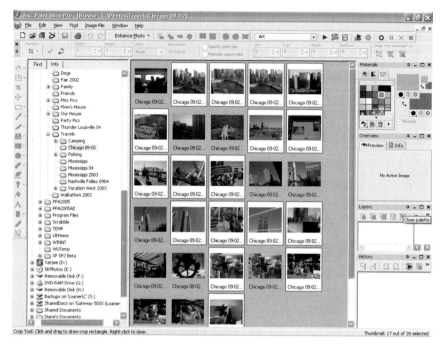

Figure 10-4 *Select the images you want to print.*

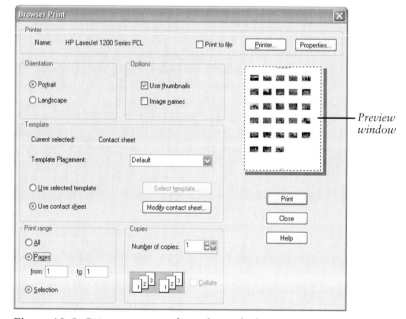

Figure 10-5 *Print a contact sheet through the Browser Print dialog box.*

As you can see, this is a very busy dialog box. The Preview window shows you how your group of selected images will look based upon the current settings. From the Browser Print dialog box, you can click the Printer button and select a different printer, and you can click the Properties button to set Printer properties. (We'll look at that more in the next section.)

You can opt to print your contact sheet in landscape or portrait orientation. When printing in portrait orientation, the longest dimension is vertical, while in landscape orientation, the longest dimension is horizontal.

Click the Image names box if you want each image's filename under the thumbnail.

In the Print Range section in the lower right corner of the Browser Print dialog box, you can choose between printing all images in the Browser window, or you can click Selection to print only the images you selected from the Browser window.

The standard contact sheet has six rows of five images, for a total of 30 images per sheet. In the Template section, you'll find two important options. If you don't want the layout of 30 images per sheet, you can click the Modify contact sheet option, which displays the Custom contact sheet dialog box (see Figure 10-6).

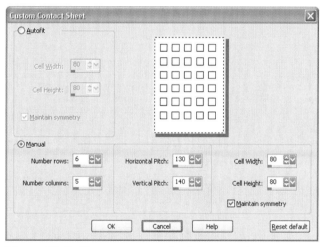

Figure 10-6 *Create a customized contact sheet.*

Here, you can specify the number of rows and columns you want for your thumbnails and optionally specify the individual cell height and width, as well as the spacing between each cell.

The other option you should check is in the Template Placement drop-down list.

This option determines how the selected images are placed in their individual cells. For example, if your images are of different sizes, clicking the Fill Cell option makes them all the same size as the thumbnail cell. Be careful of this option, though. Using this option can distort your images when printed.

After setting your options, click the Print button, and you'll see your images in a contact sheet thumbnail format.

Don't forget to close your Paint Shop Pro Browser window when you are finished with it!

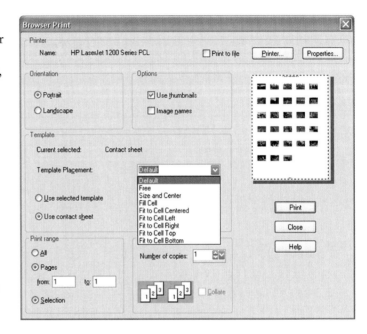

Printing Through the Print Menu

Use the Print menu if you want to print images on nonstandard size paper, such as 4 × 6 or 5 × 7. You'll need to go through a couple of steps to tell your printer what you are doing:

1. Open the image you want to print.
2. Click the File menu and select Print.
3. If needed, click the Printer button to select the printer you are going to use.

Properties button

4. You can see in Figure 10-7 that even though the print size is 6 × 4 inches, Paint Shop Pro still assumes you want to print the image on standard 8.5 × 11 inch paper. Click the Properties button.

5. The Properties dialog box will open, but the options available and the appearance of the Properties dialog box vary, depending on the printer you selected. Figure 10-8 shows two properties dialog boxes for two different printers.

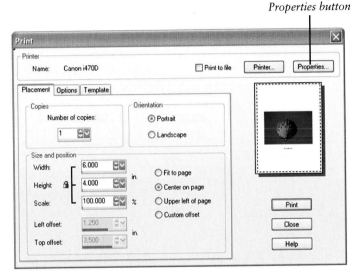

Figure 10-7 *If you are printing on a nonstandard paper size, click the Properties button.*

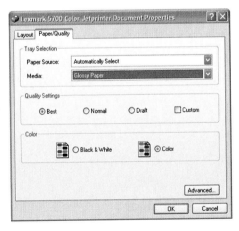

Figure 10-8 *Available options vary, depending on your selected printer.*

6. From the Media (or Media Type) drop-down list, select the type of paper you are using.

7. Somewhere in the Properties dialog box, you'll find an option to select the paper size. In our example Canon printer, we find the paper size option on the Page Setup tab, but on the Lexmark printer, we have to click the Advanced button to find the paper size option.

8. Select the paper size you want to use.

9. For the best results, make sure that the print quality is set to high. Again, the location of this option will vary, depending on the printer you are using.

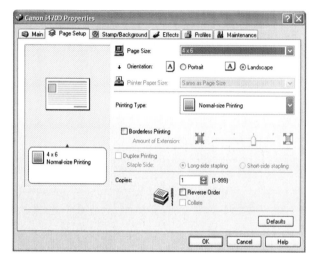

Figure 10-8 *Available options vary, depending on your selected printer.*

10. Click OK to close the Properties dialog box; then click the Print button to print your image.

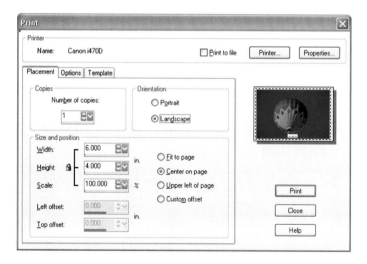

Working in Print Layout

You've already seen several ways to print your images, but the best is yet to come. Paint Shop Pro includes a comprehensive range of choices in terms of image format and placement. These choices come in the form of Print Layouts.

You can use the Print Layout templates, whether you want to print a single image, multiple images, or multiple copies of an image on a full-sized sheet of paper. The templates provided with Paint Shop Pro cover the options most of us want, but if not, you can create your own layout and save it for future use if you want to.

Click the File menu and select Print Layout, which displays the Print Layout window. The Print Layout window contains its own menu and toolbar, and any images you have open currently appear on the left side of the window (see Figure 10-9). By default, Paint Shop Pro assumes you want to print one image on the sheet.

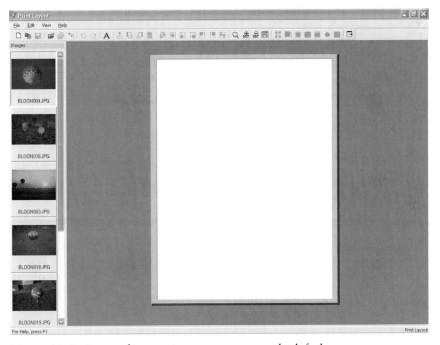

Figure 10-9 *Currently open images appear on the left, but you can open additional images.*

Click the File menu and click Open Templates, which displays the Templates dialog box shown in Figure 10-10.

The supplied templates are organized by category, mostly based on standard image sizes such as 5 × 7s or wallet sizes. After you select a category, click the template you want to use and click OK. The Print Layout window now shows the template you selected.

Drag the image you want in each of the template frames. You can use any image more than once, and you don't have to use all the frames. If you want an image that does not appear in the Images area, click File and then Open to open additional images.

Changes are made easily from the template. For example, if you place an image in the wrong holding space, simply drag it into the correct frame. If you place an image you don't want in a frame, click it and press the Delete key.

A number of options are available to help you adjust the image placements. If your images don't fit in the frame like you want, from the Edit menu you can modify the cell placement, making choices such as Size and Center or Fill cell.

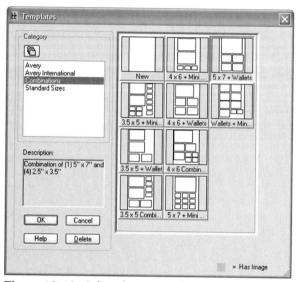

Figure 10-10 *Select from a wide variety of printing templates.*

Figure 10-11 *Drag-and-drop your images into the template.*

All the placement options are also available on the Print Layout toolbar. Pause your mouse over any tool to see its description. You'll also find options for rotating any framed image.

You'll probably need to select the appropriate paper type, so click the File menu and select Print Setup. You'll see the Print Setup dialog box (see Figure 10-12), which provides a number of options, including a Printer selection button and a Properties button, which is where you select the paper type. Refer to the previous section for a refresher on selecting paper type.

Other options on the Print Setup dialog box include the number of copies, the page orientation, and the Print Output, which is where you can print CMYK separations if you want. You can also specify a header and/or footer to print on

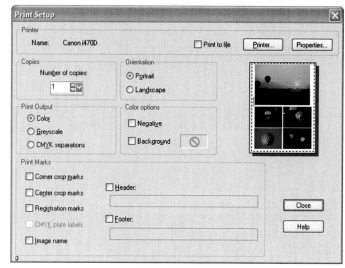

Figure 10-12 *Set the options you want for this layout.*

every page, and you can tell Paint Shop Pro to print the image filename under every image. Make your choices and then click the Close button.

Finally, when you're ready to print, click the File menu and click Print.

When you close the Print Layout box, a message box will appear asking you if you want to save the layout. If you think you want this layout for future use, such as if you need to go back and further edit an image, you should save it. Give it an easily identifiable name and check any other options in the Save dialog box.

What's Next?

Wow! We're finished. Hopefully, you have learned how to take an everyday photograph, manipulate it, improve it, and turn it into a work of art. From here, let your imagination be your guide, but be sure to take Paint Shop Pro along to do the legwork.

Take a look at Appendix A, which lists several hundred Web links where you can view artwork created in Paint Shop Pro, download lots of freebies, and learn tips and tricks from other Paint Shop Pro users.

When I was a young girl, we had a beautiful horse named Apples. We named her that because she absolutely loved to take apples from our apple tree.

One day, Apples decided to follow me to school.

A

Paint Shop Pro Web Links

The World Wide Web has thousands of sites dedicated to using Paint Shop Pro. If you have a chance, take a look at some of the links listed in this appendix. Some of them provide general Paint Shop Pro help information, whereas others are step-by-step tutorials on special tasks you can accomplish with Paint Shop Pro. Some are related to photography, and others relate to graphics in general. Still others are links to free, or mostly free, things you can download to use with Paint Shop Pro—things such as picture tubes, masks, filters, frames, and other goodies. If you enjoyed Chapter 8 about digital scrapbooking, you'll find a number of links to Web sites related to scrapbooking with downloadable fonts and backgrounds, again some that are free, some not.

Many of these sites refer to prior versions of Paint Shop Pro, but you'll find that you can use most of the information they offer with your current version of Paint Shop Pro as well.

I apologize in advance if any listed site closes or modifies its content. Although these links were active and accurate at the time of this book's publication, Web sites change frequently. Also, make sure that your anti-virus software is up to date before you download *anything* from the Internet. You cannot be too safe!

Graphics

1001 Fonts	http://www.1001fonts.com
1001 Free Fonts	http://www.1001freefonts.com
3scrapateers	http://www.3scrapateers.com/
Abstract Dimensions	http://psptips.com/
Abstract Fonts	http://www.abstractfonts.com/fonts
Adventures of Nikki and Nichie	http://catarific.com/
Alb's Tutorials	http://tutorials.thealb.de/
Alice's Nook	http://www.alicesnook.com/
Ally's Attitudes	http://allytoy.addr.com/
Always Unique	http://always-unique.net/
AmphiSoft Filters	http://photoshop.msk.ru/as/index.html
Andrew's Resource Center	http://arc.ireed.net/index.php
Andri's Websites	http://www.andri.hispeed.com/home.htm
Angie's Art	http://angiesart.tripod.com/index.html
Anita's PSP Tutorials	http://www.psp4u.tk/
Annie's Corner	http://www.msnusers.com/AnniesCorner/
AP Graphics	http://anzwers.org/free/apgraphics/index.html
Arctic Whispers	http://www.arcticwhispers.net/
Arizona Kate	http://www.arizonakate.com/
Artwork by EssexGirl	http://www.essexgirl.uk.com/
Baby's Breath	http://babys-breath.com/
Barbara's Place	http://www.barbie.thegraphicsgroove.com/
Barb's Playground	http://www.barbkermisdesigns.com/
Be's Design Treasures	http://www.besdesigntreasures.com/
Bingoware	http://www.bingoware.com/tutorials/
BJ Web Art	http://www.bjwebart.com/
Black Cat Pub	http://www.blackcatpub.org.uk/
Brovik Web Productions	http://www.brovik.com/
Carol & Graphics	http://carolsassy.topcities.com/
Chaney's Tutorials	http://chaneytuts.topcities.com/index.htm
Cheri's Corner	http://cheriscorner.topcities.com/index.html
ChrisChris Tutorials	http://ergfriends.com/chrischris/
Christian Creations	http://www.ccsite.net/resources/index.htm
CJ's Home on the Web	http://www.cjshome.com/
Country Doodlin'	http://www.countrydoodlin.com/

Cre8tive Edges	http://www.geocities.com/aushortyau/index.html
Create From Scratch	http://black_cat_designs.tripod.com/
Creating with Paint Shop Pro 7	http://www.fullerw.freeserve.co.uk/index.html
CS Green Designs	http://www.pspbuddies.com/
Cuboid Arts	http://cuboidarts.com/
Cursed Creations	http://cursedcreations.com/main.shtml
Cybia	http://www.cybia.co.uk/
DaFont	http://www.dafont.com
Dana Lea's Graphics	http://danaleasgraphics.com/index.html
Dani's Graphics	http://ydany.tripod.com/index.html
Dani's PSP Playground	http://pspplayground.fateback.com/
Darian	http://www.darianbc.com/index.html
Dawn and Sandy's Creations	http://www.geocities.com/resqur111/Index.htm
Dawn's Tutorials	http://www.geocities.com/dawnstutorials/
Daydreamer's	http://daisydaydreamer.tripod.com/
Debbie's Designs	http://iamdebbie.net/
Deb's Paint Shop Pro Tutorials	http://bis.midco.net/djlarson1/indexmidco.htm
Deb's Tuts	http://www.debstuts.com/
DeRosa's Creations	http://medlem.spray.se/derosacreation1/
Design by Astro	http://www.byastro.com/
Designed to a T	http://www.designedtoat.com/
Designs by Donna	http://designsbydonna.com/
Designs by Dozi	http://www.dozibaer.com/
Designs by Joy	http://www.designsbyjoy.net/
Designs by TraciRose	http://designsbytracirose.com/
Desktop Designs	http://www.damorrisons.com/desktop/
Dianas Tubes	http://freetubes.com/
Dia's Dimensions	http://diasdimensions.com/
Digital Aspects	http://digitalaspects.org/
Digital Scrapbook Place	http://www.digitalscrapbookplace.com/
Digital Scrapbooking	http://www.digitialscrapbooking.com
Dis and Dat	http://www.disdatdesigns.com/
Distinctively Donna	http://www.distinctivelydonna.com/
Dixie Lady's Digital Garden	http://www.dixielady.com/
Dizteq.com	http://www.dizteq.com/
Dizzinz Studio	http://dizzinz.dizz.com/index.htm
Dodo's New World	http://regretless.com/dodo/newworld/

Dream Vision Arts	http://www.dreamvisionarts.com/
Eagle Rose's Fantasy Realm	http://eaglerose.crosswinds.net/index.htm
Eagle's Rest Graphics	http://eaglesrestgraphics.com/
Ellie's Themes	http://elliesthemes.surfhoo.com/
Ellie's Treasures	http://www.ellies-treasures.com/home/home.html
Emerald's City of Tutorials	http://groups.msn.com/EmeraldsCityofTutorials/
Esda home	http://esda3.tripod.com/esda.html
ESP Concepts	http://www.espconcepts.com/
Evening Star Graphics	http://www.angelfire.com/stars4/eveningstar/
Fairy Skyla	http://fairyskyla.net/pallet.htm
Fantasy Dream World	http://home.tiscali.nl/fantasydreamworld/
Fantasy Inspirations	http://fantasyinspirations.8m.com/
Fateback Free Fonts	http://freefonts.fateback.com
Firefly Imaging	http://www.firefly-imaging.com/
Fitty's	http://www.revjim.dsl.pipex.com/
Floof's	http://www.floofs.bravepages.com/
Fluttrby Designs	http://www.fluttrbydesigns.com/
Font Diner	http://www.fontdiner.com
Font Garden	http://www.fontgarden.net
From the Cat	http://members.tripod.com/FromTheCat/index.htm
From the Heart	http://heartcrygraphics.org/
Fun Stationery Creations	http://katra.co.uk/intro.htm
Gail's Grapevine	http://members.rogers.com/gailsgrapevine/
Gallery Estazia	http://estazia.topcities.com/
Gardendale Designs	http://www.gardendaledesigns.com/
Gfx Sally	http://www.gfxsally.com/
GrafX Design	http://www.grafx-design.com/
Graphic Arts by Elle	http://graphic-and-arts-by-elle.com/
Graphic Buds	http://www.graphicbuds.com/
Graphic Butterfly	http://www.graphicbutterfly.com/
Graphic Distractions	http://littlevanillabeans.yoll.net/
Graphic Visions	http://www.angelfire.com/on2/lovelylady/
Graphical Nuances	http://graphicalnuances.com/
Graphics by CandeeKis	http://www.candeekis.com/
Graphics by Juan Perez	http://www.s88899170.onlinehome.us/
Graphics by Lady Barbara	http://graphicsbyladybarbara.com/
Graphics by Lisbeth	http://home.no.net/tindir/

Graphics by Mona	http://graphics.carverhouse.net/
Graphics by Tape	http://www.sammal.pp.fi/tape/graphics/
Graphics by the Elf	http://www.geocities.com/sue9901/
Graphics Den	http://www.actden.com/grap_den/
Graphics Galore and More	http://groups.msn.com/graphicsgaloreandmore/
GreatKris	http://www.greatkris.com/
Green Dawn	http://www.tritachion.de/
Griffin Images	http://www.griffinimages.com/
Guffy Creek	http://www.guffycreek.com/
Harold's PSP Tuts	http://www.geocities.com/harldjon/
Havasu Hideout	http://www.havasuhideout.com/index/index.html
Haylers Heavenly Creations	http://www.haylerscreations.com/
Heaven's Peace	http://heavenspeace.com/index.php
Heffy's	http://www.heffy.com/
Helen's Colorations	http://hellen5.50megs.com/
Helping Hand	http://www.angelfire.com/folk/helpinghand/
Hilda's Graphics	http://www.geocities.com/hhellin/
Holder's Computer Art	http://www.glhold.com/index.html
House of Lime	http://www.houseoflime.com
Hummingbird Meadows	http://www.hummingbirdmeadows.com/
Impressions of Shydove	http://www.geocities.com/shydove_94044/
Irene's Designs	http://d600617.u36.hosted.servetheworld.net/
Ivy's Graphics	http://ivysgraphics.topcities.com/
Jacinda's Web Design	http://www.jacindaswebdesign.com/
Jaddell's Graphics	http://www.jaddell.com/
Jaded Design	http://jadeddesign.50megs.com/
Jaguarwoman Websuite Boutique	http://www.jaguarwoman.com/
Jan's Niche on the Net	http://webistry.net/jan/
JansDesigns	http://www.jansdesigns.com/
Jennie's World	http://jenniesworld.com/Tutorials.htm
Jenn's Little Corner	http://clix.to/jlc
Jen's Place	http://members.tripod.com/jennette10/
Joyful Creations	http://www.joyfulcreationsdesigns.com/
JP's PSP Tutorials	http://jpkabala.com/paranormal/index.html
Jubilate	http://moonwolf.250free.com/index.html
Jumbo	http://www.jumbo-psp.com/
Jumpin' Jack's Flash Designs	http://loraannn.com/

Just Kiss-Graphics Tuts	http://www.justkiss.com/psp
Just Mousing Around	http://www.justmousingaround.com/
Just One Drop	http://www.justonedrop.com/
Just us Now	http://www.justusnow.com/fonts01.html
KanDu Designs	http://groups.msn.com/KanDuDesigns
Kandy'z	http://www.angelfire.com/ky/kandykizz/
Karamei's Backgrounds 'n Tubes	http://members.aol.com/_ht_a/Karamei/
Karen's Creations	http://karenscreations.infinology.net/
Karen's Kreations	http://www.karenskreations.co.uk/
Kat Korner	http://groups.msn.com/KatKorner/
Kath's Korner	http://www.kathskorner.com/
KaysKreations Stationery	http://www.kayskreations.net/
KC Graphics	http://k.cureington.tripod.com/
Keith's Creations	http://keithscreations.net/
Kelly's Web Creations	http://www.kellyswebcreations.com/
Keye's Center	http://www.keyescenter.com/
KGL Graphics	http://www.kglgraphics.net/
Kimmy Smith	http://www.kimmysmith.com/
Kim's Place	http://www.geocities.com/Heartland/Woods/2987/
Kirobu	http://kirobu.com/
KiwiNessie Webbed	http://www.nessiedesigns.com/
Koala's Pages	http://www.thekoala.com/
Krafty Kards	http://www.kraftykards.com/
KROW Workshop	http://club.coolmaps.com/krow_psp_intro.cfm
Kuntree Scrappin Designs	http://www.kuntreescrappindesigns.com/
La Faerie	http://lafaerie.com/
Lady Alba	http://members.cox.net/maggiea13/
Lady J's Creations	http://www.geocities.com/spring_bouquet/
Lady Majika	http://www.ladymagika.com/
Lady Sara	http://ladysara.org/
Lana's Place	http://lanarj.tripod.com/
Larabie Fonts	http://www.larabiefonts.com
Lazy Daze Designz	http://lazydazedesignz.com/
Letha's Designs	http://lethasdesigns.com/tutorials/
Linda at Home	http://lethasdesigns.com/tutorials/
Liss' PSP Corner	http://www.lisspspkorner.com/
Little Piece for Dreams	http://www.lpdreams.com/

Lori's PSP Tutorials	http://ljgdesign.com/
Lori's Web Graphics	http://loriweb.pair.com/
Louise's Graphics	http://louise.poppyfield.net/Tutorials.htm
Lover's Paradise	http://www.prestigiousdames.com/dee/
Luver's Tutorials	http://www.geocities.com/luverstuts/
LVS Online	http://www.lvsonline.com/
Lynn Graphics	http://www.lynngraphics.esmartweb.com/
Made by Char	http://prestigiousdames.com/char/
Madlassgrin	http://www.madlassgrin.co.uk/
Maegg Graphics	http://maegg.com/
Maeve's World	http://www.maevesstuff.netfirms.com/
Majestic Artistry	http://majesticartistry.com/
MaMaT's PSP7 Tips	http://htmlhelp.rootsweb.com/imagehelp/psp7/
Mandy's World	http://www.mandysworld.com/tutorialindex.htm
Mann Made Images	http://www.mannmadeimages.com/
Maple Creek Graphics	http://www.geocities.com/maplecreekgraphics/
Mark-Henri	http://www.markhenri.com/
Marlie's PSP	http://marliesplace.net/
Martin's Eclectic Adventures	http://martinseclectic.net/
Mary Bear's Tutorials	http://jment1.com/psp/index.html
Marylizbeth's PSP Pages	http://www.geocities.com/mary_lizbethkirwan/
Mary's Sea of Dreams	http://www.geocities.com/mcjd83/
Masterstoneman	http://masterstoneman.com/
MidLite PSP	http://groups.msn.com/MidLitePSP/
Midnite Design	http://midnitedesign.50megs.com/main.html
Mitzi's Country Christian Home	http://www.mitzi-bear.com/
Moedog's Garden	http://users.snowcrest.net/moedog/
Moms Corner 4 Kids	http://www.momscorner4kids.com/fonts/
Monarch Designs	http://groups.msn.com/MonarchDesigns
Monica's Melange	http://www.wallek.com/monica/
Moon and Back Graphics	http://www.gentlearts.net/
Moon's Designs	http://moonsdesigns.com/
Moyen Designs	http://members.lycos.nl/moyendesigns/
Mrs. Huddle's Haven	http://mrshuddleshaven.com/
Mystic's Tuts	http://mystics-tuts.tripod.com/
Nanette's Place	http://www.nanettes-place.com/
Nanson's Place	http://nansons-place.com/

ND Designs	http://www.nkuehl.com/
Nemesis Tutorials	http://www.nemesistutorials.com/
New Dawn Designs	http://www.newdawndesigns.com/linda/
Nightshadow FX	http://www.nightshadowfx.com/
No Place Like It	http://www.aunt-em.com/
NSK PSP Workshop	http://nskpsp.150m.com/index.htm
Ondrun	http://ondrun.50megs.com/
Opal's Place	http://opalplace.org/
Original Free Tubes Site	http://www.freetubes.com/
Outta My Shell Digital Studios	http://www.omsds.com/index.html
P. Ann's Place	http://pannsplace.50megs.com/opening.html
Paint Shop Potpourri	http://www.geocities.com/joflo723/
Paint Shop Pro 5.0 Tutorials	http://www.glorianon.com/psp/
Paint Shop Pro 6 Tips	http://hometown.aol.com/ronaldlvick/index.htm
Paint Shop Pro Art Resources	http://www.digitalartresources.com/PSP/ArtResources.htm
Paint Shop Pro Beginner's	http://www.angelfire.com/pop/tutorials/
Paint Shop Pro Newsgroup	http://www.egroups.com/group/PSP7Newbies
Paint Shop Pro Notebook	http://mjrb.org/tut/lecthall-index.html
Paint Shop Pro Tutorials	http://psp7tutorials.homestead.com/index.html
Painted Pixels	http://www.paintedpixels.com/
Pieces of Penny	http://www.piecesofpenny.com/
Pike Graphic	http://www.pikegraphic.com/index.htm
Pinoy 7	http://www.pinoy7.com/
PItuts.com	http://www.pituts.com/
Pixel Art by Joyce	http://www.pixelartbyjoyce.com/
PixelNook	http://pixelnook.home.comcast.net/
PJ's PSP Stuff	http://www.solarraven.com/PJs-psp8stuff.html
Plain Vanilla Graphics	http://plainvanilla.www3.50megs.com/
Playful Pixels	http://www.playfulpixels.com/
Playing with Pixels	http://www.virtuallydesigned.com/psp/
Pracken's Place	http://www.prestigiousdames.com/Pracken/
Prairie Pixels	http://prairiepixels.com/
Pretty Art PCC	http://www.homestead.com/tats1/prettyart.html
Princess Graphic Designs	http://pgd.therapids.net/index.htm
PSP Camp Ratty	http://campratty.com/questions.html
PSP Fun	http://www.pspfun.net/
PSP Gear	http://pspgear.com/

PSP Help and Hints	http://www.psphelp.com/
PSP Power	http://www.psppower.com/
PSP Toybox	http://www.psptoybox.com/index.html
PSP Tutorials by KathZil	http://kathzil.nl/tutorials/
PSP Users Group	http://www.pspug.org/
PSP Variete	http://www.pspvariete.com/english.htm
PSParadise	http://www.psparadise.co.uk/
PSP-X Mass Construction	http://psp-x.com/index.htm
Pumpkin Ridge Creations	http://www.pumpkinridgecreations.com/
Purrcat Designs	http://members.cox.net/purrcat1/index.html
Quill Signatures	http://www.quill-signatures.com/divider.html
Rainbow Pixels	http://www.rainbowpixels.us/home.html
Rainbow Row Graphics	http://rainbowrowgraphics.tripod.com/
Raven Graphics	http://www.ravensdarkside.com/
Red Prince Atelier	http://www.redprince.net/atelier/
Reindeer Graphics	http://www.reindeergraphics.com/
Ricki's House	http://www.rickishouse.com/
Riverdancer Designs	http://www.riverdancerdesigns.com/
Robins PSP Resources	http://www.putertutor.net/
Ron Lacey	http://ronstoons.com/
Ronni S.	http://www.prestigiousdames.com/ronni/
Rosecca	http://members.tripod.com/rosecca/
Rosepetal Designs	http://www.rosepetaldesign.com/
Sandee's Place	http://sandeesplace.infinology.net/
Saphire Design	http://www.weariersaphire.co.uk/
Sarah's Useful Web Stuff	http://www.sarahswebstuff.com/intro.php
SassiJulie	http://www.pspdesignsbyjulie.com/
Sassy Signatures	http://www.sassysignatures.com/
Scrapbook-Bytes	http://www.scrapbook-bytes.com/
Scrapbooking with Design	http://www.scrapbookingwithflipalbum.com/
Shala's Graphics	http://shala.addr.com/index.htm
Shell's Designs	http://shellsdesigns.co.uk/
Silkenthread	http://www.silkenthread.net/
Simply Jill	http://www.simplyjill.com/
Singing Snowmen	http://singingsnowmen.freeservers.com/
Snap's Shady Studio	http://shadystudios.250free.com/
Sparks Creations	http://www.sparkscreations.com/

Spider's Nest	http://www.bjgeiger.com/index.html
Spoonloads	http://www.spoonloads.com
Staker Family	http://www.stakerfamily.com/index.html
StarKeeper's Graphics	http://www.angelfire.com/va3/graphictuts/
State of Entropy	http://www.state-of-entropy.com/
Steve's Place	http://www.steve-mann.com/index.html
Studio 73	http://www.studio73.ca/
Studio Bean	http://www.carolynsbarrett.com/index.html
Sumrall Works, Inc.	http://www.sumrallworks.com/
Sunrise Creek	http://sunrisecreek.net/
Sunshine Suzy-Q	http://sunshinesuzyq.com/Tutorial.htm
Susan's Place	http://myweb.absa.co.za/tikburo/index.html
Sweet Dreams Digital	http://sweetdreamsdigital.com/
T Creations	http://blkbeltmom.faithweb.com/
Taiga Designs	http://taigadesigns.homestead.com/Index.html
Tau Taurea	http://www.tau-taurea.com/
Tephra's Web Studio	http://psp.tephras.com/
Terry and Amber	http://www.at-techsolutions.com/
The Bitter Old Man	http://www.thebitteroldman.com/psp/psp7.htm
The Lost Mystic	http://lostmystic.fateback.com/
The Plug In Site	http://thepluginsite.com/
The Taskbar	http://www.the-taskbar.com/
Thomas Creek Productions	http://www.thomascreek.com/
Tigger's Graphics	http://www.tiggersgraphics.com/
Tilly Garden	http://www.angelfire.com/art/tutorialsntubes/
Titanicaxx	http://www.titanicaxx.co.uk/
Toni's Place	http://www.graphicsbytoni.com/
Tracy's Graphics	http://www.tracysgraphics.com/
Traviata Place	http://www.traviataplace.nl/
Treasure Designs	http://www.treasuredesigns.net/
Two Sides Come Together	http://www.aussieus.com/tsct_tuts_main.htm
TwoPeasInABucket	http://www.twopeasinabucket.com/freefonts.asp
Typadelic	http://www.typadelic.com/free.html
Under the Fairy Moon	http://www.fairy-moon.com/
Val's Visions	http://www.valsvisions.com/index.html
Veck	http://veck.web1000.com/
Venux	http://www.venux.org/venux/

Visions Realized	http://www.visionsrealized.0catch.com/
Visual Perspectives	http://kldesigns.deep-ice.com/index.html
Wacom Graphics Tablets	http://www.wacom.com/
WBG Creations	http://www.wgbcreations.com/
Web Art by Sue	http://www.webartbysue.com/
Web Decor	http://webdecor.8m.com/
Web Graphics on a Budget	http://mardiweb.com/web/
WGA Design	http://www.wgadesign.com/
Whisper's Corner	http://www.whisperscorner.com/
Willshak's View of Things	http://www.willshak.com/
Wintermoon's Expressionz	http://www.kreative-expressionz.com/
Wompietuts	http://www.wompietuts.com/
Worth1000	http://www.worth1000.com/
Xanthic Eye	http://www.xanthic.net/tutorials.html
Yorkie's Yorkies and Stationery	http://www.geocities.com/ccgsardog/index.html
Your Webness Cyber Corner	http://www.yourwebness.com/
Yvonne's PSP Creations	http://fp.ymv13.plus.com/
Ziggy's PSP Tutorials	http://www.user.shentel.net/donazig/
Zimmertech	http://www.zimmertech.com/

Newsgroups

If you like to read newsgroups, here are a couple of them. You can post Paint Shop Pro questions and receive answers from other Paint Shop Pro users or even the Jasc programmers.

http://www/jasc.com/community/forums/
(This is the Jase Community Forum and is accessible through the Web so you don't have to use a newsreader.)
comp.graphics.apps.paint-shop-pro
(If you don't have a newsreader program, you can also access this newsgroup from google.com.)

TIP

Just a reminder that Chapter 6 includes several Web links to plug-in filters you can use with Paint Shop Pro.

A brother is a friend, defender,
listener, conspirator, a counselor
and a sharer of delights and sorrows.

B

Keyboard Shortcuts

Like most Windows applications, there's usually more than one way to accomplish a single task or access a particular feature. Included with Paint Shop Pro are a number of shortcut keystrokes that you can use to access tools or menu options without having to reach for your mouse.

Tool Shortcuts

Shortcut	Function
A	Arrow/Pan tool
B	Paint Brush tool
C	Clone tool
D	Deform tool
E	Dropper tool
F	Flood Fill tool
I	Picture Tube tool
J	Dodge tool
L	Lighten/Darken tool
M	Move tool
O	Vector Object Selection tool
P	Preset Shapes tool
R	Crop tool
S	Selection tool
T	Text tool
V	Pen tool

Tool Shortcuts (continued)

Shortcut	Function
X	Eraser tool
Z	Zoom tool
Shift+Alt+F6	Swap materials
Ctrl+Shift+F6	Reset materials palette

Menu Shortcuts

Most commonly accessed menu functions include a shortcut key combination that you can use instead of clicking the top-level menu and selecting options under that menu. These shortcuts are organized by the different top-level menu items.

File Menu Shortcuts

Shortcut	Function
F12	File, Save as
Ctrl+B	File, Browse
Ctrl+N	File, New
Ctrl+O	File, Open
Ctrl+P	File, Print
Ctrl+S	File, Save
Ctrl+F12	File, Save copy as
Ctrl+Delete	File, Delete
Shift+C	File, Import, Screen capture, Start
Shift+Alt+D	File, Workspace, Delete
Shift+Alt+L	File, Workspace, Load
Shift+Alt+S	File, Workspace, Save

Edit Menu Shortcuts

Shortcut	Function
Delete	Edit, Clear
Ctrl+C	Edit, Copy
Ctrl+E	Edit, Paste as new selection
Ctrl+G	Edit, Paste as new vector selection
Ctrl+L	Edit, Paste as new layer

Edit Menu Shortcuts (continued)

Shortcut	Function
Shortcut	*Function*
Ctrl+V	Edit, Paste as new image
Ctrl+X	Edit, Cut
Ctrl+Y	Edit, Repeat
Ctrl+Z	Edit, Undo
Ctrl+Shift+C	Edit, Copy merged
Ctrl+Shift+E	Edit, Paste as transparent selection
Ctrl+Shift+L	Edit, Paste into selection
Ctrl+Shift+Z	Edit, Command history
Ctrl+Alt+Z	Edit, Redo

View Menu Shortcuts

Shortcut	Function
Shortcut	*Function*
Num+	View, Zoom in by 1 step
Num-	View, Zoom out by 1 step
F2	Hide palettes
F3	View, Palettes, Script output
F4	View, Palettes, Tool options
F6	View, Palettes, Materials
F7	View, Palettes, Histogram
F8	View, Palettes, Layers
F9	View, Palettes, Overview
F10	View, Palettes, Learning center
F11	View, Palettes, Brush variance
Ctrl+Shift+A	View, Full screen preview
Ctrl+Shift+G	View, Snap to grid
Ctrl+Shift+T	Show hidden toolbars
Ctrl+Alt+G	View, Grid
Ctrl+Alt+N	View, Zoom to 100%
Ctrl+Alt+R	View, Ruler
Ctrl+Alt+M	View, Magnifier
Shift+A	View, Full screen edit
Shift+Alt+G	View, Snap to guides

Image Menu Shortcuts

Shortcut	Function
Ctrl+I	Image, Flip
Ctrl+M	Image, Mirror
Ctrl+R	Image, Rotate, Free rotate
Shift+I	Image, Image information
Shift+O	Image, Palette, Load palette
Shift+P	Image, Palette, Edit palette
Shift+R	Image, Crop to selection
Shift+S	Image, Resize
Shift+V	Image, Palette, View palette transparency
Ctrl+Shift+1	Image, Decrease color depth, 2 colors
Ctrl+Shift+2	Image, Decrease color depth, 16 colors
Ctrl+Shift+3	Image, Decrease color depth, 256 colors
Ctrl+Shift+4	Image, Decrease color depth, 32K colors
Ctrl+Shift+5	Image, Decrease color depth, 64K colors
Ctrl+Shift+6	Image, Decrease color depth, x colors
Ctrl+Shift+8	Image, Increase color depth, 16 colors
Ctrl+Shift+9	Image, Increase color depth, 256 colors
Ctrl+Shift+0	Image, Increase color depth, 16 million colors
Ctrl+Shift+V	Image, Palette, Set palette transparency

Adjust Menu Shortcuts

Shortcut	Function
Shift+B	Adjust, Brightness & Contrast, Brightness & contrast
Shift+G	Adjust, Brightness & Contrast, Gamma correction
Shift+E	Adjust, Brightness & Contrast, Histogram equalize
Shift+L	Adjust, Hue & Saturation, Colorize
Shift+M	Adjust, Brightness & Contrast, Highlight, Midtone/shadow
Shift+T	Adjust, Brightness & Contrast, Histogram stretch
Shift+U	Adjust, Color Balance, Red/Green/Blue
Ctrl+Shift+H	Adjust, Brightness & Contrast, Histogram adjustment

Layers Menu Shortcuts

Shortcut	Function
Shortcut	*Function*
Shift+K	Layers, Invert Mask/Adjustment
Shift+Y	Layers, New Mask Layer, Hide all

Selections Menu Shortcuts

Shortcut	Function
Shortcut	*Function*
Ctrl+A	Selections, Select all
Ctrl+D	Selections, Select none
Ctrl+F	Selections, Float
Ctrl+H	Selections, Modify feather
Ctrl+Shift+B	Selections, Select from vector object
Ctrl+Shift+F	Selections, Defloat
Ctrl+Shift+I	Selections, Invert
Ctrl+Shift+M	Selections, Hide marquee
Ctrl+Shift+P	Selections, Promote selection to layer
Ctrl+Shift+S	Selections, Select from mask

Window Menu Shortcuts

Shortcut	Function
Shortcut	*Function*
Ctrl+W	Window, Fit to image
Shift+D	Window, Duplicate
Shift+W	Window, New window

Help Menu Shortcuts

Shortcut	Function
Shortcut	*Function*
Shift+F1	Help, Context help

Light: While the Christmas cactus can adapt to low light more abundant blooms are produced on plants that have been exposed to high light intensity. Keep your plants in a sunny location indoors. Christmas cactus needs shading from the sun between May and September.

Soil: Well-drained soil is a must for Christmas cactus.

Water: Water thoroughly when the top half of the soil in the pot feels dry to the touch. When fall arrives, water the plant only well enough to prevent wilting. During the month of October, give the plant no water. Cautiously resume watering in November

Fertilizing: As tender growth appears in the spring, apply a weak solution of liquid houseplant fertilizer at 2 to 3 weeks.

Temperature: Prefers warm temperatures, although evening temperatures of 50 to 55 degrees can be used to initiate flower bud formation From October on, keep the plant where it is cool at night, keep away from drafts from heat vents, fireplaces or other sources

Christmas cactus

Scientific name:
Schlumbergera bridesii

Origin:
A group of epiphytic cacti native to the South American jungle

Glossary

15-bit image. An image that contains a maximum of 32,768 colors.

16-bit image. An image that contains a maximum of 65,536 colors.

1-bit image. An image that contains a maximum of 2 colors.

24-bit image. An image that contains a maximum of 16,777,216 colors.

4-bit image. An image that contains a maximum of 16 colors.

8-bit image. An image that contains a maximum of 256 colors.

Adjustment layer. A layer that is used to apply color adjustments to the layers below it.

Airbrush. The Paint Shop Pro tool that digitally sprays a fine mist of paint.

Ambient lighting. Nondirectional lighting that bounces off walls, ceilings, and other objects in the scene when a picture is taken.

Angle of view. The amount of a scene that a lens can capture.

Animation Shop. An application that is included with Paint Shop Pro to create animations.

Animation. A series of sequential images with an optional transition effect to create the illusion of movement.

Anti-alias. The smoothing and blending of pixel edges to eliminate jagged edges on curved and slanted lines.

Artifact. Unwanted noise added to an image, usually by digital cameras, scanners, or high compression.

Aspect ratio. The ratio of width to height.

Attribute. Items that determine the appearance of text, such as bolding, underlining, italics, font, or size.

Automatic rollups. Floating objects that open automatically as you hover your mouse in their area but then close up again when you move your mouse out of their vicinity.

AutoSave. A feature that periodically saves a temporary version of your document.

AVI. Abbreviation for Audio Video Interlaced. A Windows multimedia file format used for video and audio.

Background color. The canvas color on which graphics display.

Background layer. The bottom layer in many images.

Background. In photography, the background is the area behind your main subject of interest. In graphics, background is the canvas on which graphics display.

Backlighting filter. A Paint Shop Pro filter that darkens the bright, overexposed areas of a photo.

Batch Processing. A technique for applying the same photo-editing action to multiple images at the same time.

Bevel. A three-dimensional edge on an object.

Bit depth. *See Color depth.*

Bit. The smallest unit of digital information that a computer handles.

Bitmapped image. An image that is composed of small squares, called *pixels*, which are arranged in columns and rows. Each pixel has a specific color and location.

Black. The color formed by the absence of reflected or transmitted light.

Blend. To combine two layers or areas of an image. Often used to create a more realistic transition between image areas, as when retouching or compositing in image editing.

Blur. An effect that reduces areas of high contrast and softens the appearance of an image. Blur is achieved by reducing the contrast between pixels that form the edges.

BMP. File format abbreviation for a bitmapped image.

Brightness. The amount of light or white color in an image. Usually represented by a percentage of 0, which is black, to 100, which is white.

Browser. A feature of Paint Shop Pro that allows you to see and manage multiple thumbnail images.

Browser toolbar. Displays useful tools when you're browsing images.

Burn tool. A Paint Shop Pro brush tool used to make areas darker.

Calibration. A process used to correct for the differences in the output of a printer or monitor when compared to the original image.

Camera RAW. A file format used in Paint Shop Pro that can manipulate the unprocessed images captured by digital cameras.

Canvas size. The size of the area within an image window.

Canvas. The area on which an image is displayed.

Cast. An undesirable tinge of color in an image.

Chromatic aberration. An image defect, often seen as colored fringing around the edges of an object. Chromatic aberration is common in digital images.

Clone tool. A tool used to duplicate a portion of an image.

CMYK. Abbreviation for Cyan/Magenta/Yellow/Black, which are the four standard ink colors used in printing.

Color correction. Changing the relative amounts of color in an image to produce a desired effect, typically a more accurate representation of those colors.

Color depth. The number of bits of color information that is available for each pixel.

Color model. Any system for representing colors as ordered sets of numbers. Paint Shop Pro uses the most common color models, which are RGB, CMYK, and HSB.

Color palette. Contains a selection of available colors, styles, and textures, and it displays the current foreground and background colors and styles.

Color replacer tool. A Paint Shop Pro tool that simplifies changing all of a selected color to another hue.

Color wheel. The circular color area from which you can create a custom color.

Colorize. An effect that converts an image or selection to a uniform hue and saturation while retaining its lightness.

Composite. In photography, an image composed of two or more parts of an image, taken either from a single photo or multiple photos. Usually, composites are created so that the elements blend smoothly together.

Composition. The pleasing or artistic arrangement of the main subject, other objects in a scene, and/or the foreground and background.

Compression. A process that is applied to saved images to reduce file size. Some compression schemes, such as JPEG, discard image information.

Contract command. Shrinks a selection by a specific number of pixels.

Contrast. The difference between the light and dark areas of an image.

Crop. To remove part of an image outside a selection.

DCNR. A tool that removes digital camera noise.

Defloat. To merge a floating selection into a layer.

Deformation. To change an images appearance by moving data from one area to another.

Defringe. To clean the edges of a selection by removing pixels of the background color.

Density. The ability of an object to stop or absorb light. The less light reflected or transmitted by an object, the higher its density.

Depth-of-field. The distance between the nearest and furthest objects in focus as seen by a camera lens. Depth-of-field determines how much of an image is in sharp focus, and what parts, such as the background, are out of focus.

Desaturate. To reduce the purity or vividness of a color, making a color appear to be washed out or diluted.

Diffusion. The random distribution of grey tones in an area of an image, producing a fuzzy effect.

Digital. Electronic (non-physical) information that a computer reads and processes.

Digital camera. A camera that takes pictures and stores them in its memory or on a disk.

Distortion. A usually unwanted change in the shape of an image.

Dithering. When a computer monitor substitutes a color, it cannot display with a similar color.

Dodge tool. A Paint Shop Pro brush tool used to make areas lighter.

DPI. Abbreviation for dots per inch. Related to the resolution of a printed image, DPI is a unit of measurement that measures the number of dots that fit horizontally and vertically into a one-inch measure.

Dropper tool. A Paint Shop Pro tool used to sample color from one part of an image, so it can be used to paint, draw, or fill elsewhere in the image.

Effect. A graphics function that creates a modification to an image.

Emboss. An effect that causes the foreground of an image to appear raised from the background.

EXIF. *Exchangeable Image File Format.* Developed to standardize the exchange of image data between hardware devices and software. EXIF is used by most digital cameras and includes information such as the date and time a photo was taken, the camera settings, resolution, amount of compression, and other data.

Expand a selection. Increases the size of a selection by a specified number of pixels.

Export. The process of saving a file into a different format.

Exposure. In photography, the amount of light allowed to reach the film or sensor, determined by the intensity of the light, the amount admitted by the lens, and the shutter speed.

Feather. The process of fading an area on all edges of a selection. Measured in pixels.

File associations. A method of determining which files your computer opens automatically using Paint Shop Pro.

File format. The structure of a file that defines the way it is stored.

Fill flash. A Paint Shop Pro filter that allows you to lighten the darker, underexposed areas of a photo.

Filter. A tool that applies special effects to an image.

Filter. In photography, a device that fits over the lens, changing the light in some way. Paint Shop Pro includes many filters that change the image pixels to produce special effects.

FireWire (IEEE-1394). A fast, serial interface used by scanners, digital cameras, printers, and other devices.

Flat. An image with low contrast.

Flatten. A term used to merge multiple layers into a single layer.

Flip command. The command that reverses an image vertically.

Float command. The command that temporarily separates a selection from an image or layer.

Floating objects. Screen elements appearing in the middle of the Paint Shop Pro window that can be moved to other areas of the window. Floating objects have automatic rollup.

Focus. To adjust the lens to produce a sharp image.

Foreground color. The primary color for the painting and drawing tools.

Format. The shape and size of an image or text. Also, the method that a browser uses to display an image.

F-stop. A camera lens aperture setting that corresponds to an f-number, which helps determine both exposure and depth of field. The larger the f-stop number, the smaller the f-stop itself.

Gamma. A term given to the brightness values in an image.

Gamma correction. A correction to the display contrast between an image and the monitor.

Gamma. A numerical way of representing the contrast of an image.

Gaussian blur. A method of diffusing an image by calculating which pixels to blur, rather than blurring all pixels, producing a random look.

GIF. File format abbreviation for a *Graphic Interchange Format* image. GIF images support transparency, but only 8-bit (256) color. Commonly used with Web graphics.

Gradient Fill. A fill that is created by the gradual blending of colors.

Grey scale image. An image that uses up to 256 shades of grey.

Grid. An equally spaced series of vertical and horizontal lines to help align objects.

Handles. Control points on vector objects that are used to edit the object.

High contrast. A wide range of density in a print, negative, or other image.

Highlight. The lightest part of an image.

Histogram. A graphics representation showing the distribution of color and light in an image.

History palette. A Paint Shop Pro palette that tracks the changes you've made to your image during the current work session. The history clears when you close the image.

HSL. Abbreviation for *Hue/Saturation/Lightness*. A method of defining colors in an image.

HTML. Abbreviation for *Hypertext Markup Language*. A programming language that is used to create Web pages.

Hue. A color.

Image window. The area in which you work on your image.

Internet. A global network of computers used to transfer information.

Interpolation. A technique used to create new pixels or remove pixels whenever you resize or change the resolution of an image. It is based on the values of surrounding pixels.

Invert. In image editing, to change an image into its negative; black becomes white, white becomes black, dark grey becomes light grey, and so forth. Colors are also changed to the complementary color; green becomes magenta, blue turns to yellow, and red is changed to cyan.

Jaggies. Staircasing effect of lines that are not perfectly horizontal or vertical, caused by pixels that are too large to represent the line accurately. *See also Anti-alias.*

JPEG. Abbreviation for *Joint Photographic Experts Group*. *See also JPG file format.*

JPG file format. A file format that supports 24-bit (16,777,216) color but not transparency. Commonly used with Web graphics.

Kerning. The distance between characters of text.

Landscape. The orientation of a page in which the longest dimension is horizontal, also called *wide orientation.*

Layer palette. Lists each layer in the current image.

Layer. A level of an image that can be edited independently from the rest of the image.

Leading. The distance between lines of text.

Levels. A feature used to apply changes to image contrast and brightness.

Line art. An image that is composed of two colors only, usually black and white.

Logo. A name or symbol that many businesses use for easy recognition.

Lossless compression. An image-compression scheme, such as TIFF, that preserves all image detail. When the image is decompressed, it is identical to the original version.

Lossy compression. An image-compression scheme, such as JPEG, that creates smaller files by discarding image information, which can affect image quality.

Luminance. A physical measurement of the brightness information in an image. Luminance is determined by the amount of grey.

Magic Wand. A selection tool that works by selecting content rather than defining edges.

Marquee. A selection area that is represented by "marching ants."

Mask. A feature that allows some portion of an image to be hidden.

Midtones. Parts of an image with tones of an intermediate value. Paint Shop Pro allows you to manipulate midtones independently from the highlights and shadows.

Mirror. An exact copy of an image that is placed in reverse of the copied image.

Moiré. An objectionable pattern in an image, usually generated by rescanning an image that has already been halftoned.

Monochrome. Having a single color, plus white such as greyscale.

Negative image. A photographic image in reversed form where the light areas become dark and the dark areas become light.

Negative. *See Invert.*

Neutral color. In image editing's RGB mode, a color in which red, green, and blue are present in equal amounts, producing a grey.

Node. A control point on a vector object.

Noise. The grainy appearance in some images.

Object. A single element in an image.

Opacity. The density of a color or layer.

Overexposure. A condition in which too much light reaches the film or sensor, producing a dense negative or a very bright/light print, slide, or digital image.

Overview window. Displays entire image when zooming in to a small area.

Palette. A collection of tools providing quick access to selected Paint Shop Pro elements.

Panorama. A broad view usually created from combining together several photographs.

Path. The guiding line for a vector object.

Perspective. The interpretation of how far the foreground and background appear to be separated from each other.

Picture tubes. Fun little pictures that you paint with your brush.

Pixel. The smallest element in an image.

Pixels per inch (ppi). The number of pixels that can be displayed per inch, usually used to refer to pixel resolution from a scanned image or on a monitor.

Plug-in. An outside filter that can be accessed from within PSP.

PNG. Abbreviation for *Portable Network Graphics*. A file format designed for Web graphics that supports both transparency and 24-bit (16,777,216) color.

Portrait. The orientation of a page in which the longest dimension is vertical, also called *tall orientation*.

Posterize. Effect that replaces areas of continuous color tone with single colors.

Preferences. The area in which each user maintains customized settings for Paint Shop Pro.

Print Preview. The feature that allows you to view an image prior to printing it on paper.

Raster image. A bitmapped image made up of pixels.

Rasterize. To convert a vector image to raster.

RAW. An image file format offered by many digital cameras that includes all the unprocessed information captured by the camera.

Red-eye. A photographic effect that frequently occurs in photographs of humans and animals, giving a shiny or red appearance to eyes.

Replace Color command. The Paint Shop Pro feature that allows you to pick a specific color and replace it with any other color.

Resample. To change the size or resolution of an image. Resampling down discards pixel information in an image; resampling up adds pixel information through interpolation.

Resize. The ability to make an image or object larger or smaller.

Resolution. The measurement of the detail in an image.

Retouch. To edit an image, most often to remove flaws or to create a new effect.

RGB (Red/Green/Blue). The three primary colors that compose most images.

Rotate. To turn an image or object.

Saturation. The measure of strength of an image's color.

Scale. To change the size of a piece of an image.

Scanner. A hardware device used to translate pictures and text into digital language that a computer can interpret.

Script. A file that holds recorded steps and is used to automate those steps.

Selection. The outline that appears around an area to be modified.

Sensor array. The grid-like arrangement of the red, green, and blue-sensitive elements of a digital camera's solid state capture device.

Shadow. The darkest area of an image. Sometimes applied as an effect.

Sharpen. An effect that works by boosting contrast between adjacent pixels that form an edge.

Skew. A deformation that tilts an image along its horizontal or vertical axis.

SmartMedia. A type of memory card storage for digital cameras and other computer devices.

Smoothing. To blur the boundaries between edges of an image, often to reduce a rough or jagged appearance.

Soft focus. A Paint Shop Pro feature that creates soft outlines.

Solarization. An effect created by combining some positive areas of the image with some negative areas. It works by inverting all colors above a selected value.

Status bar. The line at the bottom of an application window that displays help and image details.

Stroke. An outline of text.

Text banner. Animations often seen on Web pages—usually at the top—that have text moving around.

Threshold. A predefined level to determine whether a pixel will be represented as black or white.

Thumbnail. A miniature version of an image.

TIFF. Abbreviation for *Tagged Image File Format*. A format that scanners commonly use.

Tint. A color with white added to it.

Title bar. The bar at the top of the application that displays the Paint Shop Pro Control icon, the application name, and the name of the active image and its format, as well as the standard Windows buttons.

Toolbar. Similar to a palette, a collection of frequently used tools.

Toggle. To switch an item back and forth from one state to another. Frequently used to turn the display of layers on and off.

Tolerance. The range of color or tonal values that will be selected with Paint Shop Pro tools.

Tool palette. Contains the image-editing tools.

Toolbar. Displays tools to manage files and commonly used menu functions.

Tool Options palette. Displays options for the currently selected tool.

Transparency. An area that lacks color.

Tripod. A three-legged supporting stand used to hold the camera steady.

TWAIN. A common computer interface among scanners, digital cameras, and computers.

Underexposure. A condition in which too little light reaches the film or sensor, producing a thin negative, a dark slide, a muddy-looking print, or a dark digital image.

Undo. The ability to reverse actions.

Unsharp masking. The process for increasing the contrast between adjacent pixels in an image, increasing sharpness, especially around edges.

USB. A high-speed serial communication method commonly used to connect digital cameras and other devices to a computer.

VCR controls. An Animation Shop toolbar that controls viewing an animation.

Vector graphic. An object that uses mathematics to create images. Vector graphics can be edited, moved, and resized easily.

Warp. The process of distorting digital images.

Watermark. Embedded information in an image that is used to mark an image with copyright and author information.

Web browser. A software program that is designed specifically to view Web pages on the Internet.

White balance. The adjustment of a digital camera to the color temperature of the light source.

White. The color formed by combining all the colors of light (in the additive color model) or by removing all colors (in the subtractive model).

Workspace. The portion of the Paint Shop Pro window where you work on your image.

Zoom. The process of viewing an image in a larger or smaller magnification.

Index

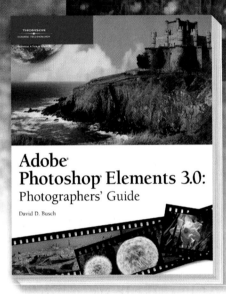
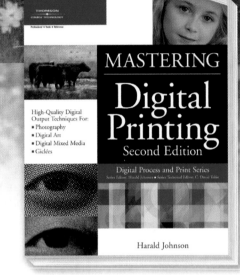

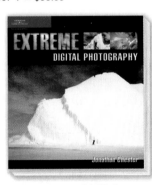
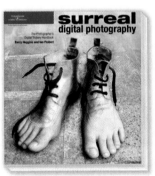
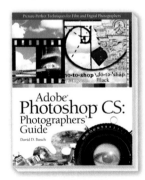